Genocide

Genocide

The Power and Problems of a Concept

Edited by

ANDREA GRAZIOSI AND FRANK E. SYSYN

McGill-Queen's University Press
Montreal & Kingston • London • Chicago

ISBN 978-0-2280-0834-7 (cloth)
ISBN 978-0-2280-0951-1 (ePDF)
ISBN 978-0-2280-0952-8 (ePUB)

Legal deposit first quarter 2022
Bibliothèque nationale du Québec

MQUP acknowledges the financial contribution of the Holodomor Research and Education Consortium towards the publication of this book.

Funded by the Government of Canada | Financé par le gouvernement du Canada | Canada

Canada Council for the Arts | Conseil des arts du Canada

We acknowledge the support of the Canada Council for the Arts.
Nous remercions le Conseil des arts du Canada de son soutien.

Library and Archives Canada Cataloguing in Publication

Title: Genocide : the power and problems of a concept / edited by Andrea Graziosi and Frank E. Sysyn.
Other titles: Genocide (Montréal, Québec)
Names: Graziosi, Andrea, 1954– editor. | Sysyn, Frank E., editor.
Description: Includes bibliographical references and index.
Identifiers: Canadiana (print) 20210306742 | Canadiana (ebook) 20210306769 | ISBN 9780228008347 (cloth) | ISBN 9780228009511 (ePDF) | ISBN 9780228009528 (ePUB)
Subjects: LCSH: Genocide. | LCSH: Genocide—History—20th century.
Classification: LCC HV6322.7 .G44 2022 | DDC 304.6/63—dc23

This book was typeset in 10.5/13 Sabon.

Contents

Acknowledgments

This volume contains essays presented at the conference "Genocide in Twentieth-Century History: The Power and the Problems of an Interpretive, Ethical-Political, and Legal Concept," which was held in October 2018 at the University of Toronto with the support of the Holodomor Research and Education Consortium (HREC) at the Canadian Institute of Ukrainian Studies, University of Alberta, and the support of the Institute for Holocaust, Genocide, and Memory Studies at the University of Massachusetts, Amherst. We are deeply grateful to Alon Confino, who worked with us in preparing the conference; to those who made its organization possible, Marta Baziuk and Anastasia Leshchyshyn of HREC first and foremost; to all the participants, including the colleagues whose papers proved unavailable for inclusion (Doris Bergen, Dani Blatman, Christian Gerlach, Alexandr Korb, Anthony Dirk Moses, Robert Cribb, Mark Kramer, Raz Segal, and Anna Shternshis); and to the many graduate students and junior scholars who contributed to making the discussions in Toronto so lively.

Genocide

INTRODUCTION

Genocide and Mass Categorical Violence

Andrea Graziosi and Frank E. Sysyn

In the last decades of the twentieth century, the study of genocide, which had mostly focused on the Holocaust, expanded into comparative attempts that more often than not pivoted around that quintessential genocide. It subsequently exploded both historically and geographically to encompass past epochs, new continents, and new cases.[1] Thus the concept of genocide, which crystallized in the 1940s, has proven to be both intellectually productive and crucial to an understanding of the past, the present, and, unfortunately, the future.

This expanded application compounded and made more visible issues that, as the debates at the United Nations revealed, were present since the introduction of the concept. It also added new ones. In particular, tensions arose from the friction between a legal and thus basically rigid concept, and the multifaceted realities explored by research in fields such as history, anthropology, law, area studies, gender studies, and the history of ideas. Furthermore, the legal and political consequences and the benefits that accrued due to "achieving genocide status" exerted a powerful push toward discussing historical events using a simplistic "genocide or not" binary mode, a process plagued by political pressures.

These problems and tensions, as well as the evolution in the use of the genocide concept, are at the heart of the essays assembled in this volume. They come from new research in fields as varied as Holocaust and Armenian studies, Soviet and Cold War history, French legal culture, and African studies. The aim is not to propose yet another redefinition of a concept that has fully proven its worth and has come to stay. By pointing to the problems deriving from its use, we seek to contribute to a more nuanced understanding and to expand our knowledge of phenomena that – as research has shown – unfortunately form an integral part of the human experience.

In the following pages, we turn first to an examination of the context in which the concept emerged in a certain, not merely "geographical," part of Europe, and to explore tendencies in its intellectual background. We then briefly discuss how the concept of genocide, differentiated and contested since its very inception, evolved and transformed in the face of a rapidly growing body of research. This research soon pointed to both the multiplicity and variety of genocidal experiences. It also brought to the fore the challenges this variety posed to the very concept that kept these experiences together and made us understand them. Besides, powerful political pressures and legal consequences related to the genocide concept generated dangers for intellectual inquiry and even scholarly integrity. We discuss these dangers in light of our authors' contributions and conclude by providing some thoughts on the options and hypotheses for solutions they offer.

The Context: State-building, Transformative Projects, Collective Categories, Mixed Territories, and the "Genocidal Century"

Our discussion of the problems raised by the genocide concept is grounded in the study of a twentieth century that starts in Africa, with the Herero and Nama extermination, and ends with the conflicts and tragedies deriving from state-building and rebuilding activities that have recently made this continent a focal point for discussions of genocide.[2] However, most contributors to this volume focus on a twentieth-century Europe that includes the Ottoman Empire. Especially in its central, eastern, and southern parts, this "Europe" was an epicentre of war, conflict, and violence: empires clashed and collapsed; social, national/ethnic, linguistic, and religious hierarchies were radically modified; dozens of new states emerged and even more tried but did not succeed; and widely different militant groups promoted and implemented, or attempted to implement, a variety of passionate but often merciless transformative projects inspired by diverse ideological principles – national, social, racial, and ideological. The events of the century thus amply and repeatedly confirmed the inadequacy of the often disproved but as often re-proposed opposition between European and world history that had cast Europe as relatively free of such cataclysmic events.[3]

Needless to say, it would be possible to discuss the strengths and problems of the genocide concept from other perspectives, such as that offered by an examination of European expansion after the fifteenth century, which has been analyzed in genocidal terms.[4] Certainly there are solid reasons to adopt this approach – that is, to interpret the conflictual and often exterminating encounters between human populations that had been separated for long periods of time and therefore were highly differentiated, and to account for the dreams, plans, and actions of many a colonist to "replace" indigenous populations. However, this is a perspective and a context much different from the perspective and context for which Lemkin created the genocide concept. For it to be able to travel over time and place, the genocide concept would need deep restructuring in terms of time spans, actors, and the meaning of intent.

However, the European twentieth century and the African post-colonial experience allow us to address directly what Raphaël Lemkin had in mind when he conceived the genocide concept: that is, mass violence exerted over a relatively short period against groups (national/ethnic and "racial," but also social and religious) that had long coexisted. The classical loci of such incidents of mass violence targeting specific groups have been the mixed territories of a Central-Eastern Europe extending east up to the Caucasus and the borders of "ethnic" Russia, or what Lewis Namier used to call the "European Middle East."[5] At the beginning of the twentieth century, these territories also extended to the south to include much of the Balkans, Anatolia, and the actual Middle East, and reached farther east to the British Raj. They also had important western counterparts, for instance, in Ireland, Spain, and Alsace-Lorraine. It was by studying them that Ludwig Gumplowicz, Ludwig von Mises, Lewis Namier, and later Arnold Toynbee, whom Namier strongly influenced, developed the basic intellectual tools we still employ to analyze and understand the social and political dynamics of mixed territories. Not incidentally, the first three of these men were Jews born in Galicia, a salient example of such territories, and it was in Eastern Galicia's capital, Lemberg (Lviv, Lwów), that von Mises and Namier were born (the latter actually in a nearby estate), and where Lemkin studied law.[6]

European (and of course also non-European) mixed territories, such as Spain during and after the *reconquista* and the fall of the Granada Emirate, Cromwell's Ireland, and Polish Ukraine, had already provided ample evidence in earlier centuries of their potential for mass violence and "cleansings" of various kinds. These were often tied to religious discourses, but were already intertwined with ethno-linguistic identities and state-building attempts, as well as with the claims and atrocities of conquest. As the outcome of the repression and expulsion of Jews and Moriscos indicates, the mobility of the populations of mixed territories as a consequence of violence had already emerged. This mobility, however, reached its peak in the twentieth century with mass killings and "cleansings" that tragically restricted these territories' geographical scope (a scope, however, that soon started to re-expand within Europe due to migration).

This peak was reached through phenomena that were already evident in the eighteenth century and had three main contributing factors: the demographic revolution, modernization, and a massive state-building wave. The population boom that originated in the countryside "objectively" furthered (e.g., through urbanization) the homogenization of languages, populations, and religions in territories whose cities, or special sub-regions, were often inhabited by people speaking languages and holding religious beliefs different from those of the surrounding countryside. The same demographic boom also created a mass of young people who could not find their place in traditional societies and who provided the extraordinary energy that fueled subsequent social and political outbursts. Modernization swept away those societies' previous social and ethnic, but also psychological and normative, equilibria. State-building, for which France, Germany, fascist Italy, and finally the USSR provide the most successful models, was intimately tied to the first two factors. It was accompanied by an extraordinary array of ambitious, and even utopian, radical transformative projects inspired by a variety of ideologies and fed by the seemingly unlimited energy, possibilities, and expectations engendered by the demographic and economic boom, modernization, and Europe's predominance in the world.

In less than two centuries, in a process that was initiated by the American and Latin American wars of independence but which soon centred on and culminated in Europe before expanding beyond its borders, the world was reorganized along state lines: hundreds of new states of many kinds were born (including a handful of more or less disguised empires), and possibly thousands more tried to emerge, coalescing around a plurality of ideologies and ideas, whose carriers were young and aggressive elites. As Mark Levene and Michael Mann note, many of these state projects, including unsuccessful ones embodied in partisan armies, had clear ideas about the "people" whom they sought to promote and represent (peoples often identified with "nations" in the Herder-Mazzini-Stalin meaning of the term,[7] but also not infrequently conceived in social, ideological, racial, or religious terms).

Some of these elites, and not just extreme nationalists, openly theorized about the need for this however-defined people to be "pure" and created blueprints for achieving such purity, thus engendering a predisposition to and a capability for what would later be termed "genocide." As Levene and many others have stressed, this capability was often sparked into action by a state "perceiving the integrity of its agenda to be threatened by an aggregate population defined by the state as an organic collectivity, or series of collectivities" in times of war, political and geopolitical tensions, and economic crises.[8]

Nonetheless, in the most aggressive variants, which were often the most ideologically motivated, the very transformative project in whose name the state-building (or re-building) elite legitimized itself was sufficient to ignite mass collective violence even in peacetime. These projects made states more prone to resort to genocidal violence in times of tension so that it could be claimed, as Robert Melson suggested, that one of the main novelties of modern "genocides" is their connection to ideologically motivated programs.[9]

In his contribution to this volume, Scott Straus stresses the role of narratives that inspire such transformative projects, while Ron Suny raises the problem of the ties of such projects to totalitarianism, a concept at least as contested as that of genocide. Discussion of totalitarianism directs our attention to the new kind of state (totalitarian/authoritarian) that emerged from the First World War, the centrality of which is stressed by Michelle Tusan. Douglas Irvin-Erickson turns our attention to the crucial role that Johan Galtung assigns to "cultural violence" in making "direct and structural violence look and feel right" by legitimizing it for a supposed superior good.

Ideas and ideologies, therefore, did count, and nationalism, socialism, and especially their hybrids (which found an ideal breeding ground in mixed territories, where social and national liberations often appeared to coincide) were the main motors of these "transformative" genocides. One of their most striking features is the pretended rationality, the paranoiac but apparently impeccable logic by which the elimination of this or that group (that is, the building, un-building, or re-building of peoples and societies) is justified, often springing from classifications improperly borrowed from the social sciences that analyze societies on the basis of their disaggregation in collective groups of various kinds.

Obviously, there were other important factors in play as well. In his work, Christian Gerlach has rightly questioned the one-sided emphasis on grand intellectual discourses and action from above, pointing to the role of agency from below, while in his essay in this volume Suny looks at the role of emotional disposition, the pathological construction of the enemy, and a delusional rationality in the decision to adhere to this or that ideology.[10]

If we look at the state- (and empire-) building wave unleashed in Europe by the French Revolution and the Napoleonic wars, clear geographical and chronological epicentres appear, most but not all accompanied by clearly marked waves of violence targeting specific groups. They arose in the Balkans starting with Greece, in the Italian peninsula, and in the German or German-dominated lands, in nineteenth-century Ireland, and then again in the Balkans and in Central and Eastern Europe, as well as in the Russian and Russian-dominated areas, in the formerly Ottoman ones, in Ireland after the First World War, in civil war Spain, and in a large part of the continent during the Second World War. The crests of these waves are found in the 1820s, 1848–49, 1859–61, 1870–71, 1878, and the periods 1912–23 and 1938–49, followed by the post-1989–91 recrudescence in the former Yugoslav and Soviet territories.

State-building then peaked via decolonization in the former colonial empires, and is today at its most active in sub-Saharan Africa, which is also undergoing a demographic boom and a speedy modernization process. Because of the much longer history of human settlement in Africa and therefore of the much denser proximity of human populations, state-building there lost some of its typical European features such as the fixation on a unique "ethnic" or linguistic core. These features might instead be revived in South Asia, should Hindu nationalism precipitate a new fragmentation along lines anticipated by India's linguistic states in what remains of the old British Raj, which had already fractured in the 1947 partition, and then again in 1971 with the birth of Bangladesh.

Europe and the European experience, given their initial centrality in this state- (and empire-) building with mass-violence activity, were the cradle of the genocide concept. We know that Johann Gottfried Herder spoke of "killers of peoples and murderers of nations,"[11] and as Irvin-Erickson has noted, Gracchus Babeuf (one the founders of modern socialism, to whom the Bolsheviks erected monuments soon after the revolution), used the term *nationicides* in 1794 to condemn the actions of Jean-Baptiste Carrier, the Jacobin sent to Nantes to quell the peasant uprising in the Vandée.[12]

Soon afterward, German anti-French nationalists such as Ernst Moritz Arndt claimed that Germany needed "a military tyrant who is capable of exterminating whole nations." And in 1848–49, while the Hungarians and Serbs sought to eliminate each other from the Banat (the beginning of a bloody trail that involved other nationalities and continued until the end of the twentieth century), even Karl Marx and Friedrich Engels wished for the extermination of "counter-revolutionary nations" (not classes) through the "terroristic" elimination of their elites, the elimination of their geographic names and languages, and the absorption of their "demographic masses" into the revolutionary nations – that is, Germany, Poland, and Hungary.[13]

A few decades later, in an interesting reversal, socialists decried the Russian Empire's nationality policies as *völkermordende*, a term Otto Bauer also used in his innovative work on the national question, and as Irvin-Erickson remarks, *Völkermord* appeared "in reports about the German colonial war against the Herero and Nama peoples and to describe the Ottoman campaign against the Armenians."[14]

Lemkin's intellectual discovery, precipitated by the cruel racial policies driving the last German imperial offensive in the East, was thus a systematization of previous thinking. Worth noting is the role his borrowings from Bauer played in perfecting the concept and in informing his reflections on the Armenian tragedy and the mass violence targeting specific groups in Europe and the Middle East in the 1920s and 1930s. Lemkin, however, did much more: by formalizing and giving a classical name to already-observed practices, he also conceptualized them. Moreover, precisely because of its evolution and oscillations, his concept of genocide was on the whole much richer than the legal formulation of 1948. In *Axis Rule*, for instance, Lemkin directly tied repression and extermination practices to the Nazi transformative political project and its "narratives," and he also later linked the Holodomor in Ukraine to Soviet ones,[15] thus establishing a direct connection between genocides and transformative ideologies, a connection that has often since been underestimated.

In the 1990s, after some decades in which genocide studies proceeded haltingly and were mostly focused on the Holocaust and the Armenian case, events in Yugoslavia and Rwanda, as well as the breaking down of the Cold War ideological framework, caused a veritable explosion of new research that proved the vitality and fertility of Lemkin's creation. Our knowledge of "genocides" grew by leaps and bounds: scores if not hundreds of group-based mass liquidations, cleansings, forced assimilations, and various kinds of "distortions" of human groups – inspired by a plethora of ideas, parties, ideologies pure and hybridized (e.g., national socialist), religions, and state and imperial projects – were discovered the world over, in war and in peacetime. This raised a classification problem and implicitly challenged the traditional sense and meaning of the concept, both the legal one enshrined in the UN definition and also the more subtle and elastic one that can be derived from Lemkin's own evolution. Soviet history is a case in point, but similar conclusions could be derived by other experiences. As one of our authors, Norman Naimark, has observed, the period from 1929 to 1953 (although Moshe Lewin has argued that the Russian civil war also presented evident "genocidal" features) hides a number of mass group "liquidations" of an extremely differentiated character, intensity, and scale, that can be interpreted in terms of the genocide category.[16]

In fact, each of these liquidations was inspired by a coherent ideology even if the ideology could abruptly change or more slowly morph,[17] and in fact these ideologies often ended up producing chaos and numerous unintended results. The methods varied greatly, and often important variations took place even within the same group of events, as one of us argues in the chapter on Soviet famines, comparing the brutal logic behind the Kazakh tragedy to the sophisticated reasoning that inspired Stalin's attempt to "unmake" and distort Ukrainian nation-building.

A "category-based" reading of society inspired all of these different liquidations, which at least formally always targeted specific ethnic or social groups: kulaks, peasants and nomads of various nationalities, ethnic Germans, Chechens, Orthodox priests, former members of the socialist-revolutionary party, "criminals" sentenced to more than three years, abandoned children, and so on. In fact, reading the lists of the categories targeted for repression in the secret *prikazy* that classified the urban population in 1933 or in those that opened and motivated the Great Terror of 1937–38 is an extraordinary voyage of discovery of an "intelligent," logical, and homicidal paranoia, as well as confirmation of Lemkin's intuition about the importance and power of "group-thinking" in the making of genocide.[18]

Genocide's Challenges and Problems

The variety, the many hybridized forms, and the continuous transformations (which can be found in the Soviet case as well as in the Ottoman/Turkish, Central-Eastern European, and African ones) raise serious problems for, and present as many interesting challenges to, a legal and ethical-political category such as genocide. This is so because legal categories, even if subjected to interpretation, tend to have relatively stable, almost fixed meanings. A similar rigidity is inherent in ethical-political judgements of the black-and-white, this-or-the-other-side-of-the-barricade type, which is the kind of judgement that the genocide category nearly always carries with it. This stability was strengthened by Lemkin's choice of the Greek root *genos*, dictated by his desire to give his concept a scientific, respectable appearance, but possibly also by his earlier education as a Herderian-Mazzinian nationalist.[19] The realities we have been discovering and the need to understand them instead call, and strongly so, for elasticity and nuance. They encourage concepts capable of subsuming and accounting for such diversity, and at the same time of capturing the general nature of these realities. The difficulties and challenges are implicit in the very category Lemkin created, whose meaning, which evolved over time, is subtler than the one that crystallized in 1948. Even Lemkin's category is nonetheless destabilized by ambiguities and inner contradictions that may point to solutions to the problems we face.

There is, first, the ambiguity of the term *genos*. The Greeks used it to describe a social group claiming a common descent, and certainly a "nationalist" century like the twentieth, with its passion for peoples and peoples' rights (self-determination first and foremost) pushed for reading *genos* as, precisely, "people." Lemkin at first intended it this way, possibly as a consequence of his Zionist education. As Irvin-Erickson reminds us in his essay, Lemkin originally conceived the concept of the *genos* "as an enlarged family unit having the conscience of a common ancestor – first real, *later imagined*."[20] However, this final specification, in line with Max Weber's intuition[21] that predates the 1980s' "subjectivist" turn, makes clear that the groups Lemkin termed as *genos* could also be culturally and politically "construed" entities, that is, by-products of human history rather than blood communities.

Possibly in part as a response to the narrowing influence exerted by the process of United Nations approval and by the legal quality it had to assume, Lemkin's concept moved away from the initial more circumscribed "ethnic" Greek *genos* and grew closer to the much wider sense of the Sanskrit *gana* ("flock, troop, multitude, number, tribe, series or class" – but also "any assemblage or association of human beings formed for the attainment of the same aims"). His "nations" thus became "families of minds," that is, human groups united by and sharing the same culture, and genocide could in theory mean the suppression of any human group intended as and feeling itself to be such, and not solely the national, ethnic, racial, and religious groups included in the United Nations' definition. The horizon of a concept that was born to defend natural, or supposedly natural, entities thus came to include, at least potentially, the suppression of any more or less stable social aggregate of individual preferences and choices, *implicitly morphing into a tool of radical criticism of any category-based mass violence.*

Problems also derive from the political strictures imposed upon the genocide category in its formalization at the United Nations, which shaped its final form and gave it the relative rigidity typical of juridical norms. The approval of the Genocide Convention itself was little short of miraculous: the defeated powers had committed terrible crimes, but the victors had just sanctioned at Potsdam the mass expulsion of millions of Germans from Central-Eastern Europe, and many victorious or neutral countries had an interest in hiding parts of their pasts, not to mention the European imperial powers' actions in the colonies, Soviet "liquidations," or the United States' Jim Crow laws and Indian deportations. To succeed, Lemkin thus embarked on an extraordinary sales campaign that, as Irvin-Erickson notes, forced him "to redefine genocide to accommodate the interests of member states who did not want to enact a broad humanitarian law that could interfere with their past or their interests." In the words of Anton Weiss-Wendt, who studied the confidential reports each power drafted in connection to its ratification, the draft convention "became a pawn in the ideological struggle between the two superpowers." The genocide category, therefore, was a "casualty of the Cold War" as well as of decolonization, which is to say, of political contingency: "No surprise, then, that the Genocide Convention proved so difficult to apply: it was meant to be a dead letter."[22]

As Weiss-Wendt notes, the United States sought to exclude provisions applicable to past and present abuses committed by the drafting nations. The United Kingdom circulated the draft among colonial governors to check for problems that could emerge from it. Even more interestingly, the Soviet Union, and Stalin personally, followed each step with great attention, but also a few contradictions. All references to *social* groups were eliminated from the initial draft (which had included a definition of physical destruction that applied to dekulakization), but Molotov approved including *political* groups, which Stalin had eliminated from the draft. Eventually the Soviet delegation was instructed not to make an issue of the inclusion of political groups (possibly in part because the Nuremberg court had already admitted political, but not social, considerations), so that eventually it was Lemkin himself, under pressure from the United States, who struck political groups from the text.

As surprising is the discovery that the Soviets also approved extending genocide to include the destruction of groups "in whole or in part," greatly enhancing the potential use of the convention against their own policies. Stalin instead confirmed the basically Mazzinian approach to the national question that, by banalizing Bauer, he had adopted with Lenin's approval in 1913: he insisted upon the connection between genocide and "Fascism/*Nazism* and *analogous racist* 'theories' that preach *racial and ethnic hatred*," and he expanded "*cultural genocide*" to "*ethno*-cultural genocide."[23]

In her essay, Caroline Fournet stresses the limitations deriving from the cultural and legal traditions and the national interests of specific countries such as France, the peculiarity of whose approach is indeed striking.

One of the first countries to sign the convention, France did not incorporate genocide into its own legislation until 1994, a perfect instance of the victors-versus-vanquished factor in the making and implementation of the genocide concept, as well as of its ambiguities and problems. Before that year, for instance, in the famous Barbie trial, French courts had recognized as crimes against humanity only those committed "in the name of a state practising a policy of ideological supremacy." In other words, as Fournet writes, they "turned what was merely a jurisdictional limitation at Nuremberg into a definitional requirement of crimes against humanity, unduly linking the latter to a particular state policy: Nazism. Practically speaking, there could be no crimes against humanity outside the very specific context of the Second World War." French home and colonial practices, from Vichy to Algeria, were thus sanitized.[24]

When, finally, genocide was transposed into French legislation, it was by introducing a number of significant changes that pointed to some of the problems in the original UN formulation while also complicating the international scenario. The enforcement of a concerted plan, for instance, was substituted for "intent," and groups "*determined by any other arbitrary criterion*" were added to the "national, ethnic, racial or religious" ones contemplated in the 1948 convention.

Given the growing variety of events that can be justifiably ascribed to the "genocide" category that researchers have been exploring, most of our authors support the need for an extension of the category. In fact, as Michelle Tusan underlines, the very way in which historians and social scientists, if not jurists, think about genocide is changing. If some fear that too widespread an application endangers the concept's analytical and legal powers, others are convinced that the expansion of our knowledge requires it, as students of colonialism have repeatedly asserted. A strong signal in the latter direction comes also from the French 1994 law, on the basis of which the liquidation of both social groups (such as in Stalinist dekulakization) and political groups (as in the 1965 Indonesian Communist massacre) would be considered genocide.

The term could and should also include the broadening of the means by which genocides are perpetrated, as well as expanding the typology of their victims (the two being of course closely related). Annette Timm makes a very strong case for expanding the category to include sexual violence. We know that during the Armenian genocide and in the former Yugoslavia of the 1990s, mass rape reached extraordinary, and most probably intentional and therefore political, dimensions. In fact, since that decade, sexual violence has been formally included in the list of crimes against humanity. Timm goes further and shows what we miss by "forgetting" to address sexual violence in the Holocaust, namely a crucial "part of the experience of survivors." She also points to the distortions that derive from this omission, such as the amazing wave in the 1960s and 1970s of pornographization of Nazi sexual practices.[25] On the basis of the study of the Kazakh tragedy and of the Holodomor, we support the inclusion of mass, willed starvation both among the crimes against humanity (where it now figures but indirectly) and in genocidal practices, a stance for which Alex de Waal recently made a powerful case.[26]

Gerlach's questioning of the role of grand discourses and action from above can be seen as an invitation to expand genocide studies to embrace a from-below approach that would include both victims and perpetrators. This valuable and appropriate claim does not seem to require, however, an abandonment of from-above perspectives, given that ideas and ideologies, grand transformative projects, and leaders grand and small have played crucial roles. Tusan proposes as a remedy the expansion of the concept "in favor of more elastic legal, economic and political conceptualizations." She suggests in particular that we put at the centre of genocide research lived experience taken in a *longue durée* perspective that encompasses how genocide is experienced/suffered after the event. This is for her also the way "to address the vexing question of comparative genocide," which would thus be given firmer foundations.[27]

Problems also arise from the opposite direction, that is, from the legal aspect of the category and the concomitant impact of trials, reparations, and the moral and ideological supremacy afforded by the recognition of genocide. Of course, this legal core is the source of much of the power and attraction of the category, exerting its influence in at least two worrying directions. On the one hand, it pushes the scientific debate onto the already-mentioned binary path – "is it genocide or not" – thus intellectually impoverishing and at the same time politically animating that very debate, while greatly simplifying and even banalizing and distorting research (a yes-or-no alternative is not, as a rule, a proper or fruitful historical approach). In addition, as Suny has noted, too great a focus on legal aspects tends to cast history as a morality play with a simplistic Manichean structure and predetermined fixed roles, which history of course is not.

Tusan contends that "a too-sharp focus on the anatomy of genocide – what qualifies and what does not, who is to blame for committing the act or failing to prosecute it – risks pushing scholarship into a corner by positing the study of genocide as a moral and political act." Straus points to another possible negative consequence. If, he asks, "among scholars of genocide, a dominant question often boils down to: 'Is it genocide or not?,'" isn't it possible, nay, probable, that "such a focus can perhaps unwittingly reinforce the idea that other forms of mass violence do not deserve similar kinds of recognition and scholarly intention, and that in turn dovetails with how histories of violence get told?" Besides, as Mark Kramer stated at the conference, one has also to consider the potential for conscious manipulation of the genocide category by political actors interested in either winning the favour of international public opinion, international organizations, non-governmental organizations, and Western powers, or silencing voices within or beyond their communities.[28]

According to Straus, recent Rwandan and Burundi history makes an interesting and compelling case for the limitations and dangers of the genocide category that implicitly extends to transitional justice and to the ideology that transitional justice risks producing. For instance, the Rwandan case is "told through the eyes of two main historical actors, the 'bad' Hutus and the 'good' Tutsi victims," reinforcing "stereotypes [as well as] the idea that ethnic groups act uniformly." This sort of narrative can be used to defend and maintain rigid structures of subordination in which a given group is doomed to remain "inferior" by the collective guilt imposed upon it. Moreover, the absolute centrality of genocide makes "marginal or even invisible other forms of mass violence," so much so that "to speak of related non-genocide crimes is tantamount to denialism," and "other crimes become justifiable in the name of stopping genocide or preventing new ones." The very power of the concept and the focus on establishing what is and is not genocide risks obfuscating everything else, including other instances of violence, and impoverishes the intellectual debate, as some discussions of, for example, Ukrainian and Israeli history confirm.

A Path Forward

Scholars, and especially historians, are thus called to wrestle with the problems raised by the genocide category, as well as "with some of the intended (and unintended) consequences of the work that the label does," to use Straus's words. Other options are of course available. One is to restrict the term's use to a very limited group of cases, the Holocaust first and foremost. Suny, for instance, proposes this approach, albeit in a qualified way. Contrary to Naimark, who labels as genocide most cases of intended mass liquidation of specific groups in the Soviet experience, Suny believes that "analysts ought to refrain from collapsing all forms of mass violence into a single type, usually titled genocide, a term that regrettably has been stretched to cover quite distinct forms of crimes against humanity." For him, "genocide and genocidal are distinct," and while "the adjective can certainly be used to describe acts of mass killing that do not strictly meet the conventional definition," the use of the term genocide to cover too wide a terrain is untenable also because "blurring categories makes it impossible to explain." However, since the supporters of this approach reject the tenet according to which only the Holocaust qualifies as genocide, the problem remains that research and scientific debate will be forced back to the binary question – is it genocide or not – that Suny himself is unhappy with, and for good reason.

A perhaps more satisfactory way to address these issues without losing sight of justifiable concerns is to follow Straus in his search for a concept better able to account for what we have been discovering in non-colonial and postcolonial societies, and to do so without renouncing the advantages of the genocide category or the accomplishments of its creator. Perhaps this can be done by going back, on the one hand, to the Lemkin who recognized the basic affinity and the equal worth of all human groups intended as and feeling themselves to be such. We would need to abandon the ethnic Herder-Mazzini-Stalin conception behind the initial *genos* option and the 1948 UN convention, as well as the naturalistic ideas of "nation" and "nationalism" that historians radically criticized in the 1980s, and which Bauer and Weber disproved more than one hundred years ago. On the other hand, we must acknowledge the strict and impressive relationship that modern state-building (including state-building attempts) has with the idea of building (and re-building, or un-building in critical moments) "peoples" by using certain groups and targeting others on the basis of more or less well-developed and apparently rational ideas and projects.

One could thus start from a category capable of encompassing all the cases of willed, mass liquidation of groups, stressing its link with ideas, ideologies, and transformative narratives and projects. Straus's "Mass Categorical Violence" (MCV) seems from this perspective a good choice precisely because it recognizes both the mass nature of the violence and its categorical and thus intended and willed nature. Clearly, we have also to acknowledge the connection between the resort to MCV and times of crisis: wars first and foremost, but also the periods in which a state, or simply a mobilized group, feels its existence and projects to be in danger, creating the conditions for emotional dispositions and delusional behaviours born out of fear (this being, perhaps, a basic human reaction that accounts for the importance of scapegoating in history). The role of crises and of objective tensions, however, must not obscure the existence and relevance of particularly aggressive narratives that promote specific transformative projects capable of mobilizing sections of the population for mass, categorical violence in times of peace.

Another crucial factor is the categorization of a population into groups endowed with collective responsibility for atrocities – that is, the abandonment of the principle that such responsibility can only be individual. Clearly, while the vulgarization of scientific thinking bears some responsibility, it seems that "collective" scapegoating is somehow embedded in human nature, especially but not solely in times of crisis (when it is all the more dangerous). Such vulgarization, a product of the eighteenth and nineteenth centuries, is behind many different beliefs that, by promoting or eliminating this or that national, racial, social, or religious group, it is possible to attain a better, superior, or safer society. Building and un-building (or making and un-making) are therefore always to be considered together, and MCV can be directed in both directions. Unfortunately, it must also be noted that results seemed to point to the "efficacy" of such beliefs: countless national (of the Herder-Mazzini-Stalin variety) and/or socialist states were built by manipulating and/or removing groups. The dramatic failures and general impoverishment brought about by such criminal attempts have become evident only in the long run.

If MCV is a more useful category for understanding and explaining the past two centuries, we must acknowledge that not all cases of MCV are equal in scale. We can reserve a special place for the extermination of significant proportions of large groups over a limited amount of time, be they social, national, or religious groups. The term genocide would be reserved for this subcategory of MCV, such as the Armenian genocide, the Ukrainian Holodomor, and the Kazakh genocide. The pinnacle of the category would be found in the intended *total* liquidation of a specific population, as is of course the case of the Holocaust, which could thus be seen (at least today and one hopes forever) as the peak of the MCV class and of its genocide subcategory – but at the same time, because of its extraordinary absolute features, as constituting a category of its own. The adoption of the MCV category might thereby allow us to transcend the unfortunate but understandable separation between Holocaust and genocide studies.

NOTES

1 It is enough to look at the diversity of the materials published in the field's main journals, *Holocaust and Genocide Studies* (1986); *Genocide Studies and Prevention* (1994); and the *Journal of Genocide Research* (1999); or at the encyclopedias edited over the past few years, both online, like Jacques Sémelin's *Encyclopédie en ligne des violences de masse* (2008), now *Violence de masse et Résistance – Réseau de recherche* (https://www.sciencespo.fr/mass-violence-war-massacre-resistance), and in print, like Israel W. Charnyi's *Encyclopedia of Genocide* (2000), Donald Bloxham's and Anthony Dirk Moses's *The Oxford Handbook of Genocide Studies* (2010), and Jens Meierhenrich's *Genocide: A Reader* (2014).

2 Jürgen Zimmerer, *Deutsche Herrschaft über Afrikaner* (Munster: Lit, 2002); Jeremy Sarkin, *Germany's Genocide of the Herero* (Cape Town: UCT Press, 2011), in itself a good illustration of the pressure arising from the genocide concept. Alex de Waal, ed., *Evil Days: Thirty Years of War and Famine in Ethiopia* (New York: Human Rights Watch, 1991), and Scott Straus, *Making and Unmaking Nations: War, Leadership, and Genocide in Modern Africa* (Ithaca, NY: Cornell University Press, 2015), are excellent studies of the conflicts arising out of state-building in Africa after decolonization.

3 Andrea Graziosi, "Il mondo in Europa. Namier e il 'Medio oriente europeo', 1815–1948," *Contemporanea* 10, no. 2 (2007): 193–228.

4 See for instance Anthony Dirk Moses, ed., *Empire, Colony, Genocide: Conquest, Occupation, and Subaltern Resistance in World History* (New York: Berghahn, 2008).

5 Lewis B. Namier, "From Vienna to Versailles," in *Conflicts: Studies in Contemporary History*, (London: MacMillan, 1942), 1–19. In interpreting the history of these regions, many important books have stressed their mixed nature and their crucial role in a twentieth-century European history that has expanded beyond much of its traditional "Western" outlook. Among them are Mark Mazower's *Dark Continent* (New York: A.A. Knopf, 1998) and *Salonica* (New York: A.A. Knopf, 2004); Andrea Graziosi, *Guerra e rivoluzione in Europa, 1905–1956* (Bologna: Il Mulino, 2001); Norman Davies's *Microcosm*, on Breslau-Wrocław (London: Jonathan Cape, 2002); Timothy Snyder's *Bloodlands* (New York: Basic Books, 2010); Omer Bartov's and Eric Weitz's *Shatterzone of Empires* (Bloomington: Indiana University Press, 2013); Mark Levene's *The European Rimlands* (Oxford: Oxford University Press, 2013), and Alfred J. Rieber's *The Struggle for the Eurasian Borderlands* (New York: Cambridge University Press, 2014).

6 Ludwig Gumplowicz, *Das Recht der Nationalitäten und Sprachen in*

Österreich-Ungarn (Innsbruck: Wagner, 1879); *Der Rassenkampf, soziologische Untersuchungen* (Innsbruck: Wagner, 1883); and *Outlines of Sociology* (New Brunswick, NJ: Transaction Books, [1885] 1980) (with an interesting introduction by Irving Louis Horowitz); Ludwig von Mises, *Nation, State, and Economy: Contributions to the Politics and History of Our Time* (New York: New York University Press, [1919] 1983); Namier, *Conflicts*; Arnold Toynbee, *The Treatment of Armenians in the Ottoman Empire* (London: Hodder and Stoughton, 1916); Andrea Graziosi, "Viewing the Twentieth Century through the Prism of Ukraine: Reflections on the Heuristic Potential of Ukrainian History," in *The Future of the Past: New Perspectives on Ukrainian History*, edited by Serhii Plokhii, 97–118 (Cambridge, MA: Harvard University Press for HURI, 2016).

7 Andrea Graziosi, "Communism, Nations, and Nationalism," in *The Cambridge History of Communism*, vol. 1, edited by Silvio Pons and Stephen Smith, 449–74 (Cambridge: Cambridge University Press, 2017). Here as elsewhere in this introduction, Mazzini was read through the deforming lenses of Pasquale Stanislao Mancini's *Della nazionalità come fondamento del diritto delle genti* (1851).

8 Mark Levene, *Genocide in the Age of the Nation State*, vol. 1 (London: I.B. Tauris, 2005), 35; Michael Mann, *The Dark Side of Democracy: Explaining Ethnic Cleansing* (New York: Cambridge University Press, 2005).

9 Robert Melson, *Revolution and Genocide: On the Origins of the Armenian Genocide and the Holocaust* (Chicago: University of Chicago Press, 1992).

10 Christian Gerlach, *Extremely Violent Societies: Mass Violence in the Twentieth Century* (Cambridge: Cambridge University Press, 2010), and oral comments at the conference "Genocide in Twentieth-Century History: The Power and the Problems of an Interpretive, Ethical-Political, and Legal Concept," University of Toronto, October 2018. See also Ronald G. Suny's essay in this volume and his *"They Can Live in the Desert but Nowhere Else:" A History of the Armenian Genocide* (Princeton: Princeton University Press, 2015).

11 Hans Kohn, *The Idea of Nationalism: A Study in Its Origins and Background* (New York: MacMillan, [1944] 1967), 436.

12 Gracchus Babeuf, *Du Système de Dépopulation ou la Vie et les Crimes de Carrier* (Paris: Franklin, 1794), 84.

13 Hans Kohn, *The Mind of Germany: The Education of a Nation* (New York: Scribner's, 1960), 278; István Deák, *The Lawful Revolution: Louis Kossuth and the Hungarians, 1848–1849* (New York: Columbia University Press, 1979), 140–1; Roman Rosdolky, *Engels and the 'Non-historic' Peoples: The National Question in the Revolution of 1848* (Glasgow: Critique, [1948] 1987), 123, 156.

14 Otto Bauer, *Die Nationalitätenfrage und die Sozialdemokratie* (Wien: Verlag der Wiener Volksbuchhandlung, 1907).

15 Raphael Lemkin, "Soviet Genocide in Ukraine," *Journal of International Criminal Justice* 7, no. 1 ([1953?] 2009): 123–30.

16 On Naimark's understanding of the role of genocides in Soviet history, see "Reappraising Mass Terror, Repression, and Responsibility in Stalin's Regime: Perspectives on Norman Naimark's *Stalin's Genocides*," *Journal of Cold War Studies* 14, no. 3 (2012): 149–89.

17 Terry Martin, in "The Origins of Soviet Ethnic Cleansing," *Journal of Modern History* 70, no. 4 (1998): 813–61, was among the first to call attention to the sliding from social to "ethnic" factors in Soviet repressions; Eric D. Weitz, "Racial Politics without the Concept of Race: Reevaluating Soviet Ethnic and National Purges," *Slavic Review* 61, no. 1 (2002): 1–65.

18 A translation of the two key *prikazy* (nos. 00447 and 00485) regulating the Great Terror can be found in an appendix to Oleg Chlevnjuk, Andrea Graziosi, Terry Martin, "Il Grande terrore," *Storica*, 18 (2000): 7–61. See also Nicolas Werth, "Les crimes de masse sous Staline (1930–1953)," *Violence de masse et* Résistance – Réseau de recherche, accessed 25 August 2020, https://www.sciencespo.fr/mass-violence-war-massacre-resistance/fr/document/les-crimes-de-masse-sous-staline-1930-1953. It is worth noting that, as its very title suggests, *Genocide in the USSR. Studies in Group Destruction*, a 1958 publication of the Munich-based Institute for the Study of the USSR, clearly presented the phenomenon in its totality, anticipating much later discoveries.

19 James Loeffler, "Becoming Cleopatra: The Forgotten Zionism of Raphael Lemkin," *Journal of Genocide Research* 19, no. 3 (2017): 340–60 (our italics).

20 Raphael Lemkin, *Totally Unofficial: The Autobiography of Raphael Lemkin*, edited by Donna-Lee Frieze (New Haven, CT: Yale University Press, 2013), 181–2; Douglas Irvin-Erickson, *Raphaël Lemkin and the Concept of Genocide* (Philadelphia: University of Pennsylvania Press, 2017).

21 Max Weber, "Ethnic Groups," *Economy and Society*, vol. 1 (Berkeley: University of California Press, [1922] 1978).

22 Besides his essay in this volume, see also Anton Weiss-Wendt, *The Soviet Union and the Gutting of the UN Genocide Convention* (Madison: University of Wisconsin Press, 2017) and *Documents on the Genocide Convention from the American, British and Russian Archives*, 2 vols. (London: Bloomsbury, 2019).

23 See Weiss-Wendt in this volume.

24 Besides the essay in this volume, see also Caroline Fournet, *Genocide and Crimes against Humanity: Misconceptions and Confusion in French Law and Practice* (Oxford: Hart Publishing, 2013).

25 See also Annette Timm, *Holocaust History and the Readings of Ka-Tzetnik* (London: Bloomsbury, 2018).

26 Alex de Waal, *Mass Starvation: The History and Future of Famine* (Cambridge: Polity Press, 2018).

27 See also Michelle Tusan, *Smyrna's Ashes: Humanitarianism, Genocide, and the Birth of the Middle East* (Berkeley: University of California Press, 2012) and *The British Empire and the Armenian Genocide: Humanitarianism and Imperial Politics from Gladstone to Churchill* (London: I.B. Tauris, 2017).

28 Oral comments, "Genocide in Twentieth Century History" conference, University of Toronto, 2018.

1

Somebody Else's Crime: The Drafting of the Genocide Convention as a Cold War Battle, 1946–48

Anton Weiss-Wendt

Introduction

A few days after the UN General Assembly had adopted the Genocide Convention, the *New York Home News Magazine* summed up the negotiation process that had preceded it as follows: "the US was indifferent; the Russians said no; British – Never!"[1] Having gone through American, Russian, and British archives, I can attest that the perception so vividly captured by a journalist in December of 1948 is quite accurate. None of the Great Powers sought a genocide treaty. Reconciled with the idea that there would be one, they came to adopt different argumentation and different strategies for how to go about it.

The United Nations Convention on the Prevention and Punishment of the Crime of Genocide was born out of a collective effort to defeat Hitler's Germany. Adopted on 9 December 1948, it was supposed to usher humanity into a better future, forestalling horrors such as those inflicted by the Nazis. The former Allies attempted to replicate their joint efforts on the battlefield in a new world organization. In reality, the United Nations effectively became a battleground for the emerging superpowers, the United States and the Soviet Union. The UN member states that participated in drafting the Genocide Convention in 1946–48 had divergent interests, which informed their respective positions. That holds particularly true for the wartime Allies: the United States, the United Kingdom, and the Soviet Union. These three countries affectively shaped the United Nations as we know it. They had a decisive say on the UN agenda and all the decisions that had followed from it.

The Genocide Convention proved a casualty of the Cold War – one of many. The ideological confrontation between the Communist bloc and the West resonates in the convention's wording. For each negotiating party – and that goes beyond the Great Powers – the issue at stake was ensuing that their own wrongdoings, some of them recent or even ongoing, would not be covered by the incipient international treaty. Consequently, the UN Genocide Convention has broad political ramifications. No surprise, then, that the Genocide Convention proved so difficult to apply: it was meant to be a dead letter.

The Genocide Convention may still be accurately described as Raphaël Lemkin's brainchild.[2] Nevertheless, the treaty that emerged from the nascent United Nations breathes realpolitik. In effect, it is a reflection of an emerging status quo in world politics, a manifestation of the balance of power theory in international relations. To rephrase a popular saying, you do not want to know how politics get made. The evidence that emerges from the archives does indeed offer a distressing reading, which emphasizes a utilitarian approach to humanitarian law by national governments.

This chapter seeks to explain *why* specific arguments were advanced by the Soviet Union, the United States, and the United Kingdom in negotiating the provisions of the UN Genocide Convention. The Great Powers chose separate paths to, and different timetables regarding, the UN Genocide Convention. The United States signed the convention immediately after it had been adopted by the United Nations, but did not formally ratify it until November 1988. The United Kingdom did not sign the convention and for several decades refused to accede to it, until January 1970. The Soviet Union signed the genocide treaty in 1949 and ratified it, with reservations, in May 1954. I will start my analysis in reverse order, beginning with the Soviet perspective on the crime of genocide.

The Soviet Perspective: Delay, Subvert, and Exploit

For the first time, Lemkin pitched his concept of genocide directly to the United Nations in late spring 1946.[3] Back from Europe in late October, he approached the sixteen members of the UN Preparatory Commission one by one about putting genocide on the agenda. In so doing, he faced opposition from the representatives of the Great Powers, including Sir Hartley Shawcross and Andrei Gromyko. Despite the general lack of interest in Lemkin's proposal, it was eventually voted in, unanimously as a matter of fact.

Moscow's decision to go along reflected a general trend in Soviet policymaking in 1945–46, namely avoiding giving the impression that the USSR was not interested in the swift implementation of the Preparatory Commission's mandate. The Soviet delegation was expected to go with the flow on minor issues but bargain hard on matters of substance.[4] In short, as of late 1946 the Soviets did not identify a prospective genocide treaty as a matter of concern. The Soviet commentary on UN resolution 96(I) betrayed no emotion. A memorandum on the origin and meaning of the word *genocide* prepared in March 1947 by Foreign Ministry official Sergei Vinogradov simply reported on the progress to date. Upon Molotov's request, the Foreign Ministry had prepared a list of Soviet laws relevant to the prosecution of genocide. Ironically, the infamous Paragraph 58 of the Russian Penal Code (so-called counterrevolutionary crimes) was all the Soviet Union could relate to international criminal law at this point in time.[5]

A series of political setbacks in the first half of 1947 made the Soviet Union reconsider its foreign doctrine. If there is any single precipitating factor in the Soviet declaration of the Cold War, Geoffrey Roberts has argued, it ought to be the launch of the Marshall Plan on 5 June and its subsequent rejection by Stalin.[6] A US diplomat saw indications that the Soviet Union might not only urge unnecessarily detailed consideration of the so-called Secretariat draft – which was released later that month – but also stall the whole process.[7] And that is exactly what happened.

The Secretariat draft had adopted the widest possible formula, which formed a basis for further discussion. Central to the Secretariat draft, and hence most contentious, was article I. The article defined genocide as intentional destruction or prevention of development of racial, national, linguistic, religious, and political groups. Physical destruction was delineated as follows:

> Causing the death of members of a group or injuring their health or physical integrity by [any of the following]: (a) group massacres or individual executions; (b) subjection to conditions of life which, by lack of proper housing, clothing, food, hygiene and medical care, or excessive work or physical exertion are likely to result in the debilitation or death of the individuals; (c) mutilation and biological experiments imposed for other than curative purposes; (d) deprivation of all means of livelihood, by confiscation of property, looting, curtailment of work, denial of housing and of supplies otherwise available to the other inhabitants of the territory concerned.[8]

The Soviet Union was not at all pleased with the Secretariat draft. It was not just the content that the Soviets disliked; they abhorred a situation in which they could not exercise direct control. Without veto power, they felt vulnerable. On 1 October the Soviet delegation suggested suspending the discussion on the draft Genocide Convention until after the UN member states had a chance to submit their comments. A few weeks later, the USSR filed a question as to whether a separate convention on genocide was necessary at all. Still better, the Soviet draft resolution of 20 November proposed codifying genocide alongside the Nuremberg Principles.[9] A Soviet delegate advanced a contentious appeal. "We know what genocide is," he said in reference to the Soviet experience of Nazi occupation.[10]

In a dramatic twist, on 19 November 1947 the Ukrainian Congress Committee of America passed a resolution calling upon the General Assembly to investigate "genocide" in western Ukraine.[11] Whether coordinated or not, three days later representatives of the former Baltic governments appealed to the United Nations to investigate genocide allegedly committed by the Soviet Union against their respective nations. The provisions of the Genocide Convention had not yet been agreed upon, but already the Soviet Union felt the brunt of them. The most ominous appeared to be the connection made between anti-Soviet insurgence and charges of genocide.[12] Would that imply that by hunting down and killing members of the resistance, the Soviet Union placed its head under the blade of international law? An editorial in the *New York Times* of 16 February 1948 appeared to indirectly suggest just that.[13] From the Soviet viewpoint, this whole episode might have enforced only one conclusion: to do anything possible to ensure that the Genocide Convention could never be used against the USSR. Ideally, Soviet representatives would work hard to put the Americans and the British on the defensive by means of the Genocide Convention.

To Moscow's chagrin, the General Assembly resolution of 23 November 1947 instructed the Economic and Social Council (ECOSOC) to go ahead with the Genocide Convention. This implied resolving several "political questions" concerning protected groups, forms of genocide, and universal jurisdiction.[14] When the ECOSOC convened at Lake Success in February 1948, Soviet opposition was in the cards. The Soviet Union seemed to recognize just one instance of past genocide, that committed by Hitler's Germany. In his opening statement Professor Amazasp Arutiunian bluntly declared the Secretariat's definition of genocide too broad. The most crucial element in the struggle against genocide, in his opinion, was combatting fascist organizations that still existed in many countries. Indeed, there was a close link between the "modern notion of genocide" and the fascist ideology.[15] On 3 March 1948 the ECOSOC established an Ad Hoc Committee on Genocide consisting of China, France, Lebanon, Venezuela, Poland, the United States, and the Soviet Union. As the basis for discussion the committee would use the document prepared by the Secretariat and comments on the draft submitted by UN member states.

The Soviet train of thought regarding genocide is at its most explicit in the documents from late March and early April 1948. As the Ad Hoc Committee on Genocide was about to begin its deliberations at Lake Success on 5 April, the Foreign Ministry in Moscow prepared detailed instructions for the Soviet representative. The Soviet position at the forthcoming session of the committee was discussed at the highest political level. Both Molotov and Stalin read through and commented on a draft. Using a blue and red pencil respectively, the Soviet foreign minister and his boss highlighted the aspects of the future Genocide Convention that they found unacceptable. They tended to agree on most, but not all, issues.

The original directive obliged the Soviet delegate on the Sixth Committee to define genocide as physical destruction of population groups on the basis of their race, ethnicity, or religion. To this list Molotov added, in parentheses, political groups. Any attempts to incorporate into genocide criminal acts committed by armed bands had to be opposed on the grounds that such crimes came under the purview of domestic legislation. The second part of the directive concerned the establishment of a permanent international court or ad hoc tribunals. The Soviet Union rejected both propositions as interfering in the internal affairs of other states and violating national sovereignty. Instead, it insisted that the perpetrators of genocide should be prosecuted by domestic courts in the country where the crime had been committed. The next segment addressed the "organic" link between genocide and fascism ("and related ideologies," added Molotov). As far as the USSR was concerned, propaganda and incitement of genocide was an element of the crime. All cases of genocide should be referred by the signatories to the Security Council. If the majority of the committee disagreed with the Soviet proposal, the delegate should stay firm and, eventually, vote against the Genocide Convention as a whole.[16]

On 2 April Molotov sent to Stalin the edited text that would serve as the guiding principles for the Soviet delegation during the debates in the Ad Hoc Committee on Genocide. He said that the Secretariat draft comprised several theses covertly directed against the Soviet Union and therefore politically unacceptable. To offset it, the Soviet Foreign Ministry prepared its own draft. According to Molotov, the document known as the Basic Provisions of the Genocide Convention rejected the sly attempts to portray as genocide the deprivation of certain groups' means of existence through the confiscation of property or the "measures associated with physical exertion, which allegedly reduce people's physical strength or cause death."[17]

In a few pencil strokes, Stalin outlined his views on both genocide and the promise of international law. He rewrote one of the sentences as follows: "the crime of genocide is organically linked with fascism/*Nazism* and *analogous racist* 'theories' that preach *racial and ethnic hatred*." The references to international crimes he replaced with "crimes *against humanity*," and the references to international law he simply struck out. The term *cultural genocide* he enhanced as "*ethno*-cultural genocide," and he set the adjective "religious" in parentheses throughout the document. Most remarkable, in bold red pencil, he crossed out the word *political* as a motivation to commit genocide. Consequently, the Soviet representative on the Ad Hoc Committee on Genocide was instructed to say "no" to the following: establishing the permanent international court; enacting the principle of universal jurisdiction; enumerating acts of genocide/expanding the notion of genocide; and qualifying as genocide penalties meted out to members of armed gangs.[18]

Elsewhere I provide a detailed analysis of the comprehensive Soviet proposal as edited by Molotov and Stalin.[19] Here I want to mention just two, interrelated, elements in the emerging Soviet discourse on genocide. The first grapples with the question of which particular Soviet practices Stalin's clique was most keen on covering up, and the second dissects the idea of *just/unjust* in the Soviet worldview. Unequivocally opposed to the provisions enumerating confiscation of property and forced labour, the Soviets obviously had in mind not the Nazi practices but their own. It was the Gulag and ethnic deportations – the latest episodes of mass violence – that the Soviets were primarily concerned about.

Aron Trainin, an internationally known Soviet scholar of criminal law who made a name for himself at Nuremberg, came the closest to admitting it. Entrusted with popularizing the Soviet proposal, in May 1948 Trainin published (in Russian) three overlapping pieces on the Genocide Convention. In his piece in the law journal *Sovetskoe gosudarstvo i pravo* (Soviet State and Law), he made what I regard as a Freudian slip. On the one hand, he made no secret as to what the Soviet Union wanted to be covered by "ethno-cultural genocide": lynching in the United States and racial discrimination in Western colonies. Trainin's remark regarding the protection of culture in the Soviet Union, however, came across as an antithesis. Naturally, contended Trainin, the problem of ethnic minorities as such was nonexistent in the Soviet state thanks to its Leninist-Stalinist nationalities policy. Otherwise, forced assimilation or forced resettlement (*prinuditel'noe pereselenie*) of a certain group did not constitute an act of genocide insofar as this transfer did not function as a means of physical destruction of that group.[20]

Staying with the notion of "cultural genocide" so dear to Molotov and Stalin, it never occurred to them to apply it to ethnic groups within the Soviet Union. Deported in their entirety, population groups such as Chechens or Crimean Tatars did not enjoy the luxury of operating museums, libraries, and newspapers in exile – as stipulated in the Basic Provisions. Within the Soviet context, the very proposition is preposterous. Deemed "enemy nationalities" by Stalin's regime, these and many other ethnic groups simply did not belong in a universe of obligation, as discussed by Helen Fein nearly forty years ago.[21] In effect, the Soviets proposed punishing the crimes they had refused to acknowledge as their own. I choose to call it ideological self-righteousness.

The Stalin-edited Basic Provisions of the Genocide Convention had become the backbone of the Soviet argumentation in the United Nations all the way through December 1948.[22] Of interest here is who was the actual author of the Soviet draft proposal of late April 1948. I strongly believe that the original, unsigned, document was prepared by Trainin. First, a comparison between the text of the proposal and the three popular/academic publications on the subject of genocide by Trainin reveals uncanny similarities.[23] Second, there simply was no other scholar in the Soviet Union at the time who knew the subject as well as Trainin did. There is an article by a certain S. Volodin that appeared in *Sovetskoe gosudarstvo i pravo* in 1954.[24] I have not been able to identify the scholar who went by that name; there are no further publications by Volodin either before or after 1954, and I suspect "Volodin" was actually Trainin's pseudonym. (Trainin passed away in 1957.)

Despite their best efforts, the draft convention prepared by the Ad Hoc Committee on Genocide failed to incorporate central elements of the Soviet Basic Provisions. The Soviet delegate Alexei Pavlov lamented that the new draft did not emphasize the link between fascism/Nazism and genocide, failed to outlaw genocide propaganda, refused to restate the Nuremberg principle rejecting the superior-order defense, and committed to establishing an international criminal court. As regards the inclusion of political groups, "that was not in conformity with the scientific definition of genocide," according to Pavlov.[25]

No matter what provision of the Genocide Convention came under discussion, the Soviet tactic was to gradually shift from the defensive to the offensive. Aligning the letter of international law with its own history became less essential than probing for legal avenues of political attack. This tendency, which had crystallized by summer–fall 1948, may explain the apparent inconsistency in Soviet argumentation. For example, while fighting tooth and nail against the element of intent/premeditation, the Soviets put forward and successfully got adopted the amendment that read: "the deliberate infliction of conditions of life calculated to bring about physical destruction of certain groups, in whole or in part." At the same time, the Soviet delegation frowned upon the Syrian proposal to subsume under genocide any action aiming to force members of a group to leave their homes.[26]

Late in the drafting process, the Soviet delegation was instructed against making a fuss about political groups. Thus, a permanent international court remained the only issue that the delegation was supposed to vote down. At the end of the day, even if the Soviet amendments had been rejected, Molotov told the delegation at Paris to support the Genocide Convention as a whole.[27]

The American Perspective: Proceed with Caution

The first signs of worry started appearing within the US State Department in the summer of 1947. Like the Soviets, the Americans had doubts about the Secretariat draft's "maximum program." The State Department related the opinion of some individuals, who claimed that the program might characterize as genocide, for example, the work of the House Committee on Un-American Activities or of American foreign missionaries. Careful study and eventual redrafting was thus necessary.[28] The official US position was worked out at a State Department meeting on 4 September 1947. The discussion exposed two significant factors that came to haunt the Genocide Convention ever since: guilty conscience and pessimism. The former response is illustrated by Ernest A. Gross's opposition to counting the forced transfer of minorities as an element of the crime. By the international accord governing such past transfers he obviously meant the 1945 Yalta and Potsdam agreements that provided for repatriation of Soviet and Yugoslav citizens and effectuated expulsion of up to thirteen million ethnic Germans from Eastern Europe. Co-signed by US presidents Franklin D. Roosevelt and Harry S. Truman respectively, it subsequently proved a source of embarrassment. The most astonishing, however, was the concluding remark of Charles H. Fahy, who said "that he did not anticipate the convention actually being invoked for fifty years, or maybe twenty."[29]

The official 30 September communication of the US government was carefully worded and quite explicit. The United States objected to the inclusion of linguistic groups, but agreed to the inclusion of political groups insofar as genocide was confined to physical destruction. Under the means by which the specific characteristics of the group could be destroyed, the United States wanted to retain only forced transfer of children. Forced exile, on the other hand, "might be interpreted as embracing forced transfers of minority groups such as have already been carried out by Members of the United Nations." The clause concerning genocide propaganda contravened the freedom of speech provided for in Anglo-American rule of law. At the same time, the US government supported universal jurisdiction, since states could potentially pursue political retribution. The United States opted for an ad hoc tribunal, leaving the decision to establish a permanent international penal court outside the purview of the Genocide Convention.[30]

The same month, for the first time, the State Department mentioned an emerging issue of concern to the US government: racial discrimination against Black Americans. Nevertheless, before the actual debates on the Secretariat draft had begun, no one was sounding an alarm yet:

> The possibility exists that sporadic outbreaks against the Negro population in the United States may be brought to the attention of the United Nations, since the treaty, if ratified, would place this offense in the realm of international jurisdiction and remove the "safeguard" of Article 2 (7) of the Charter. However, since the offense will not exist unless part of an overall plan to destroy a human group, and since the Federal Government would under the treaty acquire jurisdiction over such offenses, no possibility can be foreseen of the United States being held in violation of the treaty.[31]

As time went on, however, hate crimes became a liability for the United States. Whether the discussion centred on prospective penal court or state complicity, American diplomats watched out that no element of the Genocide Convention could be construed "in such a way as to cause us difficulties with cases such as lynching."[32]

The Americans had their own talking points when preparing for the debates in the Ad Hoc Committee on Genocide. As the State Department's memorandum of 8 April attested, many of their concerns mirrored those of the Soviets. In essence, the final text of the convention should contain no provisions applicable to past and present abuses committed by the drafting nations. The State Department also had a change of heart regarding potential reference to the International Military Tribunal (IMT). The Nuremberg Tribunal was criticized as an ex post facto law, whereas the prospective convention would form a juridical basis for future, but not past, international action against genocide. By limiting the crimes to those committed "with the complicity of the responsible officials of a state," only the offenses perpetrated as a matter of state policy (such as the Nazi extermination of the Jews) could be prosecuted. Such a definition would exclude lynching and racial discrimination generally. Perhaps most striking was the US backtracking on the idea of an international penal court. Had the Genocide Convention contained a provision for such a body, a group of countries not including the United States (read: the Communist bloc) could establish an international tribunal to try acts of genocide allegedly committed by American citizens presently in their custody. An abstract reference to "competent tribunal," however, was deemed necessary. Otherwise, the memorandum explicated, the mere statement of intent to punish a guilty party might be interpreted as permitting any one state (read: the USSR) to unilaterally prosecute acts classified as genocide committed outside its jurisdiction.[33]

The most extensive US document concerning the Genocide Convention was drafted in June 1948 by John Maktos, chair of the Ad Hoc Committee on Genocide. The confidential report testified to the draft convention becoming a pawn in the ideological struggle between the two superpowers. The very first sentence in the report drove this point home: "The basic cleavage discernible in the Committee between the United States-French-Chinese conception of a convention on the one hand and the Soviet-Polish conception on the other might be described as follows: The former were interested in drafting a legal document, whereas the latter were interested in drafting what they frankly described as an 'educational' document, not for 'jurists' but for the 'peoples of the world,' in other words, a propaganda weapon." When speaking with the "voice of humanity," the Soviets left the impression that they did not take the drafting of a convention seriously. Indeed, they proved the most strenuous critics of the convention so far.[34]

Throughout the thirty-three-page document, Maktos trained his eyes on the Soviets. By insisting on national courts over an international tribunal the USSR created a basis for charging other governments with the commission of genocide. The referral of genocide cases to the Security Council as the only means of international redress would effectively retain the power of veto with respect to potential charges against the Great Powers. The US representative further elaborated: "As a matter of fact, in view of the veto, the Soviet Union would be judge of its own cases just as much as if they were tried in the Soviet courts." The deficiency of the Soviet formula outlining specific motives in the definition of the crime of genocide was subsequently reduced, according to

Maktos, by the inclusion of "political opinion." He cited an article in *Trud*, which ominously implied – though did not directly state – that the treatment of Black Americans constituted genocide. While criticizing the inclusion of political groups among those protected by the convention, the Soviet newspaper recapitulated the official statements shaming certain countries where the propaganda of racial hatred and genocide was supposedly ongoing.[35]

After discussing the draft Genocide Convention briefly on 16 June, the CHR returned it to the ECOSOC. The ECOSOC took up the draft on 26 and 27 August, and then transmitted it without change to the General Assembly. At its 142nd plenary meeting, the General Assembly decided to refer the draft convention prepared by the Ad Hoc Committee on Genocide to the Sixth Committee. Following a general debate, which began on 30 September, the Sixth Committee resolved to consider the draft article by article. The report of the Sixth Committee came up for debate on 9 December at the 178th and 179th plenary meetings of the General Assembly.

By the time the Third General Assembly opened in Paris, Soviet-American diplomatic relations had reached a new low. On 20 July 1948 a federal grand jury indicted the leaders of the Communist Party USA (CPUSA) for promoting violent revolution. The arrest was carried out under the Smith Act, which imposed penalties on those who advocated the overthrow of the government of the United States. Soviet authorities slammed the indictment and the consecutive trial, which pronounced a guilty verdict for all eleven defendants. The fact that the Smith Act was passed in June 1940, when Nazi Germany was tightening its grip on Europe, made *Sovetskoe gosudarstvo i pravo* speak of the "fascistization" of America.[36]

Going into the final discussion in the ECOSOC in late August, the US delegation refined its position in anticipation of Soviet obstructionism. A major change in the US position concerned protected groups. At a briefing meeting earlier that month, John Foster Dulles raised the question of why draft article II should not prohibit the killing of members of an economic or social class. However, if a large number of representatives set forth that the inclusion of economic and social groups in the convention would make it unacceptable to them, the American delegation was recommended to reconsider this matter. In any event, Soviet objections to this modification could not but reflect unfavourably on Moscow. Obviously, the killing of members of the capitalist class, merely because they belong to that class, should not be tolerated – so argued the State Department position paper. Most significantly, the United States was ready to drop the ball on political groups. It was likely that, in addition to the Soviet satellites, the Latin American countries might object to the retention of political groups in article II. Hence, if this issue proved a stumbling block to accession for a sufficiently large number of representative states, the US delegation was advised to re-evaluate its stance.[37]

The Soviet position was in a sense predictable. The American and British opposition was also to be expected. What was surprising, though, is that on certain issues the former Allies had developed an understanding in the closing months of 1948. Suddenly, they found themselves in agreement that the crimes committed by Nazi Germany did constitute quintessential genocide. The incessant Soviet assault drew home the realization that the genocide treaty, once adopted, might be turned either way. US delegate Willard L. Thorp emphasized the urgent need for drafting an international treaty on genocide "before public memory of the barbarous acts committed by Nazi and fascist forces during the last fifteen years had faded." His British counterpart, H.M. Phillips, stuck to his guns that the Nuremberg Tribunal had already accomplished what the Genocide Convention was meant to achieve. Deciding on a legal definition of genocide should be left up to the International Law Commission and the lawyers entrusted with the codification of the Nuremberg Principles, he argued. Both delegates rallied against the notion of *cultural genocide*, which supposedly diluted the treaty, or worse, rendered the whole thing meaningless.[38] A permanent international court proved yet another issue on which the Communist and Western bloc seemed to have developed an understanding. For once, the delegates decided not to beat about the bush: no one wanted a permanent international tribunal. The calls to "be realistic" permeated the arguments on both sides of the ideological divide.

Moving into the fall of 1948, the UN debates turned into a shouting match between the Soviet Union and the United States. The verbal exchanges in the Sixth Committee started increasingly to resemble duels. The Berlin crisis hung like a dark cloud over the negotiating table. Beyond the legal or logical problems that the Soviet insistence on the link between fascism/Nazism and genocide entailed, the United States was concerned about what that could mean for the future status of Germany and Italy. The need to legitimize the Communist takeover of Poland, by the same token, compelled the Polish delegation to pound the West for shielding Nazi war criminals. Adopted on Polish initiative, the article of the convention that regarded genocide as a non-political crime was meant to facilitate extradition. Some of the war criminals whose extradition had been requested were given protection in the American occupation zone, insisted the Polish delegate.[39] The notion of cultural genocide found few takers outside the Communist bloc. Judging by their statements, colonial powers and Latin American countries typically viewed cultural genocide as a form of forced assimilation.[40] There was nothing in the presentations by Soviet bloc countries that would dissipate those fears. The representative of Yugoslavia did not blink when he claimed in September 1948 that genocide was committed in "colonial wars against oppressed peoples fighting for their freedom."[41]

The British Perspective: Make It Go Away

Sir Hartley Shawcross, who previously served as chief British prosecutor at the IMT, regarded a separate genocide treaty as both unrealistic and unwise. He argued – some would say pragmatically, others cynically – in the Sixth (Legal) Committee in late September 1947 that no convention would deter a state from committing genocide. Instead, he suggested relying on existing law as had been formulated and executed at Nuremberg.[42] The British maintained that a large number of UN member states would prefer that solution as opposed to drafting a separate convention.[43] When the ECOSOC took up the issue of genocide in February 1948, the first thing a UK delegate did was express his doubts as to the purported value of such a convention.[44] Only reluctantly did the British adopt a more conciliatory line, conscious of the embarrassing indifference to the crime of genocide that their posture in the United Nations had projected.

Britain's position on the Genocide Convention reflected its attitude toward the United Nations as a whole, which differed from that of the United States. British diplomats from the inception had little faith in the United Nations and criticized the American outlook on a world organization as escapist and moralistic. By the same token, British Foreign Office officials had lost their trust in Soviet goodwill sooner than their American counterparts did.[45]

The issue of colonialism, when linked to genocide, made the British feel particularly vulnerable. Pre-emptively, the UK delegate held that extending the treaty's provisions to non-self-governing territories would be unconstitutional. Even though it would technically be possible, his government took a negative view, explained Gerald G. Fitzmaurice. The Soviet delegate instantly countered that "colonial policy had been a dark page in history even in pre-fascist times." Although the UK representative might be thinking that some peoples wished to become victims of genocide, insinuated the Soviet delegate, the Sixth Committee should not fail to extend the protection to the millions languishing in the colonies. Predictably, Fitzmaurice took the reference to a "dark page in history" badly, stating that his delegation denied the moral authority of the Soviet government to make any such statement, or set itself up as a role model before the world. This exchange exposed the US-UK rift on the issue of colonies. Maktos extended the benefit of the doubt to the British, yet rhetorically asked why the United Kingdom would refuse to apply the convention to dependent territories but not to itself.[46] He also objected to the UK amendment that listed governments and states among those responsible for the commission of genocide. Fitzmaurice retorted that if the US representative denied that genocide was indeed perpetrated by states and governments, "he was living in a fool's paradise." In response, Maktos challenged Fitzmaurice whether he denied that individuals could be guilty of genocide. On this occasion, the Soviets and the British joined forces to delete the reference to a "competent international tribunal."[47]

Unlike the Americans, the British stood firm on the issue of political groups (and for that particular reason became a target of Lemkin's criticism). If national, racial, and religious groups were to be protected, argued Shawcross, why not political? Although it is true that political groups did not have stable characteristics, he reasoned, the ruling political parties in certain states might think otherwise. It was unacceptable for a fascist state to destroy the lives of persons who happened to belong to a Communist party, and vice versa; there was still much persecution on political grounds in Europe.[48]

The Soviet animus against the British, in spite of their shrinking global imprint, does not come as a surprise. The British reciprocated, taking the fight back to the Soviets, perhaps even with a greater vigour than the Americans did. At the same time, when it came to specific provisions of the draft Genocide Convention, the Soviets found themselves in agreement with the British more often than they were ready to admit. The United Kingdom was effectively the first to point out that including political groups might pose a problem to certain states engaged in the suppression of subversive groups.[49] When so arguing, Shawcross had in mind not only the Soviet Union but also the British Empire. The internal memorandum of January 1948 stated the British opposition to reopening politically sensitive issues such as the expulsion of Germans from Poland or the exile of Communists from Greece. Even worse, His Majesty's Government could potentially be charged with genocide in the cases involving the treatment of Germans in the British zone of occupation, the Jews in Palestine, or certain colonial peoples. To avoid this scenario, the British Foreign Office had taken an uncompromising position regarding "cultural genocide" and a colonial applications clause.[50] Otherwise, of all the Western delegations, the British proved the most direct when talking to the Soviets. When debating the Soviet amendment on public propaganda of genocide, Fitzmaurice declared that he would not have had any problem with it had the world situation been different. He feared that the Soviet Union would use this provision to "further aims other than the campaign against genocide."[51]

Whether he spoke his mind or followed a political script, Shawcross raised a fundamental problem of international law:

> While considering with sympathy the idea that the countries of the world should enter into a convention on genocide, Sir Hartley Shawcross did not feel particularly enthusiastic about the draft convention before the Committee. It was a complete delusion, he felt, to suppose that the adoption of a convention of the type proposed, even if generally adhered to, would give people a greater sense of security or would diminish existing dangers of persecution on racial, religious, or national grounds. Recalling the Nuremberg trials, the representative of the United Kingdom pointed out that nobody believed that the existence of a convention such as was proposed would have deterred the Nazis or fascists from committing the atrocious crimes of which they had been guilty. Those crimes were largely the crimes of totalitarian states, which would not change their methods because of the existence of a convention to which a number of nations had adhered.[52]

The United Kingdom had several reasons to oppose the Genocide Convention: the competing interests of the Home Office and the Foreign Office, the pressure exercised by the Colonial Office, the circumstances surrounding the recent ending of the Palestine mandate, the reluctance to amend domestic laws, and the unwillingness to grant extradition because of the tradition of political asylum for those involved in insurrections against repressive regimes.[53] Besides colonial policies, British diplomats confidentially came up with a number of instances that they thought may potentially be labelled genocide: the treatment of Jews in Palestine, the expulsion of ethnic Germans from Eastern Europe, the expulsion of Communists from Greece, the treatment of ethnic Germans in the British zone of occupation, the firebombing of German cities, and the atomic bombs dropped on Hiroshima and Nagasaki.[54]

The UK government almost blundered at the very end of the exhausting two-year negotiations in the United Nations. In anticipation of the Soviet abstention during the 9 December vote in the General Assembly, the British delegation was advised to do the same. Shawcross was beside himself, as manifested in the urgent cable that he had sent to Foreign Secretary Ernest Bevin just days before the final vote. Instead of "providing an excellent argument in support of our thesis that the Slav system is a backward one," wrote Shawcross, the United Kingdom was about to line up with the Soviet bloc against pretty much everyone else.[55] In haste, the Foreign Office withdrew its recommendation for abstention.

On 9 December 1948 the Genocide Convention was passed unanimously. Chairman of the drafting committee Maktos congratulated its members on the passing of the genocide treaty, without mentioning that "they had put across our position in relation to genocide so successfully."[56] The *New York Herald Tribune* hailed the signing of the Genocide Convention, describing it as an "idealistic document."[57]

Conclusion

When Lemkin originally conceived of a genocide convention, he thought that "such a treaty would take the life of nations out of the hands of politicians and give it the objective basis of law."[58] This chapter suggests the exact opposite outcome, namely the primacy of politics over humanitarian and/or legal considerations in the UN Genocide Convention.

By comparison, the Americans perhaps come out the best from the negotiations. US diplomats, particularly at the beginning of the debates, displayed a certain humanitarian streak cherished by Lemkin. There was a common understanding that the Genocide Convention was a necessary tool and a way forward on international law. At the same time, the Americans got instantly disillusioned with the Nuremberg trial and verdict – which the Soviets, British, and French hailed and consequently sought to link up with the prospective Genocide Convention. Soviet intransigence eventually prompted a similar reaction on the part of the Americans. By 1948 a realization started settling in that the Genocide Convention could, hypothetically, also be used against the United States, specifically for unwittingly signing up for what proved to be a brutal expulsion of ethnic Germans from Eastern Europe. Racial discrimination in the American South also came into question, though at that point in time US diplomats thought it was unlikely to appear under the heading of genocide. By refusing to sign up to an international criminal court, the United States effectively rendered the new international treaty inapplicable.

However much criticism the British received from Lemkin for flip-flopping on essential provisions of the draft Genocide Convention, at least they were consistent in their rejection of the treaty. For the duration of the negotiations in the United Nations, the United Kingdom remained skeptical as to the vitality and necessity of the Genocide Convention. If it had not been for Shawcross – one of the top English lawyers and the face of the British prosecution team at Nuremberg – the United Kingdom would have ended up the only country to abstain from voting on the Genocide Convention in the General Assembly on 9 December 1948. Even then, Shawcross's insistence that the United Kingdom should vote "yes" was more of a face-saving gesture. The British saw through the Soviet efforts to gut the treaty, but also had a bone to pick with the American delegation (mainly on account of the United Kingdom refusing to consider giving up its status as a colonial power). The steadfast, negative attitude of the British government toward the Genocide Convention persisted all the way through 1969, until it could no longer hold up under the weight of public opinion.

The Soviet position on the Genocide Convention came close to being sabotage – which would be an accurate description of the Soviet policy vis-à-vis the Universal Declaration of Human Rights.[59] The Soviets from the get-go rejected any humanitarian aspect of the genocide treaty in the making. They operated solely on the basis of a cost-benefit analysis tinted with ideology. It is true that the Soviet posture in the multilateral setting of the United Nations had changed from 1947 to 1948, from the defensive to the offensive. It was no different with respect to the draft Genocide Convention. The Soviets – beginning with Stalin and Molotov at the top – went from ensuring that no provision of the treaty would apply to the country of workers and peasants, to amending the existing provisions and/or introducing new ones that would target the United States and the United Kingdom, and the West generally.

Taken in the aggregate, the available sources on the Soviet conception of the crime of genocide reveal a cynical, self-serving policy. Even the ubiquitous references to Nazi crimes cannot be taken at face value. While still counting their dead, the Soviets were developing a discourse that linked the West to Hitler's Germany through the notions of fascism and racial discrimination.

While considering all three perspectives on the drafting of the Genocide Convention, the Soviet Union proved the biggest culprit. I have on numerous occasions described the Genocide Convention as a hostage of the Cold War; the evidence coming from the realm of international law reinforces an earlier analysis that pointed to Stalin and the USSR as responsible for the outbreak of the Cold War.[60] The Soviet conception of international law – a curious mixture of class ideology and ruthless realpolitik – failed by default to accommodate a multilateral treaty with no reference to specific historical precedents (read: Nazi crimes) that would come to benefit all of humanity, as Lemkin had originally conceived of it. Stalin's regime never intended a genuine rapprochement with the West; its take on the crime of genocide is but one illustration.

When surveying the UN debates on the draft Genocide Convention in 1947 and 1948, one recurrent theme was political groups. The question of whether or not to extend protection to political groups had three undercurrents: the suppression of opposition in real time, extradition of alleged war criminals, and historical precedents. Insofar as Western delegations wanted to dispose of cultural groups by delegating this issue to the Commission on Human Rights, Communist bloc countries worked hard to omit the reference to political groups.

My research puts to rest the misconception that attributes Stalin's resistance to the notion of political genocide to his guilty conscience. However much we may speculate about whether or not Stalin thought conceptually of the destruction of the peasantry and the political opposition in the 1930s he had sanctioned, he was first and foremost a ruthless politician. That is to say, he was less concerned with the past than he was with the present and the future. The subjugation of Eastern Europe, which was accompanied by the destruction of political opposition and, in the case of the annexed territories, counterinsurgency operations – that is what was on Stalin's mind when he struck out "political groups" among those potentially protected by the Genocide Convention.[61] The Americans, too, toward the end of the marathon negotiations over the draft Genocide Convention, came to the conclusion that the issue of political groups may put the US government on the spot.

NOTES

1 *The New York Post Home News Magazine*, 13 December 1948.

2 Research on Lemkin's role in passing the Genocide Convention is quite extensive. Cf. William Korey, *An Epitaph for Raphael Lemkin* (New York: The Jacob Blaustein Institute for the Advancement of Human Rights of the American Jewish Committee, 2001); Samantha Power, *"A Problem from Hell": America and the Age of Genocide* (New York: Basic Books, 2002), 17–78; John Cooper, *Raphael Lemkin and the Struggle for the Genocide Convention*

(Houndmills, UK: Palgrave, 2008); *Totally Unofficial: The Autobiography of Raphael Lemkin*, edited by Donna-Lee Frieze (New Haven, CT: Yale University Press, 2013); Douglas Irvin-Erickson, *Raphaël Lemkin and the Concept of Genocide* (Philadelphia: University of Pennsylvania Press, 2016). See also special journal issues on Lemkin: *Journal of Genocide Research* 7, no. 4 (December 2005); *Journal of Genocide Research* 15, no. 3 (September 2013); *Genocide Studies and Prevention* 13, no. 1 (2019).

3 See doc. 9, reproduced in *Documents on the Genocide Convention from the American, British, and Soviet Archives*, vol. 1 (London: Bloomsbury, 2018), 26.

4 Ilya Gaiduk, *Divided Together: The United States and the Soviet Union in the United Nations, 1945–1965* (Washington, DC: Woodrow Wilson Center Press, 2012), 43–55.

5 See doc. 19, reproduced in *Documents on the Genocide Convention*, vol. 1, 43–4.

6 Geoffrey Roberts, "Moscow and the Marshall Plan: Politics, Ideology and the Onset of the Cold War, 1947," *Europa-Asia Studies* 46, no. 8 (1994): 1371–6.

7 Doc. 26, *Documents on the Genocide Convention*, vol. 1, 51–2.

8 UN doc. E/447 (26 June 1947).

9 UN docs. A/C.6/201, A/C.6/151. Cf. a recent study of IMT by Kim C. Priemel, *The Betrayal: The Nuremberg Trials and German Divergence* (Oxford: Oxford University Press, 2016).

10 UN Official Records of the Second Session of the General Assembly, 123rd Plenary Meeting (21 November 1947): 1301.

11 "Ukraine Groups Urge U.N. Check on Soviet," *New York Times*, 9 November 1947; "Genocide Survey Urged," *New York Times*, 23 November 1947.

12 "Appeal from Lithuania," *New York Times*, 22 November 1947; "Lay Genocide to Soviet," *New York Times*, 25 November 1947; "Obrashchenie baltiitsev v OON," *Novoe Russkoe Slovo*, 26 November 1947.

13 Editorial: "Lithuania's Independence," *New York Times*, 16 February 1948.

14 ECOSOC Official Records, Third Year: Sixth Session. Annex, Agenda Item 31: Genocide (3 February 1948): 125–6.

15 ECOSOC Official Records, Third Year: Sixth Session, 140th Meeting (13 February 1948): 146–8.

16 Doc. 53, *Documents on the Genocide Convention*, vol. 1, 98–100.

17 Doc. 58, *Documents on the Genocide Convention*, vol. 1, 107–8.

18 Doc. 59, *Documents on the Genocide Convention*, vol. 1, 109–11.

19 Cf. Anton Weiss-Wendt, *The Soviet Union and the Gutting of the UN Genocide Convention* (Madison, WI: University of Wisconsin Press, 2017), 70–5.

20 Aron Trainin, "Borba s genotsidom kak mezhdunarodnym prestupleniem," *Sovetskoe gosudarstvo i pravo* 5 (May 1948): 6–7, 14–16. For recent

scholarship on Trainin see Michelle Jean Penn, "The Extermination of Peaceful Soviet Citizens" (PhD thesis: University of Colorado at Boulder, 2017); Thomas Earl Porter, "In Defense of Peace: Aron Trainin's Contributions to International Jurisprudence," *Genocide Studies and Prevention* 13, no. 1 (2019): 98–112.

21 Cf. Helen Fein, *Accounting for Genocide: National Responses and Jewish Victimization during the Holocaust* (New York: The Free Press, 1979), 4, 8–9, 30, 33.

22 Cf. doc. 96, *Documents on the Genocide Convention*, vol. 1, 189–90.

23 Cf. docs. 60 and 61, *Documents on the Genocide Convention*, vol. 1, 111–17.

24 S. Volodin, "Konventsiia o preduprezhdenii prestupleniia genotsida i nakazaniia za nego," *Sovetskoe gosudarstvo i pravo* 7 (December 1954): 125–8.

25 ECOSOC Official Records, Third Year: Seventh Session, 219th Meeting (26 August 1948), 720–2, 728.

26 UN Official Records of the Third Session of the General Assembly, Sixth Committee, 82nd Meeting (23 October 1948): 182–6. See also UN docs. A/C.6/223 and A/C.6/234.

27 Doc. 97, *Documents on the Genocide Convention*, vol. 1, 190–4.

28 Doc. 27, *Documents on the Genocide Convention*, vol. 1, 52–4.

29 Doc. 37, *Documents on the Genocide Convention*, vol. 1, 70–2.

30 "Communication Received from the USA," UN Official Records of the Second Session of the General Assembly, Sixth Committee (30 September 1947): 235–44.

31 Doc. 38, *Documents on the Genocide Convention*, vol. 1, 72–3.

32 Docs. 63 and 64, *Documents on the Genocide Convention*, vol. 1, 119–22.

33 US Department of State to John Maktos, position on Genocide Convention in ECOSOC drafting committee, 8 April 1948, National Archives and Records Administration, Department of State decimal files, 1945–49, 59/760050/2186.

34 Doc. 73, *Documents on the Genocide Convention*, vol. 1, 138–55.

35 Ibid.

36 Moisei Shifman, "Vozrozhdenie inkvizitsii (Sudebnyi protsess nad rukovoditeliami kompartii SShA)," *Sovetskoe gosudarstvo i pravo* 10 (October 1949): 43–6, 48, 51–2.

37 Doc. 79, *Documents on the Genocide Convention*, vol. 1, 138–55.

38 ECOSOC Official Records, Third Year: Seventh Session, 219th Meeting (26 August 1948), 724–7.

39 (Poland: Katz-Sachy), ECOSOC Official Records, Third Year: Seventh Session, 218th Meeting (26 August 1948): 711–12, 715.

40 (Brazil: Amado; Egypt: Raafat; France: Chaumont), UN Official Records of the Third Session of the General Assembly, Sixth Committee, 63rd Meeting (30 September 1948): 6–8.

41 (Yugoslavia: Bartos), UN Official Records of the Third Session of the General Assembly, Sixth Committee, 63rd Meeting (30 September 1948): 9.

42 UN Official Records of the Second Session of the General Assembly, Sixth Committee, 29th Meeting (29 September 1947): 21.

43 (UK: Davies), UN Official Records, General Assembly, 2nd Session, (21 November 1947).

44 ECOSOC Official Records, Third Year: Sixth Session, 140th Meeting (13 February 1948): 145.

45 Peter G. Boyle, "The British Foreign Office View of Soviet-American Relations, 1945–46," *Diplomatic History* 3, vol. 3 (summer 1979): 309–10; Hugh De Santis, *The Diplomacy of Silence: The American Foreign Service, the Soviet Union, and the Cold War, 1933–1947* (Chicago: University of Chicago Press, 1981), 116.

46 UN Official Records of the Third Session of the General Assembly, Sixth Committee, 107th Meeting (15 November 1948): 471–7.

47 UN Official Records of the Third Session of the General Assembly, Sixth Committee, 98th Meeting (10 November 1948): 373–82.

48 UN Official Records of the Third Session of the General Assembly, Sixth Committee, 69th Meeting (7 October 1948): 60.

49 UN Official Records of the Second Session of the General Assembly, Sixth Committee, 29th Meeting (29 September 1947): 34.

50 See docs. 43, 44, 74–8, 80 reproduced in Documents on the Genocide Convention, vol. 1, 81–7, 155–61, 165–6. See also A. W. Brian Simpson, "Britain and the Genocide Convention," British Yearbook of International Law 1, vol. 73 (2002): 9, 12, 14, 24.

51 UN Official Records of the Third Session of the General Assembly, Sixth Committee, 87th Meeting (29 October 1948): 251–2.

52 UN Official Records of the Third Session of the General Assembly, Sixth Committee, 64th Meeting (1 October 1948): 17.

53 Cf. Simpson, "Britain and the Genocide Convention," 83.

54 Docs. 35, 43, *Documents on the Genocide Convention*, vol. 1, 67–9, 138–55; doc. 73, *Documents on the Genocide Convention*, vol. 2, 9–10.

55 See docs. 82–9, 91, 92, 94, 95, 98–104, 106–12, *Documents on the Genocide Convention*, vol. 1, 170–88, 194–203, 204–13.

56 Oral history interview with Maktos, 28 May 1973. Available online at http://www.trumanlibrary.org/oralhist/maktosj.htm. Cf. doc. 57, *Documents on the Genocide Convention*, vol. 1, 104–6.

57 "The UN Yesterday," *The New York Herald Tribune*, 10 December 1948.

58 *Totally Unofficial*, 114.

59 For details see Weiss-Wendt, *The Soviet Union and the Gutting of the UN Genocide Convention*, 114–29.

60 See, for example, Anton Weiss-Wendt, "The Soviet Union and the Genocide Convention: An Exercise in Cold War Politics," in *Rafał Lemkin: A Hero of Humankind*, edited by Agnieszka Bieńczyk-Missala and Sławomir Dębski, 179–93 (Warsaw: The Polish Institute of International Affairs, 2010).

61 As explicated in 1961 by Mikhail Andriukhin, who had emerged as the pre-eminent Soviet commentator on genocide in the wake of Trainin's death. See Anton Weiss-Wendt, *A Rhetorical Crime: Genocide in the Geopolitical Discourse of the Cold War* (New Brunswick, NJ: Rutgers University Press, 2018), 23.

2

The Costs of Silencing Holocaust Victims: Why We Must Add Sexual Violence to Our Definition of Genocide

Annette F. Timm

When I was asked to contribute a paper reflecting on how an investigation of sexual violence in the Holocaust might contribute to a re-evaluation of the concept of genocide, the first story that came to my mind was one I heard from a Holocaust survivor. This survivor (whom I will not name in the interests of protecting her privacy) was a participant in an annual Holocaust remembrance symposium for high school students that I regularly attend. The students hear a brief lecture (I have often been one of the many academic volunteers), and they watch a documentary film as preparation for hearing from a survivor, who provides a personal narrative and then opens the floor to questions. In 2017, I joined the volunteers and survivors for the post-symposium lunch, giving me the opportunity to speak with the woman whose talk to a hall of about 250 students I had just heard. She told me the story that symposium organizers had asked her not to share with the students. A central part of this woman's Holocaust experience had been a period spent in hiding with a group of other children in a church in Poland. Several of her protectors, she said, had had ulterior motives for hiding the children, and had regularly sexually abused the children in their care. This story was deemed inappropriate for an audience of high school students. Is it?

It is perhaps provocative to say, as I do in my title, that excluding stories of sexual abuse from commemorations and education about the Holocaust is a form of silencing. But I am going to argue that in at least some respects it certainly is, and that the specific historical circumstances of Holocaust research have until very recently perpetuated this practice of silencing. We are not, in other words, simply talking about a sensitivity towards the tender ears of children. It is now virtually tradition for scholars researching sexual violence in the Holocaust to begin their articles or books with an anecdote about presenting at a conference where a senior scholar suggested that the topic was trivial, niche, or somehow unacceptable.[1] As Atina Grossmann put it in 2002,

> despite the vast archival, memoir, and testimonial evidence they have accumulated, scholars who insist upon gender's relevance in the Holocaust still operate on the defensive. They feel compelled to note the obvious: that to explore difference does not imply hierarchizing or trivializing suffering; on the contrary, the aim is to hear the voices of the victims and survivors in such a way as to deepen our understanding of events that defy comprehension. If the Holocaust is available for scholarly analysis, rather than occupying a sacred dark void in which awed silence must reign, then gender analysis of the Holocaust is as legitimate as it is for any other historical inquiry.[2]

Although more recent work on gender and the Holocaust has made progress, this "awed silence" persists in many broader narratives of the Holocaust, both in published form and in university lecture halls. Rather than simply condemning this silence, I will explain it by providing a summary of the long political, cultural, historiographical, and methodological roots of the reticence to speak about sexual violence in the Holocaust.

Even as we try to break the silence, we must be sensitive to the fact that not all survivors have been eager to tell stories about the sexual abuse they or those close to them suffered, and some continue to fiercely resist including stories about sexual trauma in their narratives of survival. But as my opening story is meant to demonstrate, these silences are impossible to understand without reference to the attitudes of the larger survivor communities and nations in which survivors have spoken. Historians remain as likely as non-historians to fall into various traps of generalization in describing the vastly different types of sexual violence that the Holocaust produced. That sexual exploitation was often intertwined with a victim's strategy for survival – that it produced an abundance of what Auschwitz survivor Primo Levi called "grey zones" – has confounded those searching for universal truths about patriarchal structures, feminine nature, or gender relations.[3]

Explaining these failures is both a historical and historiographical exercise; it requires viewing both the historians and the survivors as actors within specific cultural contexts, and it requires a discussion of the academic consensus on acceptable historical methodologies. Yet none of this can get around the more mundane fact that the first answer to the question of why we must add sexual violence to our definition of genocide is simply that it was part of the experience of survivors. It happened. This is not a trivial answer. Sexual violence in the Holocaust occurred in ways that were not merely incidental to mass murder – not merely its by-product – but rather were intertwined in its logic. For historians or other scholars to argue that some aspect of being a victim of genocide is somehow too trivial or threatening to mention is to belittle the experience of survivors; it is to perpetuate taboos and strategies of shaming that can only get in our way as we seek to avoid genocides and other crimes against humanity in our present and future.

This leads me to the second, perhaps all-too-obvious reason for including sexual violence within all definitions and historical evaluations of genocide: because it now belongs much more explicitly to the legal definition of the word. Sexual violence was *implicitly* present as a definition of genocide from the first use of the term. When the Polish-Jewish lawyer Raphaël Lemkin coined the term "genocide" in the last years of the war, he considered sexual violence to be an act of genocide, and he unsuccessfully lobbied the International Military Tribunal (IMT) at Nuremberg to include prosecutions for acts that he considered crimes against humanity in the context of the war.[4] But despite these efforts, and despite the fact that Allied Control Council Law No. 10 (which governed the occupation of Germany in 1945) included rape as a war crime, prosecutors investigating Nazi crimes for the Nuremberg Trials joined other human rights agencies of the day in not following up on Lemkin's insights.[5] As Douglas Irvin-Erikson has written, policymakers and jurists of this era tended to argue that sexual crimes occurred only in phases of "organizational anarchy" and saw military commanders as responsible only for failing to do enough to prevent it. The work of Birgit Beck reveals this argument to be a cynical mirroring of Nazi policy on the Eastern Front, where rape was *only* prosecuted when it interfered with military manoeuvres, and where the rape of Jewish women was essentially condoned.[6] Even the December 1948 UN Convention on the Prevention and Punishment of the Crime of Genocide failed to explicitly name sexual crimes, referring only to crimes "causing serious bodily or mental harm," to "inflicting ... conditions of life calculated to bring about physical destruction" of a group, and to "measures intended to prevent births." Although these words *could* be read as including sexual violence, the failure to explicitly say so allowed those who were convinced that rape is merely an incidental feature of war to continue avoiding prosecutions of this kind. It was not until the International Criminal

Tribunal for the former Yugoslavia (ICTY, 1993) and the International Criminal Tribunal for Rwanda (ICTR, 1994) that rape was prosecuted as a war crime and a crime against humanity.[7] The long delay may be one reason for historians' hesitance to view rape as a component of genocide, but the transformation of international law in the 1990s must now have consequences for how we view the genocides of the past. Historians are understandably reluctant to impose current legal concepts backwards onto history, particularly since any plausible historical interpretation must be formulated through reference to the specific context of a given time and place. But given that the very "purpose of the genocide concept and law was to prevent its recurrence," as Dirk Moses has put it, the rules against presentism must give way to our justified present-day motivations for reading history in ways that can continue to serve us. If it is, as Moses argues, "the sight of atrocities occurring today, rather than in the mists of time" that continue to motivate new questions and guide research in the history of genocide[8] – and I agree that it is – then we cannot be blind to the fact that every genocide and act of ethnic cleansing that we know of has included a visible and undeniable component of sexual violence. The war in Yugoslavia and the genocide in Rwanda occurred in an era of vastly increased media attention, making these things much more difficult to ignore. Returning to the Holocaust with our knowledge of earlier and later genocides and with the explicit influence of recent scholarship on other forms of ethnic oppression, such as exterminationary warfare, colonial subjugation, and slavery, makes trivializations of sexual violence in these cases even more difficult to defend.

My argument builds on the work of numerous historians, cited in the pages to come, who have begun to uncover extensive evidence of sexual violence perpetrated against Jewish and other victims of the Holocaust by Nazi guards and German soldiers as well as by members of persecuted groups. As I will explain in more detail below, I also draw on the work of historians who have written extensively about the extent of rape as part of battle during the Second World War (Regine Mühlhäuser and Gaby Zipfel), and those who have burst the taboos surrounding sex as a means of survival in the Holocaust (Robert Sommer and Anna Hájková) to point out that instrumentalized sex was part of the process of dehumanization that contributed to genocide.[9] That we do not yet have a comprehensive account of these experiences continues to empower those who wish to diminish their importance, and the sheer omnipresence of sexual threat – the fact that it was often taken for granted – actually presents explanatory obstacles. Moving from unpunished public reprisals in the earlier years of Nazi rule to the ever-more-organized violence of the ghettos, the killing fields, and the concentration camps, sexual violence took on a vast variety of forms. It could be violently episodic (stranger-rape under the cover of invasion and occupation), or more invisibly sustained in the form of submission to prostitution as a means of personal and familial survival. Such experiences are commonly unreported, notoriously difficult to count, and thus vulnerable to various forms of disavowal.[10] As Ayşe Gül Altınay and Andrea Pető have argued, "a feminist theorizing of genocide, almost inevitably, involves a study of silences within silences: gender within genocide, sexuality within gender, sexual violence within genocidal violence, memory within history, the methodological within the theoretical, the personal within the public and the academic, among others."[11] As with the Holocaust as a whole, the absence of or disagreement about statistics can be used as a smokescreen for denialism. For this reason, I will resist the temptation to try to quantify what cannot yet and will likely never be reliably counted. My goal is not to provide an overview of sexual violence in the Holocaust as a whole (which would be impossible at the present state of the historiography) but to explain why such an overview does not yet exist.

The logic of the argument rests on the undeniable reality that all forms of dehumanization – planned or spontaneous, politically directed or commercially driven – leave space for sexual exploitation. One could dispute whether sexual violence itself constitutes a form of dehumanization, but it is not necessary to go down the rabbit of hole of asking whether this is just an all-too-human phenomenon to recognize the unique vulnerability of victims of genocide to this form of violence. The ubiquity of sexual violence during the process of genocidal dehumanization is a fact with which we are now much more familiar and more likely to acknowledge than the first historians of the Holocaust. These historians worked in an era – the immediate postwar and Cold War period – in which specific legal and international exigencies and the cultural complexities of coming to terms with history's most deadly century had created specific explanatory challenges. I will provide historical context for the silence about sexual violence by telling the story of how certain historiographical modes and methodologies created rules for Holocaust historians with which we should no longer be content, and I will conclude by adding to the two reasons I have already cited for insisting that sexual violence must be given more attention in our broader narratives of genocide. I turn first to historians' response to the most immediate and visceral form of evidence that at least some of them encountered: the testimonies of survivors.

Early Testimony on Sexual Violence

The first step to explaining why sexual violence was virtually ignored in early narratives of the Holocaust involves a discussion of how testimony was collected and analyzed, since it is only in individual testimony that the personalized stories of sexual violence were (and are) told. Sexual violence, after all, involves person-to-person contact, and it was most virulent in the killing fields – in other words, before deportation and outside the concentration camp. Unlike the rape camps of the war in Yugoslavia, there was no coordination or even official sanction of sexual violence in the Holocaust. There was also nothing like the forced marriages and officially approved sale of children into slavery and assimilation that occurred during the early twentieth-century Armenian genocide in the Ottoman Empire.[12] The Yugoslav and Armenian genocides were gendercides in a way that the Holocaust was not. The term "gendercide" was coined by American feminist Mary Anne Warren in 1985 to refer to reproductive sex selection, but it is now commonly used to describe the genocidal strategy of first murdering the battle-aged men of a targeted community before subjecting the women and children to a slower process of dehumanization, annihilation, and sometimes – as in the Yugoslav and Armenian cases – forced reproduction, forced marriage and religious conversion, and assimilation.[13] While some separation of the genders certainly occurred in the Holocaust, most drastically in the concentration camps, the Nazis' categorical rejection of the notion that any member of the Jewish "race" could be assimilated makes the Holocaust unique. In fact, the racial logic of Judeocide and anti-Roma and anti-Sinti measures created official policies against miscegenation that provided cover for individual perpetrators and a convenient excuse for historians who were disinclined to include this topic in later investigations. Ironically, both strategies – those that included assimilation of women and children and those that did not – produced their own mechanisms of silencing. While assimilation into Muslim communities, especially in childhood, created its own taboos and inhibitions about discussing the sexual crimes that Armenian victims had experienced,[14] the assumption that Nazi miscegenation rules had been enforced made it unlikely that victims of sexual violence in the Holocaust would be believed. In both cases, those who had willingly or unwillingly used sex to survive were rendered mute out of shame. Unlike the case of Yugoslavia, where media attention on the rape camps produced immediate discussion about how sexual violence had been a mechanism of genocide, there was no systematic effort to collect testimonies about sexual violence as a particular feature of earlier genocides.

Nevertheless, more general Holocaust testimonies certainly reveal evidence of sexual violence. Efforts to collect individual stories for the purposes of both historical reconstruction and legal retribution were varied and began long before 1945.[15] The collection of survivor testimony began in late 1943, when Polish exile groups in the United States, along with prominent political figures (such as Eleanor Roosevelt and New York mayor Fiorello LaGuardia) and Jewish intellectuals (such as Albert Einstein), sponsored the collection of testimonies in Poland. The collection was published as *The Black Book of Polish Jewry* in New York in 1943 by the American Federation of Polish Jews, in cooperation with the Association of Jewish Refugees and Immigrants from Poland.[16] Around the same time, the Soviet Jewish journalist Vasily Grossman and novelist and journalist Ilya Ehrenburg, who were serving as war reporters in the Red Army, began working together with the Jewish Anti-Fascist Committee (JAC, formed in 1942) to assemble an anthology of interviews, letters, and testimonies from the survivors of Nazi massacres, ghettos, and concentration camps on Soviet soil.[17] Meant to be published as *The Black Book of Soviet Jewry*, this collection was a victim of Stalin's post-World War II censorship and antisemitism. Nonetheless, the gathering of these testimonies today provides us with evidence that the prevalence of sexual violence on the killing fields of Eastern Europe was no secret during the war.

The Russian *Black Book* contains extensive references to sexual violence, some veiled and others more direct. The collection is organized by region rather than by theme, and it is clear that some eyewitnesses were more comfortable describing rape and other forms of sexual torture than others. In many cases, we hear only about "moral torture" or "violation."[18] In other cases the allusions are even more oblique. For example, an eyewitness to the German treatment of Jews in Kyiv in September 1941 describes one of the scenes he witnessed: "I shall never forget one girl; her name was Sarra, and she was about fifteen years old. It is hard to describe the beauty of this girl. Her mother was pulling at her own hair and crying out in a heartrending voice, 'Kill us together!' They killed the mother with a rifle butt. Taking their time with the girl, five or six Germans stripped her naked, but I saw nothing more than that."[19] The implication is certainly that the girl was sexually abused, but the precise wording leaves things ambiguous. Several descriptions note that beautiful women and girls experienced repeated violations. In "the first days of the occupation," for instance, "the German officers were all over [Lina from

Stavropol], "a strong, beautiful girl and an athlete." Her uncle described to Ilya Ehrenburg how she "would come home crying over the insult done to her. Then they murdered her."[20] Death almost invariably followed rape,[21] which often took place in front of family members. In "The Story of Agronomist Sofya Glushkinka," we hear that the beautiful wife of the author's recently murdered brother was raped in front of her children and that another saved her daughter's life by telling her not to resist the sexual taunting of the SS.[22] It was also common knowledge that German soldiers frequently cut off women's breasts before murdering them,[23] and there are a few examples of genitals (of women but also of men and boys) being crushed or mutilated.[24] There are also several reports of women and girls committing suicide to avoid rape. Partisan fighter Golda Vasserman from the Tulchin ghetto tends to refer to rape rather than forced prostitution.[25]

The Polish *Black Book* also contains numerous passages referring to sexual exploitation and violence. There are several accounts of the systematic sexual abuse of Jewish women in Polish ghettos, for instance. A February 1940 deposition from survivor "I.I." describes how a truck arrived on Solna Street in the Warsaw ghetto one day, and that "Jewish women of the district were forced into it. The procedure was frequently repeated afterwards. Girls would disappear for several days and come home after having been attacked."[26] Even more controversially, *The Black Book of Polish Jewry* also contains a section titled "Brothels for the Conquerors," which describes a proposal from the German-controlled Health Department of Warsaw to force Jewish women into prostitution in a brothel for German soldiers. Henryk Szoszkies, a former member of the Executive of the Warsaw Jewish Committee (*Judenrat*), describes an exchange with the unit leader of the Gestapo in November 1939 and insists that he categorically refused to comply with an order (later postponed due the supposed lack of a suitable building) to choose beautiful inmates for the Nazi brothel.[27] The factual veracity of this account is less important for our purposes than what its publication signified in 1943. After all, given the helplessness of ghetto inmates, it was hardly necessary to set up organized brothels to satisfy the sexual whims of German soldiers.

Both of these *Black Book* collections contain evidence of sexual violence, but quite different stories of censorship explain why neither of them were taken that seriously by the early historians of the Holocaust. Although the *Black Book of Soviet Jewry* was ready for publication soon after the war, the press plates were destroyed on Stalin's orders in 1946. Stalin's personal antisemitism and his extreme distrust of all contact with foreigners made him suspicious of a project connected with Albert Einstein and other Jews in the United States. Stalin was also unhappy that Grossman and Ehrenburg had cooperated with agencies in the United States and Palestine in collecting testimonies both during and after the war. The final portions of the material collected for the *Black Book* project were not published until 1993; this volume, called *The Unknown Black Book*, was translated into English in 2008.[28] The long delay in making this material available can be explained by the insistence of successive Soviet leaders that no distinctions should be made between different groups of World War II victims in what they called the Great Patriotic War. During the war, however, the JAC and similar Jewish organizations combatting Nazi anti-Jewish measures on German-occupied territories were tolerated as useful propaganda weapons that might encourage more American Lend-Lease aid.[29]

The case of the Polish *Black Book* is more complex and more closely intertwined with specific Allied wartime policies. As the title suggests, *The Black Book of Polish Jewry: An Account of the Martyrdom of Polish Jewry under the Nazi Occupation* was carefully conceived to elicit sympathy for the Jews in the English-speaking world, but it was also influenced by the collective constituency of a fifteen-member publication committee with deep ties to the British and American governments. As Michael Fleming has demonstrated, an "Anglo-American censorship regime" motivated by fears about the growing number of refugees fleeing toward Palestine meant that the Polish *Black Book* purposely downplayed both the scale of the crisis and the details about the later phases of systematic killings. Although information about gassing and the "almost complete destruction of Polish Jewry" was known, the book relied on year-old death statistics and failed to describe Auschwitz or other death camps.[30] This form of censorship, motivated by specific wartime contingencies and directed by the official sponsors of the publication, made the book irrelevant as soon as the full extent of the Holocaust became public knowledge. The authentic stories of the individual eyewitnesses and survivors therefore sunk into relative obscurity after 1945.

Another trove of testimonies that failed to initially find its way into the broader narratives of historians writing about the Holocaust in the postwar period was the collection of approximately 7,300 testimonies amassed by the Central Jewish Historical Commission (CJHC), founded in Lublin in 1944.[31] Following a tradition of *khurbn-forshung* (destruction research) that had begun in Eastern Europe in the early twentieth century, Emanuel Ringelblum created the *Oyneg Shabes* (Sabbath Joy), an archival stash of buried documents that he hoped would document the history of the Warsaw ghetto and that was found in September 1946.[32] Isaac Schneersohn, an Orthodox Jew who fled to France in 1943, created the Centre de Documentation Juive Contemporaine, which published collections of documents about the treatment of Jews in Vichy France and gathered tonnes of material in the interests of justice after the war.[33] Similar commissions were founded in wartime Poland and in postwar occupied Germany.[34] A German Jew, Alfred Wiener, who fled to Amsterdam in 1934 and immediately started amassing a collection of documentation that would become the Wiener Holocaust Library in London. And in the summer of 1946, Chicago-based psychologist David Broder conducted over a hundred interviews with survivors in Displaced Persons (DP) camps in Europe, later making the transcripts available to at least forty-five libraries all over the world.[35] Together, these efforts produced an enormous trove of survivor testimony. Less than a decade and a half after the end of the war, Laura Jockusch tells us, the collective archive of these various commissions and collections included some 18,000 written testimonies and 8,000 questionnaires,[36] a statistic that belies the argument that it was only the Eichmann trial that allowed survivors to speak.[37]

Up until recently, these early collections were not well utilized in historical research, and discussions of testimony are more likely to rely on more recent collections of interviews, which were made long after the raw days of liberation.[38] One reason for this neglect was that the vast majority of the testimonies and interviews gathered during or immediately after the war were in Yiddish, making them inaccessible to many university-based scholars of the Holocaust.[39] Some of these documents also present challenges of evaluation, because they were recorded as narratives composed by researchers on the basis of interviews with survivors, or, as in the case of the *Black Book* collections, they were "prepared for publication" in ways that slightly obscure authorship. The early collections represent the interviewers' or editors' choices about the questions that should be asked and the information that should be preserved.[40] Yet even under these circumstances, the early interviews provide stark evidence for the prevalence of sexual violence. David Cesarani notes that these early accounts "were composed at a time when hatred of the Nazis and Germany was unrestrained and brutal images of the war filled the media. There were few inhibitions about what could be said: sexual abuse, depravity, prisoner-on-prisoner violence, cannibalism, graphic descriptions of fifth, squalor and human degradation, as well as explicit accounts of revenge are common. Reading these memoirs and testimonies it is easy to understand why, by the end of the 1940s, the public turned away."[41] In other words, survivors had not been silent but had launched a "frenetic, global effort to transmit information about the Jewish catastrophe," and "if anything, they had succeeded too well, too soon."[42] By the late 1940s, people simply did not want to hear about this suffering anymore, and it became difficult to get Holocaust memoirs published.[43] Without either a legal or media spotlight on the subject of sexual violence (as was the case following the war in Yugoslavia and the genocide in Rwanda), these earlier raw accounts failed to find resonance in public consciousness.

Once liberated and looking toward uncertain futures, survivors quickly recognized that detailed accounts of their experiences would not serve them well. They were rarely heroic in any straightforward Zionist sense, and they evoked visceral horror rather than feelings of group solidarity. They were unlikely to help anyone to navigate the bureaucratic nightmare of DP camps, immigration applications, and family reunification efforts.[44] Stories of this type of violence were neither easily politicized (in terms of contributing to efforts to create a Jewish state) nor likely to produce the benefits that DPs most urgently needed. They certainly would not help those who wanted to get to Palestine. Describing early Israeli culture, Tom Segev notes that the Holocaust was "symbolized by a prostitute." Survivors who hoped to emigrate to Israel faced the "common stereotype that depicted [the Diaspora] as weak, feminine, and passive, and the [Y]ishuv as strong, masculine and active. The sabra represented the national ideal, and the Holocaust survivor its reverse."[45] As Peter Lagrou points out, those still in Europe tended to be so conscious of their specific audience that they emphasized their role in anti-fascist resistance rather than their persecution as Jews.[46] In this context, why would they have any reason to hope that sexual violence could garner any kind of benefit in the years it took them to establish new lives? By the end of the 1940s a combination of factors – the end of the document-gathering entailed by preparations for the IMT at Nuremberg, the rising tensions of the Cold War, the emptying of the DP camps, the survivors' own struggles to establish new lives, and international pressures to reintegrate Germany into the Western alliance – had put a temporary halt to efforts to collect first-person testimonies.[47]

Pornographization

The specific political configurations of the Cold War combined with key cultural tropes to further marginalize the voices of those who had experienced sexual violence in the Holocaust. Making this case involves drawing connections between seemingly disparate and disconnected events, public perceptions, and rhetorics that nonetheless establish a cultural consensus about the limits of speech surrounding sex. It would be fairly easy to discount each isolated incident I will raise as a small and ultimately inconsequential moment. But having ourselves witnessed the sea change that the #MeToo movement has brought to public discussions of sexual exploitation, we have perhaps become particularly attuned to the incredible impact that relatively specific and isolated media stories can have on the larger public perception of how and whether sexual violence should be discussed in polite company and how these discussions are structured by historically specific gender norms and political ideologies. In this spirit, I would argue that we cannot entirely explain the disappearance of sexual violence as a theme (nor understand how victims might be silenced in the future) if we do not directly confront the disjuncture between what historians were investigating and what the broader public wanted to know.

Evidence that the public wanted to know about Nazi sexual depravity surfaced during the second half of the war. In January 1943, almost a year before publication of the *Black Book of Polish Jewry*, the *New York Times* published a brief article purporting to describe the suicide of ninety-three Jewish girls in Warsaw who had committed suicide in order to avoid being "forced into prostitution by German soldiers."[48] The story, supposedly derived from a letter written in Yiddish by one of the girls, took on mythical force through its retelling in an American Hebrew-language newspaper and a Hebrew poem by Hillel Bavli. As Pascale Bos argues, the story of the ninety-three maidens became a "religious lament" that equated female purity with Jewish martyrdom and "played an important part in the early American Jewish imagination about the Holocaust during the war."[49] In fact, the story was likely fabricated to produce outrage and public sympathy. As Bos argues,

> the story of sexual brutality ... affirmed the Nazis' purported depravity, as stories about enemy rape tend to do. The Holocaust, imagined as the scandal of brutal Nazi sexual enslavement of pious Jewish girls became a press agenda item, a subject of political engagement. Politicizing sex and sexual violence serves as a powerful ideological tool in nationalist wars, as a culturally shared ideal of "respectability" is central to the construction of modern European national identity, and a "normative" (heterosexual, consensual) sexuality is pivotal in the solidification of this respectability, as George Mosse has shown. Thus, some antifascist discourse deliberately sexualizes

> fascism and fascist nations and pronounces them sexually perverse, deviant, and sexually violent in order to politically described these nations and their politics as culturally debased.[50]

Various examples of the cultural trope of equating Nazism with sexual debasement had been evident since the rise of the Nazi party,[51] and the topic came to infuse American popular anti-Nazi propaganda. The plot of the 1943 Hollywood film *Hitler's Children*, for example, hinges on the myth that the Nazi Lebensborn homes were breeding farms where beautiful young women were matched up with SS soldiers in loveless sexual encounters for the sole purpose of reproduction.[52] Although the film itself is entirely tame, the advertising posters hinted at sexual torture, often depicting the blond female protagonist tied to a whipping post. While these popular accounts, both explicitly fictional and purportedly factual but actually concocted for propaganda purposes, were well-meaning efforts to arouse American sentiment against the Nazis, they also set the tone for how sexual violence as perpetrated by the Nazis could be discussed – with nudges and winks that alluded to but did not openly confront the actual suffering of victims, ultimately instrumentalizing their pain in exploitative ways.

Trial Spectacle and Its Effects on Popular Culture

After the war, public attention shifted from sexual depravity to the prosecution of Nazi criminals, the practical struggles of displaced persons, the reconstruction of Western Europe, and the dramatic early events of the Cold War. It was not until the 1961 trial of Adolf Eichmann in Jerusalem that public interest, particularly in Israel, turned to a focus on the experience of the survivors.[53] In the patriotic spirit of the founding of the state of Israel in 1948, remembrance had concentrated on "politically motivated narratives of well-intentioned but deeply misleading clichés" about Jewish resisters and heroes, Alon Confino writes.[54] The tone and details of the testimonies of approximately one hundred survivors at Eichmann's trial were bound to disrupt these narratives. But one witness in particular brought new attention to the theme of sexual violence, because he had already become famous for novels that contained graphic and visceral accounts of it. On 7 June 1961, Yehiel Dinur, a survivor of Auschwitz whose semi-autobiographical novels had made him famous under the pen name Ka-Tzetnik 135633, was called to the stand in Jerusalem. The presiding judge asked Dinur, whose identity had not previously been known, why he had taken the pen name Ka-Tzetnik. His answer has since become an iconic representation of the incommunicability of the experience of Holocaust survivors. "It is not a pen name," Dinur answered. "I do not regard myself as a writer who writes literature. This is a chronicle from the planet of Auschwitz." Dinur insisted that he wrote under the name Ka-Tzetnik 135633 – created out of the commonly used short form of *Konzentrationslager* (concentration camp), and the number tattooed onto forced labourers in Auschwitz – to represent all those who had lived and died under the rules of this other planet.[55] When both the prosecutor and the judge interrupted the witness to coax him away from his poetic descriptions and toward answering questions about having met Eichmann in Auschwitz, Dinur uttered a few more phrases and fell into a coma-like faint. He had to be removed from the courtroom and never continued his testimony. The scene was broadcast over Israeli radio and was later frequently shown on television, becoming the most memorable part of what was already the biggest media event in Israel's history.[56]

As Shoshana Felman has persuasively argued, Dinur's collapse has become iconic because it so succinctly symbolized the disjuncture between the juridical goal of the trial – to establish the facts of Eichmann's involvement in the Holocaust – and the impossibility of ever achieving either individual or collective closure for a trauma of this magnitude. It was a moment, she insists, "in which history as injury dramatically, traumatically spoke," transforming "an incoherent mass of private traumas (the secret, hidden, silenced, individual traumas of survivors) into one collective, national, and public trauma."[57] From the moment of their opening statement, judges Moshe Landau, Binyamin Halevy, and Yitzhak Raveh had made this disjuncture clear: "Holocaust survivors who [will appear] on the witness stand and [will present] testimony in this courtroom will open the lock to their hearts. Material of great value for the researcher and historian is contained here. But for the court, these are only byproducts of the trial."[58]

As we will see, historians had similar difficulties turning towards the hearts of the survivors, but the spectacle of the Eichmann trial and Ka-Tzetnik's role in it produced a second and far more intense explosion of *popular* interest in the theme of sexual violence in the Holocaust. Understanding something about the forms of this popular interest turns out to be a critical part of the explanation for how the silence around sexual violence became such an entrenched feature of Holocaust scholarship, since it actually discouraged scholarly interest in the subject.

The spectacle of Dinur's collapse immediately turned a specific lens towards the content of his novels, translations of which soon appeared across the globe. The novels described the violence of life in the ghettos and concentration camps in far more graphic detail than professional historians had thus far been able to stomach. Particularly in *House of Dolls* and *Piepel*, Ka-Tzetnik emphasized the centrality of sexual violence in a way that was unique and shocking in the context of his time. *House of Dolls*, first published in Hebrew in 1953, is the ostensible story of Dinur's sister, Daniella, who is forced into prostitution as a so-called *Feldhure* – a prostitute for German soldiers – in a camp that we are led to believe is Auschwitz. *Piepel*, first published in 1958, is the story of Dinur's brother, who acted as a sexual slave for a series of barrack commanders. No one has been able to determine whether Dinur really had these siblings, and the factually correct aspects of the novels are somewhat diminished by obvious fabrications. While there is considerable evidence for the sexual slavery of young boys in the camps,[59] and while, as Katarzyna Person has demonstrated, "the abuse of Jewish women was omnipresent" in the Warsaw and presumably other ghettos,[60] we can be quite certain that no Jewish women were forced or allowed to serve as prostitutes in Auschwitz.[61] And yet, we have no evidence that Dinur was purposely inventing stories in order to titillate.[62] He likely did not know that only non-German women had been forced to work in the brothel at Auschwitz, but having spent time in the Zakrau and Niedrewalden forced labour camps, the Sosnowiec and Kamionka ghettos, and the Auschwitz sub-camp Günthergrube near Lędzin, Dinur is very likely to have witnessed the sexual enslavement and debasement of Jewish women, and he is likely to have known or known of women who had used sex to survive.[63] We must therefore read this account as a reflection of Dinur's vicarious experience of the sexual violence that all Jews, but particularly women, had experienced or witnessed as part of overall strategies of dehumanization. Whether or not the details of the novels stand up to historical scrutiny, the fact that they came from the pen of a religious man absolutely committed to presenting the authentic experience of survivors means that they have to be understood as testimony about the pervasiveness of sexual violence against Jewish women in the Holocaust, from desperate sexual barter in the ghettos to rape and sexual torture in the camps.[64]

Ka-Tzetnik's books were indeed initially received as authentic testimony in Israel, where they became bestsellers, were studied by members of the Israeli Defence Forces, and were eventually (in the 1990s) even integrated into the high school curriculum.[65] When they were first published, their themes were a rarity in a society that had not yet grappled with the most violent aspects of the Holocaust. Particularly in the 1950s and 1960s, Omer Bartov argues, the novels filled two voids: a dearth of explicit investigations of the Holocaust, and a thirst for knowledge about sex. Ka-Tzetnik's graphic depictions helped satisfy "the urge of youth to be told the truth about facts of life that adults seem to be hiding from them, and their simultaneous curiosity about and fascination with matters of sex and violence." Bartov calls the sexual themes in the novels a kind of "explicit sincerity," because they amounted to a "conscious or unconscious manipulation of readers' and viewers' articulated or unspoken fears, urges, and obsessions."[66]

But the impact reached beyond Israel. Although Dinur always insisted that his books were not fiction but "chronicles" of his experience during the Holocaust and as an inmate of Auschwitz, from the 1950s until fairly recently, they were marketed in English-speaking countries as sensationalized pulp fiction. After Moshe M. Kohn's English translation first appeared with Simon and Shuster in New York in 1955, several English and American publishing houses picked up *House of Dolls* for inclusion in their series of cheaply produced reprints – at least fifty printings by 1977.[67] Through the 1950s and 1960s, these presses adorned the book with covers that played to the appetite for various forms of exploitation in the pulp fiction market of the day.[68]

English-speaking audiences unfamiliar with Ka-Tzetnik's standing as a survivor of Auschwitz could be forgiven for falling victim to this misleading classification of his work – for consigning him, as Omer Bartov has put it, "to the lunatic fringe."[69] The English-language versions of his book covers draw on visual cues from "women in prison" and sexploitation films and novels of the 1950s and 1960s that fed a slightly later trend of Nazisploitation in the 1970s and early 1980s.[70]

With this background in mind, it is not surprising that the sudden revelation about Dinur's identity and the media attention surrounding his collapse in the courtroom in Jerusalem would become a sensation. Given the puritanical atmosphere of the early years of the Israeli state, publishers of unsavoury forms of literature certainly capitalized on the attention and the taboos by increasing their production of smutty literature with Holocaust and war themes.[71] Following the example of various exploitation genres in the United States, Israeli publishers produced the *Stalags*, cheaply made novels with racy covers that turned the theme of wartime sexual violence into pornography. These novels, Amit Pinchevski and Roy Brand note, all followed a similar formula:

> The two main themes at the center of each plot are captivity and transgression. The camp is portrayed as an isolated and enclosed microcosm. Moreover, each story makes clear that the Stalag is

> unlike any other Nazi camp. Although operating under Nazi rule, it is somehow an anomaly to that rule. Hence the camp is portrayed as both an exception to and a realization of Nazism – or better, the place where the aberration and the radicalization of Nazism meet. Under its auspices are eccentricities such as a Nazi project for immortalizing Aryans, horrendous medical experiments on prisoners, or the prostitution of female prisoners by criminals turned guards. Yet the fundamental aberration of the Stalag is the unlikely presence of men and women on opposite sides of the command line. Captivity is therefore portrayed as a laboratory of extreme brutality and at the same time as an orgy waiting to happen.[72]

It is actually quite irrelevant for our purposes whether or not, as Omer Bartov and Ari Libsker have argued, mid-twentieth-century readers got the storylines of the Stalags and Ka-Tzetnik's *House of Dolls* confused.[73] It is certainly true that the Stalags do not depict sex being forced upon Jewish women, and American versions of similar novels, like *Women without Morals*, tended to depict women as sexual aggressors, wearing SS uniforms and carrying whips.[74] What matters here is that these popular responses helped create the only cultural context in which sexual violence in the Holocaust (and during the war as a whole) could be discussed at all.[75] Despite the author's stated intent, Ka-Tzetnik's books helped produce a fixation on sexual violence that found expression almost exclusively in prurient modes. This was true even in the seemingly more respectable genres of spy novels (like Ian Fleming's James Bond series) and art films, like Luchino Visconti's *The Damned* (1969) and Liliana Cavani's *The Night Porter* (1974); but it was most evident in the explosion of Nazisploitation films of the 1970s, particularly the since-iconic pornographic horror flick *Ilsa: She Wolf of the SS*.

Some will certainly find it odd that I would call such disreputable examples of Cold War culture to mind in an essay that purports to be about how sexual violence in the Holocaust should influence our understanding of genocide. But the argument is a serious one. For one thing, Nazisploitation allowed sexual violence to serve as a more comfortable stand-in for racial violence in the popular culture of the 1970s and 1980s. As Sara Horowitz has argued, "sexual violence ... domesticates the Holocaust, diminishing its horror to something more ordinary and sparing the reader a more disturbing confrontation."[76] But fear of this domestication and a general squeamishness about discussing sexual violence in the halls of academe also made it very difficult to explicitly add this form of dehumanization to scholarly definitions of genocide. Speaking only anecdotally and from my own personal experience, I will note that older male historians who demur when I argue that we should be discussing sexual violence in the Holocaust *whenever* we describe the suffering of victims have universally admitted to me that they remember reading, seeing, or at least being aware of smutty references to Holocaust porn in their youths. Those who grew up in Israel almost all remember reading Ka-Tzetnik's novels and not being able to integrate Ka-Tzetnik's message into their own understandings of the Holocaust.[77] Without naming these historians, I want to assert that their memories, generally only revealed in private conservations, inadvertently prove my point that a squeamish awareness of pornographic tropes contributed to a silence about sexual violence in the historical profession. If we want to understand the reticence of Cold War historians to include sexual violence in their definition of genocide, we have to place their decisions in the context of the popular culture that also influenced them. The explosion of smutty imagery that followed the Eichmann trial made it all the more difficult to take sex seriously as a subject of scholarly and perhaps particularly of historical investigation.[78]

So a third reason why it is so critical to add sexual violence to our definition of genocide is that if we do not, depictions of these experiences – which we now know to have been common – are likely to be passed down in the form of pornography. The social impact of this tendency is diverse. On the one hand, Carolyn Dean has argued that "pornography" in Western culture means something beyond the mere selling of sex; the word has come to describe non-sexual forms of "effaced dignity," as is clear in the tendency to use the term to describe the exploitative effect of disseminating pictures of the bodies falling out of the Twin Towers on 9/11.[79] We describe something as pornographic not only when it titillates, but when it depicts a moment of human depredation and when it creates a numbness to suffering. Dean argues that "pornography allegorizes the causes and effects of our numbness and thereby of threats to empathic identification in a wide variety of Holocaust discussions. Unlike the term 'trauma,' which performs a similar though seemingly more weighty analytic purpose in this and related contexts, pornography does not encourage but freezes discussion, and this function is arguably its most significant accomplishment."[80] To ignore sexual violence in academic historical accounts is, in other words, to cede this territory to those with far less respect for the dignity of Holocaust victims. What Bartov calls the "illegitimate" literature on the Holocaust – accounts that exploit titillating images and sensationalize suffering – produces a silencing effect on respectable scholars who do not want to be associated with it.[81]

On the other hand, we must take Bartov's point that pornographic explorations of sexual violence did fill a void. They catered to a curiosity that was not being satisfied, and they spoke to assumptions about survivors that could not be articulated in respectable venues. As Na'ama Shik notes in Ari Libsker's documentary about the *Stalags*, female survivors (particularly in Israel) had to cope with the suspicion that they had only survived through prostitution. "They were explicitly accused. 'How did you survive?' Men would usually be asked: 'Were you a Kapo?' And women: 'Were you a whore?'"[82] Since these assumptions had not been discussed or refuted in the trials or the de-emotionalized historical accounts, they found expression in both high-brow and low-brow popular culture.[83] As Silke Wenk notes, the "pornographization" of the Holocaust was *also* a means of coping with trauma. Fetishizing the female body turns out to be a convenient way of preserving a coherent historical meta-narrative in the face of the massive destructive potential of genocide.[84] Meanwhile, scholars who attempted to distance themselves from smutty depictions of the survivors' experiences risked blindly serving national narratives that rested upon heroic stories and the preservation of the heteronormative family model.

The smut, I would argue, was evidence of cultural trauma that was not being addressed elsewhere. Jeffrey Alexander defines cultural trauma as what happens when a representative of a collectivity makes a claim that goes beyond identifying guilt in order to address the broad social impact of a crime. "It is a claim to some fundamental injury, an exclamation of the terrifying profanation of some sacred value, a narrative about a horribly destructive social process, and a demand for emotional, institutional, and symbolic reparation and reconstruction."[85] In other words, Holocaust smut can be viewed as a form of testimony to a trauma with which the courts of law and the prevailing historiographical methodologies of the day were very ill-equipped to cope. In this sense, the centrality of sexual slavery and degradation in the pulp fiction and sexually explicit films of the 1970s actually reveals an aspect of the experience of the victims of the Holocaust that had then received no serious scholarly or media attention. Rather than understanding these products of popular culture as factually mistaken, we should think of them as what Lawrence Langer has called "humiliated memory": a memory that "recalls an utter distress that shatters all molds designed to contain a unified and irreproachable image of the self."[86] Ironically, even though Langer unconvincingly asserts that "the historical significance [of rape] is very small in the context of the Holocaust experience,"[87] his concept of humiliated memory nicely explains why such subjects have remained taboo in general accounts of the Holocaust despite being regularly revealed in Holocaust testimony.[88]

Testimony about Sexual Violence in Holocaust Historiography

Precisely how ill-equipped were mid-twentieth-century historians of the Holocaust to deal with sexual violence, and how far have we come? In the early years, the very personal nature of these crimes simply could not be assimilated into a discipline that prided itself on historical objectivity. This is perhaps most apparent and well researched in the Israeli case. Historians such as Ben-Zion Dinur of Hebrew University (later the first director of Yad Vashem in 1953) were convinced that the raw emotion of survivor accounts could not be woven into an objective narrative and that the professionalization of the discipline required a focus on the documents of the perpetrators. The shift toward a more survivor-centred approach came only in 1959, when agitation from survivors both within and outside of Yad Vashem forced Dinur's resignation and opened the way for what Dan Michman has called the "Israeli school" of Holocaust research, which combines attention to Jewish communities' reactions to Nazi persecution with a close reading of perpetrator documents.[89]

In Europe and North America, historians were initially even less inclined to examine survivor testimony. As Michael Geyer and Konrad Jarausch argued in 1995, the historians concerned with explaining the Holocaust from the 1950s to the 1980s were part of a rather "insular tribe" that had set itself the task of tracking the meta-narrative of Germany's political failures and catastrophes through meticulous and ideologically neutral historical research in archives. They eschewed interdisciplinary perspectives, particularly the supposed threat of postmodernism, relying instead on overarching theories of fascism and totalitarianism. A focus on the ideologies of key figures predominated, while cultural and social structures were left largely unexplored.[90] Survivor testimony was all but ignored. In his 1956 book *Harvest of Hate*, Leon Poliakov reassured his readers that "wherever possible, to forestall objections, we have quoted the executioners rather than the victims."[91] Looking back upon his role in the development of Holocaust historiography, Raul Hilberg, whose 1961 book *The Destruction of the European Jews* has become a classic, admitted in 2008 that he had taken an entirely "top-down" approach in his quest to establish what happened. Looking back on this mode of writing in 2008, Hilberg notes that the historians of the 1960s and 70s "had [presented] an incomplete picture of what was happening, and ... the victims were not properly described at all. In fact, they were not really listened to, even though they did speak in courts or publish memoirs."[92]

Many phases of historiographical debate intervened between Hilberg's first book and his 2008 reflections. The increasing sophistication of gender history and methodologies for oral history, not to mention several prominent debates about Holocaust representation, morality in history, and the moral and philosophical influences on historians' narrative techniques, would have to be explained to account for Hilberg and others' growing willingness to accept personal testimony.[93] These developments certainly opened up possibilities for understanding the history of the Holocaust in cultural terms and for taking the voices of survivors more seriously. But they were still somewhat marginal to the discipline of history as a whole, particularly in Germany. The *Historikerstreit* (historians' dispute) of the 1980s highlighted how preoccupied the profession still was with issues of military strategy, victory, and defeat, and the rancour was an indication of how defensively professional historians reacted to any challenge to their authority to monopolize historical explanation (neatly summed up in German as *Deutungsmacht*).[94] As late as the turn of the century, memory, testimony, and the contributions of eyewitnesses were still often viewed with suspicion. As Konrad Jarausch complained in 2002, many German historians viewed "the whole 'history and memory' trend as nothing but hype."[95]

But the "trend" of memory in Holocaust history did not go away. Reacting to theorists of memory such as Jan and Aleida Assmann, along with Maurice Halbwachs and Pierre Nora, German historians have been forced to accept the existence of a strong memory culture (*Erinnerungskultur*) over which they cannot exert seamless control.[96] Since the 1990s, concerted efforts have been made to engage in interdisciplinary discussions, particularly with anthropologists and scholars of literature.[97] Although historical and the literary approaches to the Holocaust have up until recently tended to travel on isolated parallel paths, a slow transformation was underway.[98]

These developments perhaps explain why the most recent comprehensive histories of the Holocaust are much more likely to make personal testimony a central feature of their accounts. The most obvious example of this is Saul Friedländer's already seminal two-volume exploration of the Holocaust, *Nazi Germany and the Jews*, and particularly the second volume, *The Years of Extermination*. Resting on meticulous archival research and a comprehensive chronological narrative of the political, military, administrative, and ideological aspects of the Nazi regime, the book is interrupted with frequent testimonies from victims. The testimonies stand virtually without comment; they are allowed to speak for themselves and to intensify what Alon Confino has called the "sensation of disbelief."[99] "By dint of its humanness and freedom," Friedländer writes, "an individual voice suddenly arising in the course of an ordinary historical narrative of events … can tear through seamless interpretation and pierce the (mostly involuntary) smugness of scholarly detachment and objectivity."[100] Confino takes Friedländer's book as marking a decisive shift in Holocaust historiography – an indication that overarching narratives of the Holocaust are no longer imaginable without testimony and the discomfort that their emotional intensity brings. Contrary to the assumptions of the 1980s and 1990s that the Holocaust was somehow unique and required specific methodological approaches, this shift actually just reveals the limits of all historical representation. There is, in other words, a new appreciation that understanding such violence requires investigating its psychological and emotional origins and manifestations. Suddenly testimonies that were previously discounted because they were too emotional and raw become key pieces of evidence in understanding human motivation and cycles of violence.[101] And yet none of Friedländer's testimonies include accounts of sexual violence or exploitation.

Unfortunately, discussions of the role of testimony in Holocaust historiography have, for the most part, operated independently of the debates within the history of gender and sexuality. Historians of gender certainly were not ignoring the Holocaust, but the most prominent historians of the Holocaust were ignoring them, sometimes with specific attempts to discount their contributions. As I have argued elsewhere, historians in the early twenty-first century who sought to explain the involvement of the Wehrmacht in the massacres of Jews on the Eastern Front introduced the concept of *Handlungsspielräume* (room for manoeuvre or scope for action) without noting that historians of gender have long debated how gender roles intersected with other aspects of Nazi society, including racial categories, to produce spheres of action (including repressive action) for both women and men.[102] In 2006, Doris Bergen noted that sexual violence is typical of all genocides but performed a specific role in the Nazi ideology of "race and space" that deserves more attention. She insisted on a very broad definition of sexual violence, "an approach that considers both men and women; and a concept that can encompass a wide range of target groups."[103] Not all sexual violence is rape, she argues, and sexual violence very much also affected onlookers and often also targeted men.

Emasculation, humiliation, the torture of gay men, and even the effects on the perpetrators are part of the larger story of sexual violence and its role in genocide. Bergen's call has certainly produced some dividends.[104] And yet, if we look at the most recent overarching histories, there is perhaps more self-congratulation about taking these subjects into account than is really warranted. Let me provide just one example: David Cesarani's 2016 opus *Final Solution.*

In a review of Cesarani's book, Mark Roseman praises the author for integrating "the long-taboo subject of sexual violence." But does Cesarani do this "prominently and well," as Roseman asserts?[105] We certainly encounter the issue of rape in Cesarani's book. We hear from Mary Berg, for instance, a resident of the Warsaw ghetto who left behind a diary describing how forced labour would often provide the pretext for sexual violence in the ghetto. "Better-dressed Jewish women have been forced to scrub the Nazis' headquarters," she writes. "They are ordered to remove their underclothes and use them as rags for the floors and windows. It goes without saying that often the tormentors use these occasions to have some fun of their own."[106] "It goes without saying." The quotation does the work here, and Cesarani does not explore how common such offences were.

In this same description of the ghetto, Cesarani then quotes Emanuel Ringelblum, the famous Warsaw ghetto archivist. Ringelblum's notes describe how women were frequently abducted: "no one knows where to; it is said that about one hundred came back a few days later, some of them infected."[107] There are hints in how these episodes are presented that such experiences were widespread and central to the lives, deaths, and vicarious witnessing of ghetto inmates. Rape is similarly included in Cesarani's descriptions of the Nazi "Jew hunting" efforts in the killing fields of Eastern Europe. But we hear nothing about how it might have figured in the persecutions of Jews in Western regions. We learn that Ukrainian guards at Treblinka chose Jewish women from the transports to rape before sending them to the gas chambers, but nothing about rape or forced prostitution in other camps.[108] There are only sixteen entries for "rape" in Cesarani's index for a thousand-page book. They are all short passages – no more than a paragraph – and most list rape within a list of physical humiliations and torture leading up to mass murder. While we do hear about the sexual vulnerability of women in hiding, there is no sustained thematization of the role of sexual violence, and there are not even index entries for non-rape forms of it, such as sexual humiliation (of both women and men), forced prostitution, or the sexual molestation of children. The Ringelblum account gives us a hint that men might have been traumatized by witnessing the sexual abuse of women, but there is little to no mention of the sexual abuse of men themselves.[109] In sum, Cesarani has certainly deployed testimony evidence in ways that make it impossible to avoid the sexual violence that these eyewitnesses report, but he does not situate it within the spectrum of genocidal strategies or explicitly contextualize it as an inevitable and widespread aspect of processes of dehumanization.

It seems clear that work still needs to be done. The early historians, focused as they were on the archival evidence, found few references to sexual violence, particularly against Jews, in German documents.[110] Up until recently, and perhaps up to the present, even the mention of this topic can still prompt denials that it occurred. When Rochelle Saidel raised the issue of rape at a workshop at Yad Vashem in 2006, for instance, literary scholar Lawrence Langer interrupted her with the demand that she provide evidence.[111] This evidence is less rich than it might be simply because historians have rarely looked for it, a failure of imagination that can be explained with two somewhat contradictory assumptions: that sexual violence accompanies war as a matter of course; and that the laws against sexual intercourse between Jews and "Aryans" – the prohibitions against *Rassenschande* (race defilement) – were actually obeyed.[112] But the combination of a long tradition of historical disinterest in testimony and historians' unwillingness to take sexuality seriously as a subject of historical research has left a large gap in our knowledge of this aspect of the experience of Holocaust victims. Even historians, like Norman Naimark and Atina Grossmann, who have written groundbreaking accounts of rape in the Soviet invasion of Germany and (in Naimark's case) the war in Yugoslavia, have not projected their insights back into World War II, or referred to the particular vulnerability of Jews or their trauma about this afterwards.[113] We are only now beginning to see the subject of sexual violence during the Holocaust take a more prominent role in research.[114]

Since historians have begun looking for it in more creative places, the evidence that sexual violence and other forms of less violent exploitation were common, particularly in the killing fields of Eastern Europe, has begun to surface. For example, there are frequent references to sexual violence in the secretly recorded conversations between German POWs in British and American detention uncovered by Sönke Neitzel and Harald Welzer in 2001. These soldiers frequently spoke, with a casual nonchalance, about witnessing or participating in sexual violence, humiliation, and instrumentalized consensual sex. These recordings therefore provide evidence of the frequency and quotidian nature of this aspect of soldiers' military experience. The transcripts of the interviews themselves are instructive in explaining why we knew nothing about this sooner. One of the British transcribers of the tapes found soldiers' discussions of incidents of sexual violence so trivial and repetitive that he stopped typing out the details, noting only the word "women" four times with time stamps at half-hour intervals.[115] One can only wonder what other examples of this kind of thing we might find if we actually look. Understanding precisely how ubiquitous this type of violence was comes *not* only from looking for its extreme or organized forms but rather from paying attention to how knowledge of it seeped into culture and social practice. Given the tendency to erase the evidence for this kind of violence, we might need to experience some of the discomfort of our peers who work on long-past centuries by basing our cases on relatively small amounts of evidence. Elissa Mailänder has recently demonstrated how much one can glean from a single photograph; she convincingly explains what a group of laughing soldiers can tell us about their likely exposure to rape on the Eastern front.[116]

In other cases, the archival evidence is richer than one might expect and is finally beginning to be analyzed. We now have studies of forced prostitution, sexual enslavement, rape, and the various forms of coerced sexual barter in both the killing fields of Nazi-occupied Europe and the concentration camps – enough to claim that there is irrefutable evidence that sexual violence was ubiquitous in every phase of the Holocaust.[117] It was also, as Regine Mühlhäuser has demonstrated, widespread in the German military (Wehrmacht), particularly on the Eastern front, a fact that cannot easily be disentangled from the progression of Holocaust violence.[118] Up until quite recently, historians simply had not developed the theoretical or narrative techniques to describe these scenes of sexual degradation with the appropriate sensitivity and understanding of culturally contingent causality.[119]

This explanation of why it took so long for sexual violence to be integrated into the history of the Holocaust leads me to suggest a fourth reason why it should be: because doing so highlights the blurred boundaries between complicity, victimhood, and perpetration that characterized the quotidian functioning of genocidal social and interpersonal structures. It is uncomfortable to acknowledge that the heightened emotions of conflict and persecution could also produce sexual release for those most threatened by the war and its racialized violence. Analogous to the complexities of describing the relationship between victim and perpetrator in the concentration camps, there were grey zones where consensual sex took place in a context of extreme repression. While the desire to survive and the need to barter for food played a role in most decisions to engage in sexual activity in the concentration camps and ghettos, Anna Hájková notes that this did not preclude the formation of love relationships. She quotes Otto Bernstein, a survivor of Theresienstadt ghetto, who reminisced that "many a passionate love began with a double portion of potatoes."[120] Even entirely instrumentalized relationships, where sex was offered in return for a hiding place or other forms of aid, could involve positive emotions. In the diary of Molly Applebaum, we learn that when she and her cousin Helen were hiding on a Polish farm, they viewed having sex with their protector not only as the price to be paid for his willingness to hide them in a pit under his barn, but also as a pleasant and even necessary distraction from the fear that might otherwise have destroyed them.[121] The sexual aspect of Applebaum's experiences, including what was clearly a passionate if unconsummated lesbian love affair with a friend who did not survive the Holocaust, receive only oblique mention in Applebaum's recently published memoir. This inability to articulate sexual experiences even late in life underlines the points about silence and taboos that I have made throughout this chapter.[122] It is not surprising that survivors felt no encouragement to tell such stories immediately after the war, when neither early welfare efforts to help them nor legal or scholarly investigations to contextualize their experiences were taking sexual violence or exploitation seriously as a central component of the dehumanizing strategies of genocide. That this silencing persists, however, is an indication of how important it is to start making this theme a more central part of education efforts.

Conclusion

This chapter has demonstrated that understanding the various stages of historiography on sexual violence requires an archaeological approach to historians' own methodologies and socio-political lifeworlds.[123] They were themselves influenced by taboos against speaking publicly about sex and sexual violence in eras when all portrayals of sex could too easily descend into or be categorized as porn and when laws against rape and efforts to counteract sexual violence in Western societies were not exactly advanced. The pornographization of the history of sexual violence in the Holocaust is a symptom of cultures that view almost any depiction of sex as porn, whether or not it conforms to Carolyn Dean's definition of "effaced dignity." To avoid this effect, we have to accord dignity to survivors by speaking about their experiences without flinching and without succumbing to taboos. We have to understand the process of silencing these voices as having arisen from both the methodological predilections of postwar historians and the fears of survivors – their reticence to break taboos, their feelings of shame and trauma, and the threat of social rejection. Given our current exposure to stories of sexual abuse, we should not find it so difficult to muster a sympathetic understanding of why many survivors quickly stopped speaking about these experiences. To reveal such stories, after all, would have done very little to contribute to the prosecution of Holocaust perpetrators, especially given the priorities of Allied justice. Telling the stories, on the other hand, certainly would have increased the pain of family and community members, both those who lived through the war in more protected circumstances and those who were born after it.

We now have enough distance from these direct relationships to move forward with less trepidation. Historians today have the methodological tools to tackle sexual violence more directly,[124] and they have become far more aware of the types of violence perpetrated in the less-regulated killing fields outside of the more well-studied concentration camps. This rich new scholarship has made it impossible to ignore that sexual violence was so rampant on the Eastern Front of World War II that it might even be considered a weapon of war, as Regina Mühlhäuser has argued.[125] This recognition will make it easier to draw comparisons between the Holocaust and other genocides, such as those I have already mentioned,[126] but also to compare it to the violent suppression of indigenous culture and its genocidal implications in the Americas and Australasia. The Canadian "sixties scoop," the Australian "stolen generation," and the sexual violence perpetrated against American Indians in various phases of their dispossession all provide examples of how genocidal goals produce opportunities for sexual abuse by stripping individuals of community protections. This fact, it bears restating, is not simply an incidental by-product of genocide; it is central to its logic of dehumanization.

In her Human Rights Watch/Africa report on sexual violence during the Rwandan genocide, Binaifer Nowrojee notes that rape was not simply an attack on an individual Tutsi woman but rather an attempt to "strip the humanity from the larger group of which she is a part." The shame that it produced was meant to disrupt families in a way that contributed to community breakdown. Hutu propagandists had "identified the sexuality of Tutsi women as a means through which the Tutsi community sought to infiltrate and control the Hutu community," an argument that justified rape as a weapon of war.[127] Without claiming that anything quite as calculated occurred during the Holocaust, I would say that the sexualized propaganda of Nazi publications like *Der Stürmer* has received too little attention as integral to the logic of the Nazi-orchestrated campaign of hate.

Nonetheless, we have enough research to demonstrate that both sexual violence and semi-consensual and exploitative forms of sexual gratification were omnipresent in the forms and practices of Holocaust violence. The fact that this subject is slowly becoming more central to the overarching narrative of the Holocaust is apparent in the plans at the United States Holocaust Memorial Museum (USHMM) in Washington, DC, to integrate this subject into its teaching activities and permanent exhibition.[128] As a museum, the USHMM is perhaps more cognizant of its role in speaking directly to the present. Curators are aware that their visitors will be making links to more recent genocides and, indeed, to the exhibitions they might have recently visited across the Mall: the Museum of African American History and Culture and the National Museum of the American Indian. I would argue that this awareness of debates going on about other cases of ethnic subjugation can only enhance our knowledge of Holocaust history.

One final point, and one last reason for this focus on sexual violence. When I first heard the story with which I began, about a child saved from the Holocaust who still bears the scars of being molested by her protectors, I could not help but be a little angry at those who would not let her tell it. Holocaust history is not so disconnected from the present that we cannot see analogies between the crimes of the past and the incredible vulnerability of vast populations of refugees in our present. By not integrating sexual violence into the history of the Holocaust as a whole, we are saying that its dangers are simply ubiquitous and unaffected by historical circumstances and human decisions about who deserves protection. And yet the extraordinary reports we are hearing about the sexual exploitation of unaccompanied minors in refugee or migrant camps really needs to give us pause. How can we hope to protect the most vulnerable from sexual exploitation in our present if we cannot face up to its reality in the past?

NOTES

1 I have done this myself: Annette F. Timm, "The Challenges of Including Sexual Violence and Transgressive Love in Historical Writing on World War II and the Holocaust," *Journal of the History of Sexuality* 26, no. 3 (2017): 351. Another

example can be found in: Zoe Waxman, *Women in the Holocaust: A Feminist History* (New York and Oxford: Oxford University Press, 2017), 1.

2 Atina Grossmann, "Women and the Holocaust: Four Recent Titles," *Holocaust and Genocide Studies* 16, no. 1 (2002): 94.

3 Primo Levi, *Survival in Auschwitz: The Nazi Assault on Humanity*, trans. Stuart Woolf (New York: Collier, 1961).

4 For detailed descriptions of Lemkin's views on this subject and the reasons they failed to become influential, see: Douglas Irvin-Erickson, "Prosecuting Sexual Violence at the Cambodian War Crimes Tribunal: Challenges, Limitations, and Implications," *Human Rights Quarterly* 40, no. 3 (2018): 570–90; and Douglas Irvin-Erickson, "Sixty Years of Failing to Prosecute Sexual Crimes: From Raphaël Lemkin at Nuremberg to Lubanga at the International Criminal Court," in *A Gendered Lens for Genocide Prevention*, edited by Mary Michele Connellan and Christiane Fröhlich (London: Palgrave MacMillan, 2018), 83–109.

5 Irvin-Erikson, "Prosecuting Sexual Violence," 574.

6 Birgit Beck, *Wehrmacht und sexuelle Gewalt: Sexualverbrechen vor deutschen Militärgerichten 1939–1945* (Paderborn: Ferdinand Schöningh, 2004).

7 "Background Information on Sexual Violence Used as a Tool of War – Outreach Programme on the Rwanda Genocide and the United Nations," accessed 24 September 2018, http://www.un.org/en/preventgenocide/rwanda/about/bgsexualviolence.shtml.

8 A. Dirk Moses, "The Holocaust and Genocide," in *The Historiography of the Holocaust*, edited by Dan Stone (Houndsmills and New York: Palgrave Macmillan, 2004), 547.

9 The most recent contribution of Mühlhäuser and Zipfel arrived too late to be integrated into this account. See the exceptionally rich collection of essays in Gaby Zipfel, Regina Fritz, and Kirsten Campbell, eds., *In Plain Sight: Sexual Violence in Armed Conflict* (New Delhi: Zubaan, 2019). I will return to this subject and to Sommer's and Hájková's work below.

10 Elizabeth Heineman, "Gender, Sexuality, and Coming to Terms with the Nazi Past," *Central European History* 28, no. 1 (2005): 41–74; Elizabeth D. Heineman, "Sexuality and Nazism: The Doubly Unspeakable?," *Journal of the History of Sexuality* 11, no. 1 (2002): 22–66.

11 Ayşe Gül Altınay and Andrea Pető, "Europe and the Century of Genocides: New Directions in the Feminist Theorizing of Genocide," *European Journal of Women's Studies* 22, no. 4 (2015): 380.

12 Katharine Derderian has argued that "rape, kidnapping, sex slavery, and forced re-marriage became de facto instruments of genocide" in the Armenian genocide. See "Common Fate, Different Experience: Gender-Specific Aspects of the Armenian Genocide, 1915–1917," *Holocaust and Genocide Studies* 19, no. 1 (2005): 1.

13 Mary Anne Warren, *Gendercide: The Implications of Sex Selection* (Totowa, NJ: Rowman and Littlefield Publishers, 1985). On gendercide in the Armenian case, see Matthias Bjørnlund, "'A Fate Worse than Dying': Sexual Violence during the Armenian Genocide," in *Brutality and Desire: War and Sexuality in Europe's Twentieth Century*, edited by Dagmar Herzog, Genders and Sexualities in History, 16–58, esp. 17–18 (London: Palgrave Macmillan UK, 2009). On gendercide in the Yugoslav war, see Adam Jones, "Gendercide and Genocide," *Journal of Genocide Research* 2, no. 2 (2000): 185–211. C. Carpenter has offered a convincing critique of the overapplication of the concept of genocide, which does not, I would argue, undermine my use of the concept to underline the difference between the Holocaust and other genocides. See C. Carpenter, "Beyond 'Gendercide': Incorporating Gender into Comparative Genocide Studies," *The International Journal of Human Rights* 6, no. 4 (2002): 77–101.

14 Forced marriage saved the lives of many Armenian women, and it was common knowledge in interwar Turkey, but as Derderian has argued, it was a mechanism for the destruction of Armenian culture, and the stigma of its violent implementation convinced its victims to remain silent. Derderian, "Common Fate," 11, 13.

15 Laura Jockusch, *Collect and Record!: Jewish Holocaust Documentation in Early Postwar Europe* (New York: Oxford University Press, 2012), 19.

16 Jacob Apenszlak et al., eds., *The Black Book of Polish Jewry: An Account of the Martyrdom of Polish Jewry under the Nazi Occupation* (New York: The American Federation of Polish Jews in cooperation with the Association of Jewish Refugees and Immigrants from Poland; Roy Publishers, 1943).

17 Antony Beevor and Luba Vinogradova, "The Battle of Kursk," in Vasily Grossman, *A Writer at War: Vasily Grossman with the Red Army 1941–1945*, edited by Antony Beevor and Luba Vinogradova (London: Pimlico, 2006), 251.

18 See for example Ilya Ehrenburg and Vasily Grossman, *The Complete Black Book of Russian Jewry*, edited by David Patterson (London and New York: Transaction Publishers, 2002), 42, 164, 346.

19 This is from an excerpt that is described as "An article based on documentary materials and depositions from the people of Kyiv. Prepared for publication by Lev Ozerov," from Rubenstein and Altman, eds., *The Unknown Black Book*, 9.

20 Ehrenburg, *The Complete Black Book*, 218.

21 For more examples, see ibid., 166, 183, 354, 382.

22 Ibid., 212–13.

23 Ibid., 18, 61, 130, 205, 428.

24 A report compiled by the author and journalist Vladimir Lidin describes an incident in Talne, Ukraine, where an SS officer pulled "a boy's pants off and

crushed his genitals with the heel of his boot. 'Try reproducing now!' he said to the laughter of other German soldiers." Ehrenburg, *The Complete Black Book*, 21. Vasily Grossman's report of the evidence compiled from Treblinka also describes how one of the commandants, Kurt Franz, had "specially trained [his] dog to pounce on the doomed people and tear out their genitals" (473).

25 Ehrenburg, *The Complete Black Book*, 149.

26 Apenszlak, *The Black Book of Polish Jewry*, 28.

27 Ibid., 26–9.

28 Rubenstein and Altman, eds., *The Unknown Black Book*.

29 Antony Beevor and Luba Vinogradova, "Afterword," in Grossman, *A Writer at War*, 344–5. As Irving Louis Horowitz notes in the preface to *The Complete Black Book of Russian Jewry*, the documents assembled by Grossman and Ehrenburg "later became a weapon in the hands of Soviet anti-Semitism" when the "Jewish Anti-Fascist Committee was [declared] a 'center for nationalistic and espionage activity'" and wartime Jewish activists were caught up in Stalin's postwar purges. See Horowitz, "The Totalitarian Collusion: The Complete Black Book of Russian Jewry," in Ilya Ehrenburg and Vasily Grossman, *The Complete Black Book of Russian Jewry*, edited by David Patterson (London and New York: Transaction Publishers, 2002), ix. In January 1948, Solomon Mikhoels, the chairman of the JAC who had cooperated with Grossman and Ehrenburg on the *Black Book*, was hit by a truck and killed. Grossman's suspicions that this was a KGB hit were likely correct. Beevor and Vinogradova, "The Lies of Victory," in Grossman, *A Writer at War*, 346. Timothy Snyder reports that by 1952, thirteen members of the JAC had been killed. "Timothy Snyder on the Forgotten Holocaust," *Truthdig*, 15 February 2008, accessed 7 May 2019, https://www.truthdig.com/articles/timothy-snyder-on-the-forgotten-holocaust.

30 Michael Fleming, *Auschwitz, the Allies and Censorship of the Holocaust* (Cambridge: Cambridge University Press, 2014), 190–1.

31 These testimonies are housed at the Jewish Historical Institute, Żydowski Instytut Historyczny, ŻIH in Warsaw, and are now also available at Yad Vashem and the US Holocaust Memorial Museum. See Beate Müller, "Trauma, Historiography and Polyphony: Adult Voices in the CJHC's Early Postwar Child Holocaust Testimonies," *History and Memory* 24, no. 2 (2012): 157–95.

32 The archive is variously known as the Ringelblum Archive, Oneg Shabbat, Oyneg Shabes, or Oyneg Shabbos. It is now housed at the Jewish Historical Institute in Warsaw (www.jhi.pl/en/archives), and selections have been made available in an online exhibition at Yad Vashem, "Let the World Read and Know," accessed 15 August 2016, www.yadvashem.org/yv/en/exhibitions/ringelbum/intro.asp. For general accounts of the archive, see Samuel D. Kassow, *Who Will Write Our History? Emanuel Ringelblum, the Warsaw*

Ghetto, and the Oyneg Shabes Archive (Bloomington: Indiana University Press, 2007). See also Zoë Waxman, "Testimony and Representation," in *The Historiography of the Holocaust*, edited by Dan Stone (Houndsmills and New York: Palgrave Macmillan, 2004), 490.

33 David Cesarani, "Challenging the 'Myth of Silence': Postwar Responses to the Destruction of European Jewry," in *After the Holocaust: Challenging the Myth of Silence*, edited by David Cesarani and Eric J. Sundquist (London and New York: Routledge, 2012), 15.

34 See ibid. for details.

35 Alan Rosen, "'We Know Very Little in America': David Boder and Un-Belated Testimony," in *After the Holocaust*, edited by David Cesarani and Eric J. Sundquist, 102, 110. Rosen notes that even combined with other efforts to interview 7,000 survivors in Poland, 3,500 in Hungary, and 2,500 in Germany, only about 2–3 per cent of DPs were ever interviewed and that most did not want to speak.

36 Jockusch, *Collect and Record*, 11. By way of comparison, she writes that the Shoah Visual History Foundation holds 52,000 testimonies (48,361 from Jews); and the Fortunoff Video Archive holds 4,400 testimonies (12).

37 On the myth of silence, see also Hasia R. Diner, "Origins and Meanings of the Myth of Silence," in *After the Holocaust*, ed. David Cesarani and Eric J. Sundquist, 192–201; and Hasia R. Diner, *We Remember with Reverence and Love: American Jews and the Myth of Silence after the Holocaust, 1945–1962* (New York: New York University Press, 2010).

38 More recent collections include: the Fortunoff Video Archive at Yale, founded in 1981, Steven Spielberg's Shoah Visual History Foundation, founded in 1994, and the various collections of Yad Vashem and the US Holocaust Memorial Museum.

39 Mark L. Smith, "No Silence in Yiddish: Popular and Scholarly Writing about the Holocaust in the Early Postwar Years," in *After the Holocaust*, edited by David Cesarani and Eric J. Sundquist, 55–65.

40 For a discussion of the "polyphony" of these narratives – the fact that the interviewers' voices, questions, and intentions are somewhat obscured and can overshadow the voices of the interviewees – see Müller, "Trauma, Historiography and Polyphony."

41 Cesarani, "Challenging the 'Myth of Silence,'" 29.

42 Ibid., 32.

43 For instance, in the late 1940s six Italian publishers rejected Primo Levi's superb and now-classic memoir *Se questo è un uomo* ("If this is a man," but most often published in English under the title *Survival in Auschwitz*). See Alon Confino, "Fantasies about the Jews: Cultural Reflections on the Holocaust," *History and Memory* 17, nos. 1–2 (2005): 315.

44 Atina Grossmann, *Jews, Germans, and Allies: Close Encounters in Occupied Germany* (Princeton, NJ: Princeton University Press, 2007).

45 Quoted from Segev, *The Seventh Million*, 121, in Pascale Bos, "Sexual Violence in Ka-Tzetnik's House of Dolls," in *Holocaust History and the Readings of Ka-Tzetnik*, edited by Annette F. Timm (London: Bloomsbury Academic, 2017), 117.

46 Pieter Lagrou, "Facing the Holocaust in France, Belgium, and the Netherlands," in *Lessons and Legacies VI: New Currents in Holocaust Research*, vol. 6, edited by Jeffrey M. Diefendorf, 482–3 (Evanston, IL: Northwestern University Press, 2004). For examples of how Jewishness was downplayed, see accounts by resisters like David Rousett, Eugen Kogon, and Pelagia Lewinska, who barely mention Jews in their books. See also Janusz Nel Siedlecki, Krystyn Olszewski, and Tadeusz Borowski, *We Were in Auschwitz*, trans. Alicia Nitecki (New York: Welcome Rain, 2000) – the Polish original was published in 1946 under the title *Byliśmy w Oświęcimiu*; Tadeusz Borowski, *This Way for the Gas, Ladies and Gentlemen*, edited by Barbara Vedder, trans. Barbara Vedder and Michael Kandel (New York: Penguin Classics, 1992) – originally published under the title *Pożegnanie z Marią* in 1959.

47 See Jockusch, *Collect and Record*, 45; Lawrence Douglas, *The Memory of Judgment: Making Law and History in the Trials of the Holocaust* (New Haven, CT: Yale University Press, 2005), 12; and Cesarani, "Challenging the 'Myth of Silence,'" 29.

48 Quoted from "93 Choose Suicide before Nazi Shame," *New York Times*, 8 January 1943, 8, in Pascale Bos, "Sexual Violence in Ka-Tzetnik's *House of Dolls*," in *Holocaust History and the Readings of Ka-Tzetnik*, edited by Annette F. Timm, 110.

49 Ibid., 111.

50 Ibid.

51 Particularly useful explorations of this theme can be found in: George L. Mosse, *Nationalism and Sexuality: Middle-Class Morality and Sexual Norms in Modern Europe* (Madison: University of Wisconsin Press, 1985); and Laura Frost, *Sex Drives: Fantasies of Fascism in Literary Modernism* (Ithaca, NY: Cornell University Press, 2002).

52 I have written about this in detail elsewhere. See Annette F. Timm, "Titillation in the Guise of Authenticity: Myths of Nazi Breeding from *Hitler's Children* to *The Kindly Ones*," in *'Holocaust'-Fiktion. Kunst jenseits der Authentizität*, edited by Iris Roebling-Grau and Dirk Rupnow, 271–94 (Paderborn: Wilhelm Fink Verlag, 2015).

53 For a description of standard assumptions about the "silence" of the survivors before 1961, see David Cesarani and Eric J. Sundquist, "Introduction," in *After*

the Holocaust, edited by David Cesarani and Eric J. Sundquist, 1–2. On the impact of the Eichmann trial, see Tom Segev, *The Seventh Million: The Israelis and the Holocaust*, trans. Haim Watzman (New York: Henry Holt and Company, 1991), 70–1, 424, 440, 479–80.

54 Alon Confino, *Foundational Pasts: The Holocaust as Historical Understanding* (New York: Cambridge University Press, 2011), 19.

55 Quoted in Shoshana Felman, *The Juridical Unconscious: Trials and Traumas in the Twentieth Century* (Cambridge: Harvard University Press, 2002), 136.

56 For descriptions of the impact of the event, see Felman, *The Juridical Unconscious*, 127; Anita Shapira, "The Eichmann Trial: Changing Perspectives," in *After Eichmann: Collective Memory and the Holocaust since 1961* (London: Routledge, 2005), 20; and Segev, *The Seventh Million*, 4.

57 Felman, *The Juridical Unconscious*, 7, 164.

58 Quoted in Hanna Yablonka, "The Development of Holocaust Consciousness in Israel: The Nuremberg, Kapos, Kastner, and Eichmann Trials," *Israel Studies* 8, no. 3 (2003): 3. Yablonka's English translation contained grammatical problems, which I corrected.

59 For a summary, see Robert Sommer, "Pipel: Situational Homosexual Slavery," in *Lessons and Legacies XI: Expanding Perspectives on the Holocaust in a Changing World*, edited by Hilary Earl and Karl A. Schleunes (Evanston, IL: Northwestern University Press, 2014).

60 Katarzyna Person, "Sexual Violence during the Holocaust: The Case of Forced Prostitution in the Warsaw Ghetto," *Shofar* 33, no. 2 (2015): 107.

61 Robert Sommer has demonstrated that none of the ten "Sonderbauten" (special buildings) where women were forced into sexual slavery in concentration camps housed Jewish women. He has found evidence that approximately two hundred women acted as prostitutes at Auschwitz. Robert Sommer, "Sexual Exploitation of Women in Nazi Concentration Camp Brothels," in *Sexual Violence against Jewish Women during the Holocaust*, edited by Sonja M. Hedgepeth and Rochelle G. Saidel, 46–60, esp. 52 (Hanover: University Press of New England, 2010); and Robert Sommer, *Das KZ-Bordell: Sexuelle Zwangsarbeit in nationalsozialistischen Konzentrationslagern* (Paderborn: Schöningh, 2009).

62 For the most detailed biography of Dinur in English, see Dina Porat, "An Author as His Own Biographer – Tzetnik: A Man and a Tattooed Number," in Timm, *Holocaust History and the Readings of Ka-Tzetnik*, 13–36.

63 There is considerable, if scattered, evidence that the sexual enslavement of Jewish women was common in such places, though we still await individual case studies and a comprehensive overview. For telling examples of what historians are beginning to find, see: Steven T. Katz, "Thoughts on the Intersection of Rape and Rassenchande during the Holocaust," *Modern Judaism – A*

Journal of Jewish Ideas and Experience 32, no. 3 (2012): 293–322; Person, "Sexual Violence during the Holocaust"; and Sinnreich, "And It Was Something We Didn't Talk About," 9. That there is still much more to uncover is clear. See Elizabeth Anthony, "Sexual Violence as Represented in the ITS Digital Archive: Concentration Camp Brothels," in *Freilegungen: Spiegelungen der NS-Verfolgung und Ihrer Konsequenzen*, edited by Rebecca Boehling et al., 49–60 (Wallstein Verlag, 2015).

64 On this subject, see Bos, "Sexual Violence in Ka-Tzetnik's House of Dolls"; Regina Mühlhäuser, *Eroberungen: Sexuelle Gewalttaten und intime Beziehungen deutscher Soldaten in der Sowjetunion 1941–1945* (Hamburg: Hamburger Edition, 2010); Dalia Ofer, "Gender Issues in Diaries and Testimonies of the Ghetto: The Case of Warsaw," in *Women in the Holocaust*, edited by Dalia Ofer and Lenore J. Weitzman, 143–68 (New Haven, CT: Yale University Press, 1998); and Katarzyna Person, "Sexual Violence during the Holocaust."

65 Bos, "Sexual Violence in Ka-Tzetnik's House of Dolls," 105. Yad-Vashem still offers a "Ka-Tzetnik Prize for Holocaust Consciousness." This is, however, not without controversy. Dan Miron has argued that his work should be removed from the "Reference Guide" for Israeli teachers and students. See the summary of his 1994 (vol. 10) article in the Israeli journal *Alpayim* in Jeffrey Wallen, "Testimony and Taboo: The Perverse Writings of Ka-Tzetnik 135633," *Dapim: Studies on the Holocaust* 28, no. 1 (2014): 4. Bartov writes that the Ka-Tzetnik prize was created when a father, grateful after a son's reading of Ka-Tzetnik helped pull him out of drug addiction, donated a sum of money to Yad-Vashem. Omer Bartov, *Mirrors of Destruction: War, Genocide, and Modern Identity* (New York and Oxford: Oxford University Press, 2000), 284n129.

66 Omer Bartov, "Kitsch and Sadism in Ka-Tzetnik's Other Planet: Israeli Youth Imagine the Holocaust," *Jewish Social Studies* 3, no. 2 (1997): 47.

67 This is Jeremy D. Popkin's estimate in "Ka-Tzetnik 135633: The Survivor as Pseudonym," *New Literary History* 33, no. 2 (2002): 343.

68 I briefly discuss these covers in the introduction to *Holocaust History and the Readings of Ka-Tzetnik*. Pascale Bos will discuss this subject in more detail in a forthcoming book.

69 Bartov, "Kitsch and Sadism in Ka-Tzetnik's Other Planet," 54.

70 For a useful collections of essays exploring these links, see Daniel H. Magilow, Elizabeth Bridges, and Kristin T. Vander Lugt, eds., *Nazisploitation! The Nazi Image in Low-Brow Cinema and Culture* (New York: Continuum, 2011). See also Insa Eschebach, "Sex-Zwangsarbeit in NS-Konzentrationslagern. Geschichte, Deutungen und Repräsentationen," *L'Homme* 21, no. 1 (2010): 65–74; and Silke Wenk, "Rhetoriken der Pornografisierung: Rahmungen des Blicks auf die NS-Verbrechen," in *Gedächtnis und Geschlecht: Deutungsmuster*

in Darstellungen des Nationalsozialistischen Genozids, edited by Insa Eschebach, Sigrid Jacobeit, and Silke Wenk (Frankfurt/Main: Campus Verlag, 2002), 269–96.

71 Whether or not these publications were directly inspired by Ka-Tzetnik's collapse is a matter of contention. Pascale Bos disagrees with Dan Miron on this point, as she will argue in a forthcoming article. See Bos, "Sexual Violence in Ka-Tzetnik's House of Dolls," 138n88.

72 Amit Pinchevski and Roy Brand, "Holocaust Perversions: The Stalags Pulp Fiction and the Eichmann Trial," *Critical Studies in Media Communication* 24, no. 5 (2007): 394.

73 See the documentary film, *Stalags [Stalagim]* (Heymann Brothers Films, Yes Docu, New Israeli Foundation for Cinema and TV, Cinephil, 2007). As Bos notes, one could also argue that Bartov and Libsker unjustifiably project the pornographic themes of the Stalags back onto the work of Ka-Tzetnik. Bos, "Sexual Violence in Ka-Tzetnik's House of Dolls," 138n88.

74 See in particular Richard F. Gallagher, "Lebensborn Was Hitler's Dream of Love," in *Women without Morals* (New York: Avon Book Division: The Hearst Corporation, 1962).

75 Guido Vitiello argues that "the Stalag as a genre constituted an early response to the trauma of the Holocaust and to the emotional impact of the Eichmann trial." Vitiello, "The Eroticization of Witnessing: The Twofold Legacy of Ka-Tzetnik," in Timm, *Holocaust History and the Readings of Ka-Tzetnik*, 142.

76 Sara R. Horowitz, "Mengele, the Gynecologist, and Other Stories of Women's Survival," in *Judaism since Gender*, edited by Miriam Peskowitz and Laura Levitt (New York: Routledge, 1997), 210.

77 That Dinur did not intend to sensationalize but rather to produce empathy for those whose suffering included sexual torture is apparent in his choice of depicting his main characters as his (possibly fictional) siblings. See the various contributions to Timm, ed., *Holocaust History and the Readings of Ka-Tzetnik*.

78 I would submit that even sensitive scholars like Bartov were influenced by this smut to describe Ka-Tzetnik's work (which he otherwise took very seriously) as pornography. See Barov's reflections on the impact of his experiences as a teenager in *Stalags [Stalagim]*.

79 Carolyn J. Dean, "Empathy, Pornography, and Suffering," *Differences* 14, no. 1 (2003): 92–8.

80 Ibid., 93.

81 Omer Bartov, "Kitsch and Sadism in Ka-Tzetnik's Other Planet," 49.

82 *Stalags [Stalagim]*. Note that I have translated from the German subtitles of her statement because there are errors in the English version. See also Na'ama

Shik, "Sexual Abuse of Jewish Women in Auschwitz-Birkenau," in *Brutality and Desire*, edited by Dagmar Herzog, 221–46.

83 While Foucault and other commentators on Nazi kitsch – most prominently Saul Friedländer and Susan Sontag – have insisted on distinguishing between the cultural work performed by high culture and the sensationalization of sexual themes in low culture, Laura Frost has convincingly demonstrated that these lines are not so easily drawn. She argues that indisputably pornographic depictions of Nazism in both literature and film (like *Ilsa* or even more extreme Nazisploitation flicks with titles like *Nazi Sadist* or *Captured Virgins of Nazi Terror*) share many characteristics with anti-fascist highbrow literature of the 1930s and 1940s, such as works by Christopher Isherwood, Klaus Mann, or Marguerite Duras. Both genres rely upon "sexuality as an index of truth, an essential indicator of ideology." Laura Frost, *Sex Drives: Fantasies of Fascism in Literary Modernism* (Ithaca, NY: Cornell University Press, 2002), 153–5, 159.

84 Wenk, "Rhetoriken der Pornografisierung: Rahmungen des Blicks auf die NS-Verbrechen," 269–96, esp. 290.

85 Jeffrey C. Alexander, "Toward a Theory of Cultural Trauma," in *Cultural Trauma and Collective Identity*, edited by Jeffrey C. Alexander et al., 1–30, esp. 11 (Berkeley: University of California Press, 2004).

86 Lawrence L. Langer, *Holocaust Testimonies: The Ruins of Memory*, new ed. (New Haven, CT: Yale University Press, 1993), 77.

87 He was interviewed by Jessica Ravitz, "Silence Lifted: The Untold Stories of Rape during the Holocaust," CNN, 24 June 2011.

88 It is striking that Langer seems to feel quite differently about the taboos surrounding another form of violence that is notable in the testimonies he explores, but is rarely discussed in general accounts of the Holocaust: cannibalism. In this case, he accepts that witnesses' refusal to talk about things "too terrible to describe" should not distract us from the fact that cannibalism was a central component of the overall experience of the Holocaust – in this case, "the disruptive effects of hunger in the extreme camp situation." Langer, *Holocaust Testimonies*, 213n28, 208n18.

89 Jockusch, *Collect and Record*, 197–8.

90 Michael Geyer and Konrad H. Jarausch, "Great Men and Postmodern Ruptures: Overcoming the "Belatedness" of German Historiography," *German Studies Review* 18, no. 2 (1995): 255, 262–3, 273.

91 Leon Poliakov, *Harvest of Hate: The Nazi Program for the Destruction of the Jews of Europe* (London: Elek Books, [1951] 1956), xiv. Quoted in Tony Kushner, "Saul Friedländer, Holocaust Historiography and the Use of Testimony," in *Years of Persecution, Years of Extermination: Saul Friedlander and the Future of Holocaust Studies*, edited by Christian Wiese and Paul Betts (London and New York: Continuum, 2010), 67.

92 Raul Hilberg, "The Development of Holocaust Research – A Personal Overview," in *Holocaust Historiography in Context: Emergence, Challenges, Polemics and Achievements*, edited by David Bankier and Dan Michman, 25–36, quotation from 29 (New York: Berghahn Books, 2008).

93 A seminal text in the history of these debates is: Saul Friedländer, ed., *Probing the Limits of Representation: Nazism and the Final Solution* (Cambridge and London: Harvard University Press, 1992). See also Saul Friedländer, "The 'Final Solution': On the Unease in Historical Interpretation," *History and Memory* 1, no. 2 (1991): 61–76. Summaries of the debates about representation can be found in: Dan Diner, ed., *Ist der Nationalsozialismus Geschichte? Zu Historisierung und Historikerstreit* (Frankfurt am Main: Fischer Taschenbuch Verlag, 1987). For a more recent and invaluable discussion of the meaning-making role of the Holocaust see Confino, *Foundational Pasts.*

94 For a very useful summary of this topic, see Dirk Rupnow, "Beyond Boundaries: History, the Holocaust and Literature," in Timm, ed., *Holocaust History and the Readings of Ka-Tzetnik*, 183–202.

95 This was something that he and Martin Sabrow at the Centre for Contemporary History at Potstdam made an effort to correct in a March 2001 conference entitled "The Historicisation of the Present." Konrad H. Jarausch, "Zeitgeschichte und Erinnerung: Deutungskonkurrenz oder Interdependenz?," in *Verletztes Gedächtnis: Erinnerungskultur und Zeitgeschichte im Konflikt*, edited by Konrad H. Jarausch and Martin Sabrow (Frankfurt and New York: Campus Verlag, 2002), 34.

96 Rupnow, "Beyond Boundaries." See also Rudolf Jaworski, "Die historische Gedächtnis – und Erinnerungsforschung als Aufgabe und Herausforderung der Geschichtswissenschaft," in *Verflochtene Erinnerungen: Polen und seine Nachbarn im 19. und 20. Jahrhundert*, edited by Martin Aust, Krzysztof Ruchniewicz, and Stefan Troebst (Cologne, Weimar, and Vienna: Böhlau Verlag, 2009), 19.

97 See, for example, the three-volume study: Etienne François and Hagen Schulze, *Deutsche Erinnerungsorte* (Munich: C.H. Beck, 2001–03); Aleida Assmann and Ute Frevert, *Geschichtsvergessenheit, Geschichtsversessenheit. Vom Umgang mit deutschen Vergangenheiten nach 1945* (DVA: Stuttgart, 1999); and Christian Gudehus and Michaela Christ, eds., *Gewalt: Ein interdisziplinäres Handbuch* (Stuttgart: J.B. Metzler, 2013). The work of Lawrence Langer has been particularly influential. See for example, Langer, *Holocaust Testimonies.* These are just a few examples of a very rich literature that cannot be explored in detail here.

98 See also Allan Megill, "Two Para-Historical Approaches to Atrocity," *History and Theory* 41 (2002): 104–23. A concerted recent effort to bring historical and literary approaches into dialogue can be found in Iris Roebling-Grau and Dirk Rupnow, eds., *‚Holocaust'-Fiktion: Kunst jenseits der Authentizität.*

99 Confino, *Foundational Pasts*, 53–4.

100 Saul Friedländer, *Nazi Germany and the Jews, 1939–1945: The Years of Extermination* (New York: HarperCollins, 2007), xxv–xxvi.

101 The history of emotions has also taken hold in German academia, as Ute Frevert's "History of Emotions" institute at the Max Planck Institute for Human Development in Berlin makes clear. For a description of methodological developments, see Monique Scheer, "Are Emotions a Kind of Practice (and Is That What Makes Them Have a History)? A Bourdieuian Approach to Understanding Emotion," *History and Theory* 51, no. 2 (2012): 193–220; and Barbara H. Rosenwein and Riccardo Cristiani, *What Is the History of Emotions?* (Malden, MA: Polity, 2018).

102 Susanne Lanwerd and Irene Stoehr, "Frauen- und Geschlechterforschung zum Nationalsozialismus seit den 1970er Jahren. Forschungsstand, Veränderungen, Perspektiven," in *Frauen- und Geschlechtergeschichte des Nationalsozialismus: Fragestellungen, Perspektiven, neue Forschungen*, edited by Johanna Gehmacher and Gabriella Hauch (Vienna: Studien Verlag, 2007), 22–68. Lanwerd and Stoehr are referring to the use of the term in the revised (2003) version of the Hamburg Institute for Social Research's "Crimes of the Wehrmacht" exhibition. For a longer discussion of the developments in gender history in Germany and amongst English-speaking German historians, see: Annette F. Timm, "Mothers, Whores or Sentimental Dupes? Emotion and Race in Historiographical Debates about Women in the Third Reich," in *Beyond the Racial State*, edited by Mark Roseman, Devin Pendas, and Richard F. Wetzell, 335–61 (New York: Cambridge University Press, 2017).

103 Doris L. Bergen, "Sexual Violence in the Holocaust: Unique and Typical?" in *Lessons and Legacies VII: The Holocaust in International Perspective*, edited by Peter Hayes and Dagmar Herzog (Evanston, IL: Northwestern University Press, 2006), 180–1.

104 See, for instance, the work of Bergen's former doctoral advisee, Anna Hájková, who is fast becoming one of the most important voices in this field: Anna Hájková, "Sexual Barter in Times of Genocide: Negotiating the Sexual Economy of the Theresienstadt Ghetto," *Signs: Journal of Women in Culture and Society* 38, no. 3 (2013): 503–33; and *The Last Ghetto: An Everyday History of Theresienstadt* (New York: Oxford University Press, 2020).

105 Mark Roseman, "The Last Word," *The Times Literary Supplement*, 10 August 2016, http://www.the-tls.co.uk/articles/public/the-last-word. This is a review of David Cesarani, *Final Solution: The Fate of the Jews 1933–1949* (London: Macmillan, 2016).

106 Quoted in Ibid., 276–7.

107 Ibid., 277.
108 Ibid., 516.
109 In his preface, Cesarani notes that "perhaps the most distressing aspect of the latest research is the light it throws on the rape of Jewish women and the sexual exploitation of Jews in ghettos and camps, in hiding and on the run" (ibid., xxxviii). He then goes on to discuss only the abuse of women and to bracket out the persecution of homosexuals, because his focus in the book is only on Jews.
110 Sonja M. Hedgepeth and Rochelle G. Saidel claim that there is virtually no reference to sexual violence in German documents. See their introduction to *Sexual Violence against Jewish Women during the Holocaust*, 2. In light of more recent research, this claim certainly requires revision. See the various accounts of documented sexual violence in David Cesarani, ed., *The Final Solution: Origins and Implementation*, new ed. (London and New York: Routledge, 1996); and Sönke Neitzel and Harald Welzer, *Soldiers: On Fighting, Killing and Dying: The Secret Second World War Tapes of German POWs* (London: McClelland and Stewart, 2012), esp. 164–75.
111 The experience prompted Saidel and Sonja Hedgepeth to begin work on their collection of essays, *Violence against Jewish Women during the Holocaust*. For an account of this experience, see Marisa Fox-Bevilacqua, "Silence Surrounding Sexual Violence during Holocaust," Haaretz, 16 July 2014, http://www.haaretz.com/jewish/features/.premium-1.599099.
112 Ruth Seifert has argued that "one rule of the game [of war] has always been that violence against women in the conquered territory is conceded to the victor during the immediate postwar period." See Seifert, "War and Rape: A Preliminary Analysis," in *Mass Rape: The War against Women in Bosnia-Herzegovina*, trans. Marion Faber, edited by Alexandra Stiglmayer (Lincoln: University of Nebraska Press, 1994), 58. On rape as a weapon of war, see Regina Mühlhäuser, "Reframing Sexual Violence as a Weapon and Strategy of War: The Case of the German Wehrmacht during the War and Genocide in the Soviet Union, 1941–1944," *Journal of the History of Sexuality* 26, no. 3 (2017): 366–401. On the myth that *Rassenschande* laws prevented rape, see Helene Sinnreich, "'And It Was Something We Didn't Talk About': Rape of Jewish Women during the Holocaust." On *Rassenschande* in general, see Patricia Szobar, "Telling Stories in the Nazi Courts of Law: Race Defilement in German, 1933 to 1945," *Journal of the History of Sexuality* 11, nos. 1–2 (2002): 131–63; and Alexandra Przyrembel,

'Rassenschande': Reinheitsmythos und Vernichtungslegitimation im Nationalsozialismus (Göttingen: Vandenhoeck and Ruprecht, 2003). That the racial-state paradigm has perhaps hidden certain truths from view is well demonstrated in the various contributions to Roseman, Pendas, and Wetzell, eds., *Beyond the Racial State*.

113 The two most influential explorations of the rapes perpetrated by Soviet soldiers in the context of the battle for Berlin, are: Norman M. Naimark, *The Russians in Germany: A History of the Soviet Zone of Occupation, 1945–1949* (Cambridge, MA and London: Belknap Press of Harvard University Press, 1995); and Atina Grossmann, "A Question of Silence: The Rape of German Women by Occupation Soldiers," *October* 72 (spring 1995): 42–63. Both of these scholars also discuss rape in more recent books more directly relevant to the topic of genocide: Norman Naimark, *Fires of Hatred: Ethnic Cleansing in Twentieth-Century Europe* (Cambridge, MA: Harvard University Press, 2001); and Grossmann, *Jews, Germans, and Allies*. In the *Fires of Hatred*, Naimark provides a section on rape in his chapter on Yugoslavia but nothing equivalent for the Holocaust. Similarly, Grossmann's book about race relations in postwar Germany spends considerable time on the trauma of German (including Jewish) women who had been raped by invading Soviet soldiers but does not explore lingering traumas of Jewish survivors of sexual violence during the Holocaust. In both cases, a dearth of existing scholarship is certainly part of the explanation, but both instances also represent a missed opportunity.

114 There are a few exceptions, such as: Andrea Dworkin, *Scapegoat: The Jews, Israel and Women's Liberation* (London: Virago Press, 2000); and Christa Paul, *Zwangsprostitution: Staatlich errichtete Bordelle im Nationalsozialismus* (Berlin: Edition Hentrich, 1995). I relied upon Paul's arguments in my two articles: Annette F. Timm, "The Ambivalent Outsider: Prostitution, Promiscuity and VD Control in Nazi Berlin," in *Social Outsiders in the Third Reich*, edited by Robert Gellately and Nathan Stoltzfus, 192–211 (Princeton, NJ: Princeton University Press, 2000); and Annette F. Timm, "Sex with a Purpose: Prostitution, Venereal Disease and Militarized Masculinity in the Third Reich," *Journal of the History of Sexuality* 11, nos. 1–2 (2002): 223–55. Important work on sexual violence as part of the occupation of Eastern Europe (as opposed to within the concentration camps) has been conducted by Regina Mühlhäuser: *Eroberungen: Sexuelle Gewalttaten und intime Beziehungen deutscher Soldaten in der Sowjetunion 1941–1945*; and "The Unquestioned Crime: Sexual Violence by German Soldiers during the War of Annihilation in the Soviet Union, 1941–45," in *Rape in Wartime*, edited by Raphaelle Branche and Fabrice Virgili, 34–46 (London and New York: Palgrave Macmillan, 2012). See also Dagmar Herzog, ed., *Brutality and Desire: War and Sexuality in Europe's Twentieth Century*.

115 Neitzel and Welzer, *Soldiers*, 170.

116 Elissa Mailänder, "Making Sense of a Rape Photograph: Sexual Violence as Social Performance on the Eastern Front, 1939–1944," *Journal of the History of Sexuality* 26, no. 3 (2017): 489–520.

117 See, for example, Helga Amesberger, Katrin Auer, and Brigitte Halbmayr, *Sexualisierte Gewalt: Weibliche Erfahrungen in NS-Konzentrationslagern* (Vienna: Mandelbaum, 2004); Bergen, "Sexual Violence in the Holocaust"; Christa Schikorra, "Forced Prostitution in the Nazi Concentration Camps," in *Lessons and Legacies VII: The Holocaust in International Perspective*, edited by Dagmar Herzog, 169–78 (Evanston, IL: Northwestern University Press, 2006); Anna Hájková, "Sexual Barter in Times of Genocide"; Person, "Sexual Violence during the Holocaust"; Maren Röger, *Kriegsbeziehungen: Intimität, Gewalt und Prostitution im besetzten Polen 1939 bis 1945* (Frankfurt am Main: Fischer, 2015); Sommer, *Das KZ-Bordell*; and Zoë Waxman, "Testimony and Silence: Sexual Violence and the Holocaust," in *Feminism, Literature and Rape Narratives: Violence and Violation*, edited by Zoë Brigley and Sorcha Gunne (New York: Routledge, 2010), 117–29.

118 See, in particular, Regine Mühlhäuser, *Eroberungen: Sexuelle Gewalttaten und intime Beziehungen deutscher Soldaten in der Sowjetunion 1941–1945*; and Regina Mühlhäuser, "Between 'Racial Awareness' and Fantasies of Potency: Nazi Sexual Politics in the Occupied Territories of the Soviet Union, 1942–1945," in *Brutality and Desire*, edited by Dagmar Herzog, 197–220.

119 Indeed, before the 1980s, historians had no methodology for even understanding the history of sex. It took the writings of Michel Foucault and other thinkers of the late twentieth century for us to begin historicizing sexuality, and it was not until the late 1990s that these insights were systematically employed in histories of the Third Reich. See Dagmar Herzog, "'Pleasure, Sex and Politics Belong Together': Post-Holocaust Memory and the Sexual Revolution in West Germany," *Critical Inquiry* 24, no. 2 (1998): 393–444; and Dagmar Herzog, *Sex after Fascism: Memory and Morality in Twentieth-Century Germany* (Princeton, NJ: Princeton University Press, 2005).

120 Hájková, "Sexual Barter in Times of Genocide," 503.

121 See Document 2016.442.1, Melania Weissenberg Collection, United States Holocaust Memorial Museum. I describe these aspects of the diary in more detail in "The Challenges of Including Sexual Violence."

122 Molly Applebaum, *Buried Words: The Diary of Molly Applebaum*, Azrieli Series of Holocaust Survivor Memoirs (Toronto: Azrieli Foundation, 2017). Other women who told their stories late in life have been less reticent about including accounts of how sex became a tool of survival. See, for instance, the gripping memoir: Marie Jalowicz Simon, *Underground in Berlin: A Young*

Woman's Extraordinary Tale of Survival in the Heart of Nazi Germany, trans. Anthea Bell (Toronto: Knopf Canada, 2015).

123 For an indispensable summary of the historiographical landscape in the late twentieth century, see Heineman, "Sexuality and Nazism."

124 These methodologies drew inspiration from the insights of feminist theory, a subject explored in detail in Mühlhäuser, "Reframing Sexual Violence as a Weapon and Strategy of War."

125 Mühlhäuser, "Reframing Sexual Violence as a Weapon and Strategy of War." See also Beck, *Wehrmacht und sexuelle Gewalt.*

126 See for example, Beverly Allen, *Rape Warfare: The Hidden Genocide in Bosnia-Herzegovina and Croatia* (Minneapolis: University of Minnesota Press, 1996).

127 Binaifer Nowrojee et al., *Shattered Lives: Sexual Violence during the Rwandan Genocide and Its Aftermath* (Human Rights Watch, 1996), 2.

128 In January 2017 Dagmar Herzog and I co-taught the Jack and Anita Hess Faculty Seminar at the Mandel Center of the USHMM, and we were told that our theme, "Gender and Sexuality in the Holocaust," had been chosen as part of this initiative.

3

Frames and Narratives: How the Fates of the Ottoman Armenians, Stalin-Era Ukrainians, and Kazakhs Illuminate the Concept of Genocide

Ronald Grigor Suny

The fraught and emotionally charged word *genocide* has been deployed as a polemical weapon by journalists and even scholars to condemn incidents of mass killing under a rubric that has acquired a particularly powerful resonance. While some would limit the term to the Judeocide by the Nazis during World War II, others extend the meaning of genocide to any incident of mass killing. The first practice narrows the term too drastically; the latter unnecessarily dilutes the concept and clouds explanation of why genocide occurs. The argument in this chapter is that analysts ought to refrain from collapsing all forms of mass violence into a single type, usually titled genocide, a term that regrettably has been stretched to cover quite distinct forms of crimes against humanity. As defined by the United Nations Genocide Convention, genocide is about the killing of a people, not the killing of people. That is, in the case of genocides, intentional mass murder is directed against a culturally defined group. In the exact words of the convention, genocide involves "acts committed with intent to destroy, in whole or in part, a national, ethnic, racial or religious group." Genocide, in other words, in legal terms and international law, is a particular instance of crimes against humanity, and that larger category certainly would include the Armenian genocide, the Holocaust, the Holodomor, the Kazakh famine, and other state-directed attacks on social or political groups. In order to make state-induced famines a genocide under the UN definition, it would be necessary to demonstrate that they were ethnocides rather than simply mass killings.

Intention, as well as the principal target, is key. In many cases, class and nationality, the social and the ethnic, cannot easily be disentangled, as in the case of Ukrainians (overwhelmingly peasant) and Kazakhs (nomads); in the Armenian genocide, Armenians and Assyrians of all classes, without social distinction, were subject to the same forced deportations, mass killing, and forced assimilation into Islam. While the Holodomor and the Kazakh famine were imperial assaults of the centre against distinct peripheries, they cannot be reduced to the intentional mass killing of Ukrainians or Kazakhs designed to either eliminate them as a people or render them unable to reproduce themselves as a nationality. Genocide, as has been pointed out by Dirk Moses, is the ethnicization of violence. As the "crime of crimes," it appears particularly horrific, because unlike the mass killing of political actors, who have some agency in choosing their identity, the ethnic or "racial" victims of genocide have no choice. They are killed simply because of who they are by birth.

In this chapter I examine the Armenian genocide and the Holodomor as two events that differed significantly enough to demonstrate how the concept of genocide and other historical framings can illuminate and explain why mass killings take place. I will also reference the Kazakh famine and forced settlement of nomads to refine further my understanding of genocide. In such mass crimes, motive and intentions must be specified. Before the Armenian genocide of 1915, there were other instances of mass killing of Armenians in the Ottoman Empire, most importantly the Hamidian massacres of the 1890s and the pogrom in the city of Adana in 1909. In much of my work I have tried to disaggregate these disastrous events, even though there are connections and similarities between them.[1]

Violence and even mass killing had long been part of the governing practices of successive governments in the Ottoman Empire and later in the Turkish Republic. Understandably, social scientists, most particularly historians and anthropologists, have concentrated their investigations on the seeming ubiquity and normality of state violence, punctuated by extraordinary outbursts of killing on a massive scale by governments and ordinary people. The violence against the Kurds today, which in the minds of many in the academy and in the towns of eastern Anatolia is often linked to the Armenian genocide (as Kurds themselves put it, "the Turks had you for breakfast, and they will have us for lunch") might be more precisely seen as closer to the systematic repression and the occasional use of military force during the Hamidian massacres than to the genocide.

While to the victims and to moral observers the effects of violence are similar in pain and consequence no matter what the intentions or motivations of the perpetrators, for social scientists and historians, distinctions among cases of mass killing are made in order to understand their causes. For analytical purposes I distinguish between three different forms of intentional and non-intentional mass violence. *Exemplary violence*, deployed to terrorize people into submission and obedience, should be distinguished from *excisionary* or *exterminationist violence*, which aims to eliminate special kinds of people, in the case of genocide a designated ethno-national, religious, or "racial" group, a "people."[2] These are different types of violence from *residual violence*, what American officials call "collateral damage," caused by policies or actions intended for other purposes than the actual killing of people, as in state-induced famines. The Hamidian massacres of Armenians and Assyrians in the mid-1890s, in which hundreds of thousands of people lost their lives, would be an example primarily of exemplary violence. The Armenian genocide was an extraordinary and singular example of a new regime of violence when exemplary violence gave way to excisionary violence, the state effort to eliminate whole peoples – in this case, Armenians and Assyrians – from the imperial territory, or at least to disperse them, Islamize them, or marginalize them ("Let them live in the desert but nowhere else") in order to destroy them as a coherent and conscious people able to maintain a social, political, or even cultural existence. The Ukrainian Holodomor, catastrophic as the death from famine was (an estimated four to five million people), is in my reading an example of residual violence, massive death from ill-formed and vicious policies directed toward a different end than the elimination of a people or a given category of people. While Norman Naimark sees Stalin's policies of the 1930s, which included dekulakization and the *Ezhovshchina* (both politically motivated killings of politically defined groups) as genocide, I share the view expressed by Michelle Tusan that genocide and genocidal are distinct. The adjective can certainly be used to describe acts of mass killing that do not strictly meet the conventional definition (that is, the definition in the UN Convention on Genocide), but which are akin to, that is, have an affinity with or similarity to, genocides.

Blurring categories makes it impossible to explain why mass killing occurs. As a lapsed political scientist, but one still infected by the virus of rigour, I also take seriously the historian's tendency to make careful distinctions, to split rather than lump, and believe that making such distinctions is the best path to analysis and meaningful explanation. In an attempt to salvage the concept of genocide from both unhelpful narrowing and broadening, I suggest that we look carefully at a variety of alternative frames within which to place our narratives. One of the most productive trends in both Russian/Soviet and Ottoman historiography has been the effort to rescue history from the nation and nationalism and from us-and-them histories, the very kind that have plagued narratives employing the charged term genocide. The denationalization of history has led to very fruitful engagements with the concepts of empire and imperialism, which in the case of the Armenian genocide introduces more integrated and powerful explanations of why the ruling Young Turk elite decided in 1915 to eliminate two of its constituent peoples from the realm. Turning the lens of empire to Soviet history also suggests that, rather than eliminating a whole people or even a part of it, Stalin's misguided and vicious policies were facilitated by an imperial framing of a subordinated people and were carried out with the intention of suppressing opposition and obtaining inordinate quantities of grain from a resistant peasantry. The Soviet empire was a dedicatedly modernizing empire, committed to moving its diverse peoples through an imagined evolutionary progression from one mode of production upward to urbanity, industrialism, and socialism. The regime's ambitions required in the minds of the ruling elite the crushing of peasant independence and the forced sedentarization of nomads. Those who carried out these policies, brutal and inhumane as they were, convinced themselves that they were fulfilling the historical role of social emancipation. Assisted often reluctantly by local collaborators, the outsiders sent to collect the grain were extraordinarily cruel. As true believers, they tortured people and watched them die, convinced that they were building a better world. The future dissident Lev Kopelev, then an enthusiastic Communist, remembered, "We were realizing historical necessity. We were performing our revolutionary duty. We were obtaining grain for the socialist fatherland. For the five-year plan."[3] This was a war between city and country, of Communist zealots against peasants desperate to survive, each with opposing visions of who the other was.

Besides the move from nations/nationalisms to imperial contexts, I suggest that a serious effort should be made to de-essentialize the master narratives that characterize the regimes in which the violence took place. In the case of the Ottoman Empire the move away from notions of "the terrible Turk" or the inherent violence of Islam opens analysis to more contingent, contextual, and conjunctural factors. In dealing with the Holodomor or other mass killings under Stalin, the specificity of that regime – which to my mind differs significantly from the periods before 1928 and after 1953 – must be rescued from the prevalent, deductive anti-Communism and anti-Sovietism that has marred much of Western historiography of the Soviet Union. The unquestioned normality of liberal assumptions has produced a tendency to condemn rather than critically examine the Soviet experience. Following my intellectual mentor, Moshe Lewin, I proudly, perhaps defiantly, declare myself "an anti-anti-Communist." This does not mean pro-Communist, which is the default accusation, but insists on a critical engagement with the Soviet experiment without prejudgement, prejudice, or prior indictment. Anti-Communism, which to many Western liberals and conservatives is unreflectively equated with objectivity, neutrality, and moderation, has often judged the whole of Soviet history as a condemnation or refutation of Marx or Lenin or the revolutions of 1917, and has led many to the facile equation of Stalinism with socialism *tout court*. A less condemnatory approach, which must at the same time avoid the pitfall of apologetics, makes distinctions between the revolutionary ambitions of ordinary people in 1917, the practices of Lenin, and the extraordinary cruelties of Stalinism. Many of those closest to Lenin, who later suffered prison, exile, or death, saw Stalinism as a counter-revolution against the original Bolshevism and the aspirations of 1917.[4]

If the Armenian genocide and the Holocaust are archetypical of genocide, why then is the Holodomor or the Kazakh famine not a genocide? After all, the horrendous loss of life at the hands of a brutal state was certainly genocidal. Here intentions and targets are key. Stalin's campaign of collectivization was an assault on Ukrainians and Kazakhs as peasants and nomads, on their traditional way of life, even as the intentions of the regime were not to deliberately kill them but to secure high grain requisition and consolidate the state's power over the village. The "economic" campaigns accompanied other attacks on tradition and custom, on religion, and on the national (even national-Communist) intelligentsia. The mass deaths were the consequence of horrific policies aimed at fulfilling a particular concept of socialist modernization, brutally applied; while they do not fit the UN definition of genocide, they unquestionably were crimes against humanity.

Although the intention to annihilate or render impotent a people is central, genocide is not only about intentions. It is also about consequences. The Soviet state had the power to destroy Ukraine and Ukrainians, and the Kazakhs as a people, but it neither intended to do so nor came anywhere close to annihilating these peoples or their culture. Throughout the famines there were secret relief efforts, and in the end grain was sent to Ukraine. After the famine years Ukrainians continued to benefit from Soviet nationality policies even as they were severely restrained, unable to express openly nationalist sentiments. Their sense of oppression was completely justified, yet at the same time millions in Ukraine supported the Soviet Union and its peculiar idea of socialism, and fought and died on the Soviet side during World War II.

The Hamidian Massacres, 1894–96

The particular framing that an analyst deploys illuminates some things and obscures other things. While a frame based on the nation explains much about the Armenian genocide – the nationalist rhetoric of Young Turk ideologues, ethnic cleansing and demographic engineering as a prerequisite for an ethnonational state – an imperial frame illuminates other aspects and offers a more complex explanation. During the reign of Abdül Hamid II (1876–1909), and indeed for much of Ottoman history before and after the 1890s, the use of state violence and the deployment of military force, whether regular or irregular, was part of the governing regime: mechanisms to keep *Herrenvolk* (ruling people) in positions superior to the simple *reaya* (the "flock" or ordinary people). Occasionally the normal, everyday violence used to maintain order, obtain revenues, and fight crime or rebellion metastasized into much more systematic massacres and deportations.

While some Ottoman historians have praised the degree of tolerance provided by the autonomy granted to the *millets* (religious communities), given the persistent Ottoman policy of using violence as a form of governance, it is understandable that many historians have relied on a "continuity theory," rather than a "rupture theory," emphasizing the connections of the Hamidian massacres to the genocide. Without doubt there were connections, continuities, and parallels between these two events. The perpetrators were state actors and their agents; the victims were Christian Armenians and Assyrians; the state disguised its involvement and denied its responsibilities; habits and practices of mass killing became routine and were thought to be justified; similar arguments about state security against treacherous, rebellious people were used in both cases; and both the Hamidian and Young Turk governments sought to "nationalize" – that is, Islamize or even Turkify – Anatolia as a secure base for the ruling people of the empire as they lost the imperial territories in the Balkans. Without effacing the different contexts and motivations between the Hamidian massacres and the genocide, it is notable that the architect of the genocide, Talat Paşa, pointed out that the Young Turks who came to power in 1908 were much more ambitious and determined than Abdül Hamid to "solve" the Armenian question, much more thorough and ruthless than the Red Sultan to eliminate Armenians as much as possible. The regime's ambitions and achievements were so unique, so radical, so extreme that a new word would eventually be coined to describe this particular form of excisionary violence against a designated ethnic, religious, racial group. That term was "genocide."[5]

The continuity theory linking relatively discrete instances of Ottoman violence into a narrative of genocidal intent over many decades has a long pedigree. One might note that the dedicated liberal parliamentarian James Bryce was convinced that massacres were not simply singular acts of repression but in Abdül Hamid's empire had become a long-term policy of extermination of Christians. As early as his 1889 parliamentary speech, Bryce told the House that "the whole policy of the Turkish Government would make one believe that they were following out the principle laid down by a Turkish Prime Minister some years ago, when he said that the way to get rid of the Armenian question was to get rid of the Armenians." There were certainly not only exemplary but also excisionary aspects to the Hamidian massacres, which included the removal and murder of village populations, but these excisions were not carried out as systematically as they would be in the genocide. There was far less direction from the centre in the 1890s than there would be in 1915–16. Much of the violence under Abdül Hamid was generated locally, by zealous valis (provincial governors) or infuriated crowds of armed Muslims. The picture that has emerged from recent local studies is one of separate points of violence initiated or breaking out in different times at different places. Coordination from the centre appears to be absent, but what links the various massacres is, first, the generalized fear of change that anticipated reforms would bring, change that would disadvantage Muslims and give privileges, perhaps autonomy, to Armenians. A second common thread tying together the local cases of killing is the permissiveness, even encouragement and participation in many cases, of state authorities and military in the violence against Armenians and Assyrians. Abdül Hamid encouraged and permitted officers and ordinary people to rise against the Armenians and was happy to reduce the Armenian presence in Anatolia. But his modernizing program contained within it a conservative restorationist agenda that sought order above all. Even when he fashioned himself as a modernizer of the empire, centralizing the government and building clock towers throughout the land, his personal paranoia reflected his own and broader social anxieties about unregulated change, the loss of status of Muslims domestically and of the empire internationally, and the special position of the Armenians within and outside Ottoman lands – a people whose talents he and others recognized and resented. Armenians had to be controlled, taught a lesson, reduced in influence and numbers, but not erased from the multicultural mosaic of the empire. Abdül Hamid was an empire preserver, not a demographic radical and ethnic cleanser like Talat and the Young Turks, or an ethnonational nation-maker like Kemal Atatürk.

After the Hamidian massacres of the 1890s, the Muslim opposition to Abdül Hamid, known abroad as the Young Turks, uneasily allied with Armenian and other revolutionary forces, but over time they adopted Abdül Hamid's vision of imperial preservation only to carry it to a more extreme conclusion. After taking power in a military coup in 1908 and initially resurrecting the constitutionalism, inclusion, and egalitarianism of the pre-Hamidian Tanzimat period, they abandoned the path to a more liberal multinational empire and gravitated toward a Muslim-Turkish dominated empire. Ottoman Armenians embraced the promises of constitutionalism, disbanded their revolutionary bands, and declared that they would work within the law. But promises were not fulfilled; the Young Turks failed to redress the ills that had befallen their Armenian subjects, most importantly returning Armenian lands seized earlier by Kurds and other Muslims. Instead, like Abdül Hamid before them, the Young Turks allied with the Muslim Kurds against the Armenians. After the January 1913 coup, which catapulted the most radical Turkic nationalists into power, Talat and Enver set out to realize their "nationalizing" aspirations, which included the expulsion of Aegean Greeks in 1914 and the mass deportation and massacre of Armenians and Assyrians in 1915–16.

When one considers the effects of the Hamidian massacres along with their causes, a dismal picture emerges. The government decided to permit, even encourage, lawlessness, targeting some of the most productive of the empire's subjects. Those who had long exploited the peasantry and lived off the rents of those who produced agricultural goods, those who drove the productive into debt and extracted lands from those who worked it, were given free rein to terrorize the Armenians and Assyrians. Tens of thousands of Christians pragmatically converted to Islam; other tens of thousands (among them my mother's mother's family from Diyarbakır [Tikranagert in Armenian]) emigrated. Lessons were learned by the state: Europeans might protest but there will be little consequence. Violence works. The powerful win, and there is little retribution. Not only are the victims deprived – at least for a time – of a voice, but they can be constructed as the architects of their own destruction – as terrorists, rebels, subversives, traitors.

This "provocation theory," as political scientist Robert Melson called it, blames Armenian revolutionaries for the killing, and indeed there were radical activists in some places who helped to create tensions between Christians and Muslims.[6] But scholars have concluded that there were no examples where the revolutionaries provoked the initial violence. Rather they attempted to avoid violence. Massacres were more likely to occur where there were no revolutionaries than in places (like Van) where

Armenian activists were more numerous. While Armenians were being killed in the hundreds and thousands, the world watched. Reactions varied from Christian and humanitarian outrage at the appalling, deliberate acts against ordinary, largely defenseless people, to a realpolitik response that the states of Europe were not responsible for protecting subjects of another empire. Realism, rather than humanitarian intervention, usually won out, and there was no crusade against the crescent. Instead of empathy for the Armenians, indifference reigned. Closely allied to realism was the hybrid position based on the superiority of some (Turks and Germans) and the inferiority of others (in this case, the Armenians) that perversely justified mass murder. In Wilhelmine Germany many bought into the provocation thesis and blamed the Armenians for the disorder, or the Great Powers for fanning the flames of chaos. A singular but powerful oppositional voice, that of Protestant pastor Johannes Lepsius, bucked the tides and advocated, unsuccessfully, for meaningful intervention. He was met by a backlash of Armenophobic and racist responses. Armenians were seen by some as "just the same as the European Jews" or bloodsucking Orientals. While Great Britain equivocated, the German Empire positioned itself as the staunchest defender of the Ottomans and Abdül Hamid's regime. In the decades leading up to World War I, the Armenian question and the fate of the Ottoman Empire became major pivots around which the Great Powers formed two hostile alliances.

The Genocide of 1915–16

The scale and intended effects of the massive expulsions of 1915 made the genocide a far more radical, indeed revolutionary, transformation of the imperial set-up than the Hamidian massacres. Genocide was not planned long in advance, and nor was it continuous with the earlier policies of conservative restoration through massacre or the brutal killing and deportation (*surgun*) that regimes had used to keep order or change the demographic composition of towns and borderlands. As in earlier and later massacres of Armenians, victims and victimizers were of different religions, but these mass killings were not primarily driven by religious distinctions or convictions. Rather than spontaneously generated from religion or even ethnicity, the motivations for murder arose from decades of hostile perceptions of the "other" exacerbated by a sense of loss of status, insecurity in the face of perceived dangers, and the positive support and encouragement of state authorities for the most lawless and inhumane behaviour. In order to understand the mentality and motivations of the Young Turk leaders, as well as ordinary people, to engage in mass murder, it is necessary to explore the affective dispositions of these state actors and ordinary perpetrators: the fear, resentment, and hatred that shaped their understandings and led to their strategic calculations to eliminate what they perceived to be an existential threat to the empire and to the Turks.

In my book *"They Can Live in the Desert but Nowhere Else": A History of the Armenian Genocide*, I set out to uncover the etiology and evolution of that affective disposition, the emotional universe within which things were understood and in which decisions were made. A cascade of social, political, and international destabilizations battered older ways of thinking, feeling, and acting, and generated a particularly pathological interpretation of the Armenians. Rather than religion or nationalism in isolation being catalysts to genocide, a toxic mix of past experiences, conflicts over land and status, and anxiety over their future all contributed to the disposition of the Young Turks that led them to genocide. At a moment when the Ottoman Empire was in danger – its very existence was at stake – and the Russians on one front and the British on another launched attacks, the Young Turks acted on the fears and resentments that had been generated over time. They directed their efforts to resolve their anxieties by dealing with those they perceived as threatening their survival – not their external enemies, but a perceived internal enemy, the Armenians, whom they saw as allied to the Entente. Turkic nationalist ideology, inconsistent and ill-defined as it was, both fed into and was nourished by the emotional perceptions of their lived "reality." What to denialists and their sympathizers appears to be a rational and justified strategic choice to eliminate a rebellious and seditious population can be seen as the outcome of a pathological construction of the Armenian enemy, a mental picture of the Ottoman world based on an emotional disposition that led to distorted interpretations of social reality and exaggerated estimations of threats.[7]

Most analysts agree that in the first decade of the twentieth century there was a significant shift among the Young Turks from an Ottomanist orientation, in which emphasis was on equality among the *millet*s within a multinational society that continued to recognize difference, to a more nationalist position in which the superiority of the ethnic Turks (already implicit in Ottomanism itself) and their privileged position within the state were more explicitly underlined.[8] In the early twentieth century a Turkic nationalism based on linguistic ties among Turkic peoples and notions of a common race spread among Turkic intellectuals, like Yusuf Akçura (1876–1935), both within and outside the Ottoman Empire.

A conception of a Turkish nation extended far beyond the Ottoman Turks or Anatolian Turks to a pan-Turkic ideal celebrating the ties between all the Turkic peoples, stretching from Anatolia through the Caucasus to central Asia. Ziya Gökalp (1876-1924) vividly expressed such a view in his famous poem *Turan*: "The fatherland for Turks is not Turkey, nor yet Turkestan, The fatherland is a vast and eternal land: Turan!" Many of the Turanists argued for a purified Ottoman Turkish language, freed of Arabic and Persian words, that would serve as the language of this Turkic nation and also as the official language for the non-Turkic peoples of the empire, those that made up the Ottoman *millets*. Not only Greeks and Armenians, but Arabs as well, resisted some of the modernizing programs of the Young Turk Committee of Union and Progress (CUP) that at one and the same time attempted to universalize rules and obligations for all peoples of the empire and threatened to undermine the traditional autonomies enjoyed under the *millet* system that privileged certain religious communities.

Four choices were possible for the empire after 1908: either to remain an empire dominated by Turks, subordinating the non-Turks, and perhaps expanding eastward to integrate other Turkic peoples into a Turanian empire; to transform the empire along pan-Islamic lines, allying Turks with Kurds and Arabs; to adopt the program of the liberal Ottomanists and become an egalitarian multinational state with the different religious and ethno-national communities within it constituting a single civil nation of Ottomans; or, finally, to cease to be an empire altogether and become an ethno-national state of the Turks. This last option was not clearly envisioned by political leaders until after the world war, for it would require both the dismemberment of the empire state, the loss of the Arab territories, and the physical removal from Anatolia or assimilation of millions of Armenians, Greeks, and Kurds. Though the Ottomanist option remained part of the official rhetoric up to 1914, leading Young Turk theorists and activists gradually abandoned the liberal, multicultural approach for more intensive Turkification. That move away from liberal Ottomanism and towards Turkism, the pan-Turanian form of Turkish nationalism, and pan-Islam accelerated after the coup of 1913.[9]

The Armenian genocide was the central event in the last stages of the dissolution of the Ottoman Empire. The traditional imperial paradigm that had reigned in the empire was steadily undermined by a number of factors: the revolutionary changes in the West that rendered the empire a backward and vulnerable society; the attempt to modernize along Western lines by the *Tanzimat* reformers; the differentially successful adaptations to modern life by different *millets*, with the Christians and Jews ahead of the Muslims; and the discourse of the nation that created new sources of political legitimization and undermined the traditional imperial ones. After centuries of governing the Armenians as a separate ethno-religious community, the *Ermeni millet*, and conceiving of them as the "loyal *millet*," the Ottoman state authorities and Turkish political elites, including the Young Turks, began to see Armenians as an alien people, as disloyal, subversive, "separatist," and a threat to the unity of the empire, which now required greater homogenization. This perception was compounded more broadly by anxiety about the relative economic success of Armenian businessmen and craftsmen, the competition for limited economic resources (particularly land) between Kurds, Turks, resettled Muslim immigrants from the Caucasus and the Balkans, and Armenians in eastern Anatolia, and a sense that Armenian progress was reversing the traditional imperial status hierarchy in which Muslims were positioned above the *dhimmi*, the non-Muslim "protected people." A hostile disposition towards the Armenians made Muslims more likely to see their actions not as defensive but rebellious, not as loyal but treacherous, and state permissiveness allowed Muslims to take vengeful action against these traitors.

When in the first year of the First World War the Young Turks suffered a series of defeats in the east and anticipated an Allied breakthrough in the Dardanelles, their sense of an imminent Armenian danger became acute, and they decided to carry out a vicious policy of deportation and massacre to clear Anatolia of Armenians. Initiated by the state in the brutalizing context of war, the removal of the Armenians soon became a massive campaign of murder. Social hostilities between Armenians and Turks, and Kurds and Armenians, fed the mass killings, which the state encouraged (or at least did little to discourage). More than any other instance of *surgun*, the genocide came to be seen as an opportunity to rid the empire of the Armenian problem, which had been used as a wedge by Russians and other Europeans to interfere in the Ottoman Empire. While fear and resentment, anger and hatred contributed to the disposition of the leaders who ordered the deportations, so did a perverse sense of justice and revenge against a supposed internal threat.

Given their strategic aim of preserving the empire and their conceptualization of the Armenians as internal traitors threatening its existence, Young Turk leaders initiated ethnic cleansing combined with mass annihilation. Salvation of the decaying empire required, in the minds of the Young Turks and many of their German allies, the elimination of the Armenians. Both the radicalization of their intentions and the final implementation of their plans occurred in the context of a deepening political and military crisis and the near destruction of the Ottoman state at the hands of external enemies – a crisis that consolidated a hostile affective disposition that led the Young Turks to believe the Armenians presented a mortal danger to the empire.

But these attitudes, seemingly confirmed by isolated instances of Armenian behaviour (sporadic attempts by Armenians at resisting massacre; the defection of a few leading Armenians to the Russian cause; and the organization of volunteer units of Armenians across the border in Russia), were exaggerated, sometimes deliberately, to highlight the image of Armenian treachery. These pathological constructions of the other led to a misrepresentation of the actual political and social environment in the Ottoman Empire. In reality most Ottoman Armenians were neither disloyal nor interested in separatism. They were productive subjects of the empire. Thousands of young Armenians served in the Ottoman army, and some died fighting the Russians. The very actions taken by the Young Turks pushed Armenians to act in ways that conformed to the CUP's image of treacherous Armenians. Defence, as in Van, became rebellion. Turkish state violence against Armenians then put the empire in greater danger and helped to bring about its defeat. In one aspect genocide was instrumentally irrational, based on self-deception, driven by a distorted emotional disposition and web of beliefs that constructed an Armenian enemy – the same Armenian enemy that the current Turkish deniers and their pseudo-scientific allies claim actually existed and was engaged in a civil war against the empire. Only in another, retrospective perspective would ethnic cleansing and mass murder appear more rational – the founding crime on which the succeeding regime, the Republic of Turkey, a relatively homogeneous nation-state, would be built.

Mass murder in and of itself does not a genocide make. Although legal definitions do not capture the full range of historical examples, I am arguing that there is utility in restricting the term "genocide" to what might more accurately be referred to as "ethnocide." Ethnocide is the deliberate attempt to eliminate a designated group defined by the cultural characteristics – language, imagined biological origins ("race"), religion – that have historically bound them together as a community and appear to distinguish that people from others. The term "ethnocide" is here used synonymously with "genocide," though some scholars have made an important and useful distinction that ethnocide is the destruction of a culture while genocide is the physical destruction of a people. "If the term genocide recalls the idea of 'race' and the will to exterminate a racial minority," writes Philip Clastres, "the term ethnocide gestures not toward the physical destruction of people ... but towards the destruction of their culture. Ethnocide moves then toward the destruction of their culture. Ethnocide is the systematic destruction of modes of life and of thought of different peoples ... To sum up, genocide murders the bodies of peoples, ethnocide kills their spirit. In either case, it is always a question of death, but of a different kind of death."[10] In my definition, genocide involves both the physical and the cultural extermination of a people. While other forms of crimes against humanity – war, massacres, induced famines, the Great Purges, Hiroshima and Nagasaki – involve death on a horrendous scale, the motivations and intentions of the perpetrators are different enough from ethnocides that they require distinct explanations.

In his first publication using the term he had coined, the lawyer Raphaël Lemkin explained: "The practice of extermination of nations and ethnic groups as carried out by the invaders [the Nazis] is called by the author 'genocide,' a term deriving from the Greek word *genos* (tribe, race) and the Latin *cide* (by way of analogy, see homicide, fratricide)."[11] As difficult as it is to discern, intentionality is key as the starting point, and death is the result of the intention to eliminate or render impotent. Genocide, thus, is "ethnically inspired violence" but should be distinguished from ethnic cleansing, which may entail killing but more immediately involves displacement and deportation, the physical moving of a distinct population.[12] Ethnic cleansing – whether of the American Indians or Aboriginal Australians; Chechens, Kalmyks, Crimean Tatars, Volga Germans, and other Soviet peoples; Palestinians or Kurds – is accompanied by loss of life, and killing is often an instrument to force people to move. The physical removal of people because you want the land but not its inhabitants is closely related to genocide, but may or may not require mass murder. The imperial ambitions of Europeans and the subsequent settler colonialism, beginning immediately after the discovery of the Americas in the fifteenth century and continuing into the twenty-first, resulted in horrendous violence and the forced movements of peoples, brutal precedents to the policies carried out by the Young Turks and the Nazis. Indeed, the American clearing of the continent and dispossession of the lands of its native peoples inspired Hitler's plans for the future of Eastern Europe. Ethnic cleansing and genocide bleed into one another, points on a tragic real-world spectrum, but they are usefully kept distinct for analytical purposes.

According to the UN definition, the genocidal elimination need not be total, but it should render the "people" impotent, politically and possibly culturally. Here Stalin's goals may be seen to approach genocide if one accepts that moving from a traditional, patriarchal, religious, village-centred culture is equivalent to the destruction of the nation. But in the imperial modernizing project of the Soviet regime, an older national culture was to be replaced by a higher form of civilization, a socialist nation with the features of a modern secular, more egalitarian industrial and urban society. That goal proved to be elusive, even contradicted by the viciousness of Stalinism, yet the effort transformed the cultures and societies of the Soviet peoples fundamentally. Similarly, in the cases of the Armenian and Jewish genocides, destruction of the peoples and their cultures were only partial. Those genocides eventually led to new states being formed and populated with survivors and their descendants. But the mass of Armenians never returned to the historic homeland in Anatolia they had inhabited for three thousand years, and the Jews, while hardly totally erased, never reconstituted the vibrant Yiddish culture that they had evolved over many centuries in Central and Eastern Europe. Those genocides had results; they were genocidal in the physical, political, and cultural sense. Both Jews and Armenians survived and were eventually able to establish their own independent states. And as nation-makers with imperial ambitions, they would prove to be capable of their own programs of ethnic cleansing.

Ethnic cleansings and genocides not only are catastrophes for the victims, but also impoverish the perpetrators. The ruined churches, the burnt-out homes, the decaying medreses in the Ottoman East all testified to a policy that made the country poorer, less educated, and less productive. Such policies, first in the 1890s and later repeated on a grander scale in 1915–16, continued in the repressions of Armenians, Greeks, and Kurds in the Kemalist period. And even today, in the Turkey of Recep Tayyip Erdoğan, a program of authoritarian homogenization, aimed primarily at millions of Kurds, drives a country of great potential backwards into a dark future.

Insidious Comparisons: The Armenian Genocide and the Holodomor

Because mass killings vary so greatly in origin, perpetrator, intention, scale, and intended outcome, no explanation can cover all or even most of the cases. Too many dependent variables make it impossible to come up with the principal causal factors. Stalin's intentions and actions during the Ukrainian famine, no matter what sensationalist claims are made by nationalists and anti-Communists, were not the extermination of the

Ukrainian people but were related perversely to the collectivization campaign, the destruction of any form of resistance to the dictates of the ruling party, and the absurdly high targets for requisitioning grain. Ukraine, like Kazakhstan, was a frontier zone, and fear of nationalist, anti-Communist Poland and memories of peasant revolts during the civil war of 1918–19 compounded the anxiety about Ukrainian resistance to the writ of the Kremlin.[13] Incompetence and callousness were as much the culprits as were fear of potential resistance, anger at the failure to deliver grain, and deep-seated hostility toward peasants and nationalists.[14] Like the Irish Famine of 1845–52, the Bengal Famine of 1943, and the Chinese Famine of 1958 to 1961, government was culpable in the deaths of millions in Ukraine. It is understandable that such horrific occurrences should be thought of as genocidal both in scope and intention, given that the foreseeable consequences of state policy resulted in mass death. But since they were not directed at the extermination of a definite ethnic, religious, or cultural group, a different set of explanations is required, as is necessary for the Great Purges, the Gulag, and the ethnic cleansing of the "small peoples" of the USSR. The value of the term "genocide" in the public sphere may be moral condemnation, but for historians and social scientists its salience stems not simply from establishing a category, but from the explanatory potential of that category. Historians must ask the questions "*when* genocide" and "*why* genocide."

By the early 1930s Ukrainians had gone through a world war, repeated revolutionary turnovers, a series of invasions, civil wars, Sovietization, and the nationalizing policies of the early Soviet state. While historians differ over the national sensibilities of ordinary Ukrainians in the first decades of the twentieth century, those writing on the Holodomor agree that peasants in Ukraine identified with their way of life before collectivization, and were ready to defend their homes, livestock, and families. When attacked by outsiders – Communists, Russians, and Ukrainian collaborators – they resisted as much as they were physically able. Soviet nationality policy in the 1920s had promoted Ukrainization, and identity with Ukraine and the idea of a nation had become stronger. The onslaught of collectivization produced an even tighter sense of us and them, of peasants as Ukrainians being battered by the Soviet state and of Communists who could easily be conflated with Russians.

Collectivization was an assault on Ukrainians, Kazakhs, Russians, and others as peasants and nomads, an attack on their traditional way of life, even as the immediate intention of the regime was to secure high grain requisitions, not to deliberately kill them. Stalin's ferocious policy of collectivization and the seizure of grain created a mammoth human catastrophe.

In the drive to collectivize the peasants of the Soviet Union and collect the grain required to feed the cities and export abroad, Stalin's government ruthlessly confiscated the produce, food, and even seed grain from its peasants and precipitated a devastating famine in Ukraine, the North Caucasus, the lower Volga region, Kazakhstan, and elsewhere. Millions died; people resorted to cannibalism; and the regime turned a blind eye to massive suffering for several years.

While I contend that the Holodomor was not a genocide, there was a connection between Stalin's campaign against Ukrainian nationalist intellectuals and the simultaneous assault on the peasants. Stalin was convinced – or had convinced himself – that Ukrainian peasants, along with Ukrainian party officials, were resisting the absurd, unreasonable quotas imposed on them. He considered their recalcitrance to be nationalist resistance to Soviet power and ordered that the last grain reserves be requisitioned, well aware that millions would die. The famine was not an act of nature but a deliberate human creation. The regime callously watched as people starved to death, and only in 1933, when the crisis threatened the loyalty of Soviet soldiers (many of them Ukrainians), did the government send grain into Ukraine and end the destructive policies. This was a case of repressive exemplary violence aimed at ending any resistance of Ukrainians to the policies of the central state – not the physical and cultural elimination of Ukrainians.

Here the frame of empire is helpful. The Soviet state was an imperial regime that maintained, even promoted, social and ethnic distinctions that made it easy and acceptable to differentially punish parts of its population. The Holodomor and the Kazakh famine were imperial assaults of the centre against distinct peripheries, though it would be going too far to reduce them to Russia versus Ukraine/Kazakhstan, part of a series of colonial impositions undifferentiated over time.

The imperial frame helps us move away from national and nationalist narratives and from liberal anti-Communist moralizing. Scott Straus has stressed that genocide is a political concept. The genocide frame creates one class of victims and another class of perpetrators. It makes reconciliation difficult if not impossible. States like this frame because it sets up a Manichaean view of history and contributes to the invisibility of alternative narratives. In this way it functions like the reductionist, simplifying narratives of nationalism.

Nationalisms gain their shape and strength from the particular discourses within which the nation is imagined, the styles and affective tones that link the people of the nation together in solidarity, and the ways they distinguish themselves from the alien other. Ukraine, Kazakhstan, or Armenia can be imagined as connected and coherent internally through their painful and destructive historical experiences, and distant and hostile to other peoples nearby. Alternatively, these countries can be imagined to share traditions with their neighbours and be reconceived in less exclusivist forms. Holding tight to images of the eternal "Terrible Turk" or the colonizing Russian separates peoples whom geography has fated to be together. Even humanistic intellectuals like the poet Ivan Drach have expressed such sentiments. In 1993 he wrote, "The first lesson which is becoming an integral part of Ukrainian consciousness is that Russia has never had and never will have any other interest in Ukraine beyond the total destruction of the Ukrainian nation."[15] More recently, journalist Anne Applebaum concludes that the Holodomor has become central to the perceptions (what I call the "affective dispositions") of post-Soviet Ukrainians, who believe they have experienced "centuries of Russian imperial colonization and decades of Soviet repression" and "the USSR's systematic destruction of Ukrainian culture and memory."[16] Such categorical simplifications of complicated and fraught histories only harden what is in fact fluid and should be made even more so. The death famines and the genocide have become central sources of national identities for Ukrainians, Kazakhs, and Armenians. Instead of a shared, complexly interwoven history, these visions separate and distance peoples from neighbours, relating their fates as fundamentally hostile and antagonistic, an image that seems confirmed by the current conflicts between the countries bordering one another. But serious, balanced historical exploration belies such a consistently Manichean picture. Other ways of imagining the past, present, and future remain open. Scholars have the difficult task of providing the kinds of knowledge that their readers have of history and assisting them to imagine a past more truthful and useful for the future.

NOTES

1 See, for example, Ronald Grigor Suny, *"They Can Live in the Desert but Nowhere Else": A History of the Armenian Genocide* (Princeton, NJ: Princeton University Press, 2015).

2 I have borrowed this distinction from the work of David Hoffman on Stalinism with his permission.

3 Cited in Anne Applebaum, *Red Famine: Stalin's War on Ukraine* (New York: Doubleday, 2017), 232.

4 For a critique of the anti-Communist framing of Soviet history, see Ronald Grigor Suny, "Debating Famine and Genocide" [a review essay on Anne

Applebaum, *Red Famine*], in *Contemporary European History* 27, no. 3 (2018): 476–81.

5 Much of what follows in my discussion of the Hamidian massacres comes from my introductory essay, "The Hamidian Massacres, 1894–1897: Disinterring a Buried History," *Etudes arméniennes contemporaines*, no. 11 (2018): 125–34.

6 Robert Melson, "A Theoretical Inquiry into the Armenian Massacres of 1894–1896," *Comparative Studies in Society and History* 24, no. 3 (July 1982): 481–509.

7 For interpretations of the genocide that are compatible with my own analysis see, e.g., the thoughtful essay by Stepan Astourian, "The Armenian Genocide: An Interpretation," *History Teacher* 23, no. 2 (February 1990): 111–60; Michael Mann, *The Dark Side of Democracy: Explaining Ethnic Cleansing* (Cambridge: Cambridge University Press, 2005); Mark Levene, *Genocide in the Age of the Nation State*, 2 vols. (London: Bloomsbury, 2005); Benjamin A. Valentino, *Final Solutions: Mass Killing and Genocide in the Twentieth Century* (Ithaca, NY: Cornell University Press, 2005); and Donald Bloxham, *The Great Game of Genocide: Imperialism, Nationalism, and the Destruction of the Ottoman Armenians* (Oxford: Oxford University Press, 2005).

8 See, e.g., Ernest Edmondson Ramsaur, Jr, *The Young Turks: Prelude to the Revolution of 1908* (Princeton, NJ: Princeton University Press, 1957); and Feroz Ahmad, *The Young Turks: The Committee of Union and Progress in Turkish Politics, 1908–1914* (Oxford: Clarendon Press, 1969).

9 This position is reflected in Cemal Paşa's statement: "Speaking for myself, I am primarily an Ottoman, but I do not forget that I am a Turk, and nothing can shake my belief that the Turkish Race is the foundation stone of the Ottoman empire … In its origins the Ottoman empire is a Turkish creation." Djemal Pasha, *Memories of a Turkish Statesman, 1913–1919* (London, n.d. [1922]), 251–2, quoted in Jacob Landau, *Pan-Turkism in Turkey: A Study of Irredentism* (London, 1981), 50. For a strong statement that emphasizes the burgeoning Turkic ideology, see Hans-Lukacs Kieser, *Talaat Pasha: Father of Modern Turkey, Architect of Genocide* (Princeton, NJ: Princeton University Press, 2018).

10 Pierre Clastres, "De l'Ethnocide," *L'Homme* 14, nos. 3–4 (1974): 102 (my translation).

11 Raphael Lemkin, *Axis Rule in Occupied Europe: Laws of Occupation, Analysis of Government Proposals for Redress* (Washington, DC, 1944), 79. Lemkin would later broaden his concept of genocide to include political and other groups.

12 Norman Naimark, *Fires of Hatred: Ethnic Cleansing in Twentieth Century Europe* (Cambridge, MA: Harvard University Press, 2001), 12.

13 See Andrea Graziosi, "The Uses of Hunger: Stalin's Solution of the Peasant and National Questions in Soviet Ukraine, 1932 to 1933," in *Famines in European Economic History: The Last Great European Famines Reconsidered*, edited by Declan Curran, Lubomyr Liucuk, and Andrew G. Newby, 223–60 (New York: Routledge, 2015).

14 In a provocative synthesis elaborating why Stalin's crimes should be considered genocides, Norman Naimark claims, "Political and social groups become 'invented' nations. The argument about whether the Ukrainian killer famine was directed against peasants or Ukrainians in this sense misses the point that these categories blended so easily with each other. At the very best, Stalin was determined to destroy their culture and traditional way of life." *Stalin's Genocides* (Princeton, NJ: Princeton University Press, 2010), 29. Ultimately, the argument becomes circular: by changing the definition to include what you want to call genocide, that phenomenon then becomes genocide.

15 Cited in Applebaum, *Red Famine*, 345.

16 Ibid., 345, 357.

4

The Holodomor in the Context of Soviet Mass Killing in the 1930s

Norman M. Naimark

There are many ways of thinking about the Holodomor in historical context, none of which necessarily excludes the others. Some historians have dealt with the Holodomor using comparative analysis, counterposing its genocidal characteristics to other genocides in modern history.[1] Others have looked more specifically at its properties as the product of a man-made famine in a Communist society, comparing it, in particular, to the Chinese Great Leap Forward, which cost – even at conservative estimates – some 30 million lives.[2] Comparing the Holodomor to the contemporaneous and devastating Kazakh famine, which killed more Kazakhs in terms of percentage of the targeted population than did the Ukrainian famine, can also produce instructive insights, since the Kazakh tragedy, with 1.2–1.5 million dead, shares the same political context but played out in different ways. The Soviet campaign of de-nomadization in Kazakhstan produced similar genocidal results.[3] Ukrainian historians more often than not emphasize the national/ethnic character of the Holodomor, pointing out that the genocide of the early 1930s was directed against the Ukrainian nation above all, not just at Ukrainian peasants.[4] The national/ethnic perspective makes the case easier for calling the Holodomor genocide, since it then conforms rather more neatly to the December 1948 UN Convention on the Prevention and Punishment of the Crime of Genocide.

For historians of the Soviet Union, a common and productive way of approaching the Holodomor is through the lenses of "the Great Soviet Peasant War," as Andrea Graziosi has called it: the Bolshevik attack on peasants in general and on Ukrainian peasants in particular, which began soon after the "Great October Revolution" and the institution of "war communism."[5] Anne Applebaum starts her justifiably acclaimed book *Red Famine* in this way, with an examination of the Civil War and the assault against the Ukrainian peasants during the period 1918–21. What happened to the Ukrainian peasantry in 1932–33, in her account, needs to be understood against both the backdrop of the Civil War and the collectivization campaign of 1929–30.[6]

In this contribution, I argue that the Holodomor can be profitably examined within the context of Soviet mass killing in the 1930s – what I called in my 2010 book "Stalin's genocides."[7] Here I want to focus more concertedly than in the book on the question of the continuity of Stalin's mass killings in this period. Although the seeds of mass murder were planted in the Bolshevik Revolution and the Civil War, I would suggest that the actual carrying out of genocide required a series of actions and reactions on the part of the perpetrators that was specific to Stalin's tyrannical rule, which one can date from the year 1930, when, in Oleg Khlevniuk's words, "the Stalinization of the Politburo was completed" and Stalin was "confirmed as the sole leader of the Politburo."[8] The disastrous policies of forced industrialization and collectivization were also completed in the main by 1930, which included a fierce campaign of "dekulakization" that led directly to the famine of 1932–33 throughout the Soviet Union and in Ukraine in particular. In 1932, the authorities conducted operations in towns and cities against "criminally, socially dangerous, and parasitic elements," which were intertwined with the introduction of the passport system in early 1933.[9] Hundreds of thousands of innocent people were expelled from the major cities to seek sustenance elsewhere. Then the 7 August 1932 law on the protection of socialist property created a draconian reality for peasants in which the minor theft of collective farm grain or food could be punished by execution. Combined with famine and the vengeful requisitioning of remaining peasant supplies in the winter of 1932–33, these measures (and others about restricting movement and limiting entrance to urban centres) brought about the Holodomor. One Ukrainian party chieftain described the control of the 1933 harvest as a "struggle to the death. This year was a test of our strength and their [the peasants'] endurance. It took a famine to show them who is master here. It has cost millions of lives, but the collective farm system is here to stay. We've won the war."[10] This was a mistake; the war was far from over. Instead, the famine initiated a period of mass murder that, punctuated by short periods of relaxation and retreat, continued until 17 November 1938, when the Politburo prohibited all "mass arrest and banishment operations," followed a week later by the removal of NKVD chief Nikolai Yezhov.[11]

Throughout the 1930s, it seemed as if the system needed periods of calm to absorb the spasms of bloodletting before engaging in another round of violent repressions. Mass killing in the pre-World War II period became part and parcel of securing Stalin's murderous despotism against its domestic and foreign enemies, both real and, more often than not, imagined. The failure of his policies meant the Soviet people would suffer. The coming of the war in late 1938 and 1939 disturbed the pattern of intense repression and brief relaxation of the previous decade.

The way I would like to go about exploring the linkages between the Holodomor and the mass violence in the 1930s is to use the fundamental characteristics of the history of genocide as a way to guide our understanding of the process as a whole. The major stages in the story of Soviet genocide include: (1) the dekulakization campaign that began in January 1930, when some 30,000 alleged kulaks were shot and another 2 million sent into exile, and Ukrainian kulaks (kurkuls) were designated, in Hiroaki Kuromiya's words, "particularly dangerous";[12] (2) the Holodomor and the attack on the Ukrainian intelligentsia, 1932–33, when some 3.5–4 million Ukrainian peasants in Ukraine and the Kuban died of starvation and related diseases, and tens of thousands of urban Ukrainians were "repressed;" (3) the Polish and German operations, the largest of the nationality repressions, which were begun already in 1932–33 when the borderlands were cleansed of some 15,000 Polish and German families – meaning roughly 50,000 people, who were arrested and deported to the special settlements – but reached their apogee during 1937–38, when the NKVD executed 105,485 Poles and 75,331 Germans; (4) order no. 00447, due to which at least 680,000 members of a variety of targeted groups were shot (some estimates go up to a million);[13] and (5) the Great Purges, which saw hundreds of thousands of alleged "enemies of the people" and political oppositionists eliminated. This does not exhaust the list of episodes of mass murder in the 1930s that totalled, in Robert Conquest's estimate in the revised version of *The Great Terror*, 10 million people killed.[14] And the number of dead does not in any way capture the bitter suffering and travails of those who survived the dekulakization, the famine, the purges, and the terror.

The issue of numbers needs to be adumbrated before continuing with a history of the repressions. Since the early 1990s, a large number of Soviet documents have been declassified and made available to researchers by the Russian archival service. Especially the reports from the OGPU and NKVD – the Soviet security police organizations – list in striking detail and with suspicious precision the numbers of arrested, executed, and deported in the period under consideration. These numbers need to be used very carefully and should not be considered the final word on how many Soviet citizens were repressed in the 1930s and how many were executed, killed, and perished from maltreatment, hunger, disease, torture, and the physical hardship of internment.[15] The fact that the columns of numbers always add up and that the numbers themselves are always provided to the last digit – 496,460 Chechens and Ingush deported in 1944, 1,803,392 dekulakized peasants in 1931–32, or 681,692 people shot in 1937–38 – leads one to believe that this impossible accuracy may reflect deeper problems with their veracity.

Sometimes, the incentive of the police and prosecutors was to ratchet up the numbers of arrested and executed as a way to prove their diligence to their superiors. More often, their incentive was to underreport and not report at all, especially when it came to "extraneous" deaths in the Gulag or the special settlements, and when dealing with famine or dekulakization. Alexander Yakovlev, who was head of a commission to investigate the Stalinist repressions in the early 1990s and had extraordinary access to archival sources, warned against accepting the NKVD figures as recorded. "These [NKVD figures] are false," he states. "They do not take account of the number of people confined in the internal prisons of the NKVD, and those prisons were jam-packed. They do not break down the mortality rates in camps of political prisoners, and they ignore the numbers of arrested peasants and deported peoples."[16] A good example comes from an incident related by the German historian of the terror Jörg Baberowski. At the beginning of 1934, NKVD chief Genrikh Yagoda sent an order to his Ukrainian subordinates that he needed 20,000 able-bodied prisoners to work on the Moscow-Volga canal. Many simply disappeared. Baberowski writes: "No one counted the prisoners who starved, froze to death or were shot in their labors."[17] The false precision of the NKVD data, plus the constantly shifting political agendas of the agencies charged with political repression, should be enough to insert a note of skepticism into the confident use of NKVD numbers by contemporary historians.

The Political Leadership

Genocide is not a spontaneous event. It is almost always initiated by governments, political leaders, and their bureaucratic chiefs, and is purposeful in its planning and execution. Stalin – without doubt – was the author of mass murder in the 1930s. This is pretty much agreed upon by all of those recent historians who have used the Stalin archive (fond 558) in their work, among them Oleg Khevniuk and Steven Kotkin.[18] Stalin developed the targets, provided the justification, initiated the actions, even sometimes set and adjusted the quotas of those who would be sent into the Gulag and those who would be killed. (Usually, he adjusted upwards the quotas for those who were subjected to the "highest penalty.") He also closely monitored the work of his OGPU/NVKD chiefs, Genrikh Yagoda and Nikolai Yezhov.[19]

In the trial of the Trotskyite-Zinovievite Terrorist Centre, Stalin raised the number of defendants to sixteen, including five Germans, and edited the testimony of the accused. In the second trial of the Anti-Soviet Trotskyite Centre, he hand-edited the charges.[20] He urged his adjutants to treat their prisoners with harshness and brutality, sometimes recommending torture. The method of "beat, beat, beat, and beat again," as Khrushchev noted at the 20th Party Congress, came directly from him.[21] Stalin was convinced that a "fifth column" of enemies existed in the Soviet Union and that they had to be eliminated for the revolution to survive. There could be no mercy shown to the groups of traitors and potential traitors that he identified and then proceeded to destroy, either by shooting them or exiling them to the Gulag. They were to be treated the same way as the former oppositionists in the party.

Genocide is never simply a matter of the will of a tyrant. It reflects the desires and complicity of larger numbers of perpetrators, without whom genocide could not be carried out. There was not only continuity in the supreme author of genocide in the 1920s, but in the lieutenants who oversaw the killing and sometimes carried it out. In Ukraine, the chief culprit was Vsevolod Balitskii, who was brought back to Ukraine at the end of November 1932, to quote *Izvestiia*, "in a period of brutal kulak resistance to collectivization … to help millions of *kolkhozniki* overcome kulak sabotage and secure the peaceful development and flourishing of the young Ukrainian kolkhozes."[22] As an important member of the Politburo of the Ukrainian party and the people's commissar of Internal Affairs, Balitskii turned Ukraine into a secret police dictatorship, which saw the repression of millions of Ukrainian peasants, intelligentsia members, and city dwellers, in the spirit of Lazar Kaganovich's observation that "every Ukrainian is potentially a nationalist," meaning that every Ukrainian was a likely police target.[23] Balitskii himself was removed from Ukraine by Yezhov in May 1937, ostensibly for the purpose of cleaning up the troubled Far Eastern Territory where the Ukrainian police chief was initially sent. Like so many of his OGPU cohort under Yagoda, Balitskii was implicated in a "terrorist-fascist conspiracy," sentenced to death in secret, and shot in July 1937. He was soon replaced in Kyiv by A.I. Uspenskii, who claimed in 1938 not only that 75–80 per cent of Ukrainians were bourgeois nationalists, but that "all Germans and Poles living in Ukraine are spies and saboteurs."[24]

Balitskii oversaw a group of younger mid-level perpetrators, whose political biographies dated for the most part from the dekulakization campaign of 1930–31. As Lynne Viola demonstrates in her recent book *Stalinist Perpetrators on Trial*, these were very rough-and-tumble characters, whose sense of right and wrong was warped by the violence of forced grain requisition, the shooting of kulaks, and the deportation of millions of peasants from their home villages. Caught up in the Yezhov trials like their boss Balitskii, these local NKVD chieftains' trial documents give a nasty picture of the bloody tortures carried out in their interrogation chambers and of the complete lack of honesty of the confessions in the protocols that they were charged with producing.[25] Gratuitous violence suffused the increasingly brutish repressions of the 1930s, from the dekulakization through the Great Terror, and provided a powerful element of continuity to the genocides that took place in that era. The ethics of NKVD persecution were clear: the ends justified the means, any means. When one head of the Chernihiv regional NKVD asked what to do with the arrested elderly and invalids, Yezhov rebuked him: "Ekh, you are a Chekist! Take them all to the woods and shoot them."[26] (It is unlikely, of course, that these deaths would be recorded.)

Historians cite 681,692 victims of NKVD executions in 1937–38. But it is well worth remembering that many hundreds of thousands more – we don't know exactly how many – died of beatings, torture, and suicide while interned, and of hunger, exposure, and disease in the unbearably overcrowded and under-provisioned camp system.[27] The transport of prisoners always involved high death rates, also frequently unreported or underreported by the NKVD. Even after Yezhov was dismissed as NKVD chief in December 1938, the security services continued to arrest a large number of alleged enemies. Between 1938 and 1940, the Ukrainian NKVD seized an additional 165,565 people for a variety of alleged political crimes.[28]

The Ideology

Another aspect of continuity in the various episodes of mass killing during the 1930s was the ideological backdrop to the violence. Ideology and ideas drive genocide, even if they are frequently primitive and self-contradictory. They form a set of mental precepts that infuse the actions of the perpetrators, though it takes politicians and policemen to implement them. The backdrop in this case was Marxism-Leninism-Stalinism that predicted war and intervention, given the fact that capitalism and imperialism would inevitably strike at the socialist usurper. Therefore, the Soviet Union was to be placed on a constant war footing, which justified treating alleged opponents as heinous traitors. In addition, the campaigns of the 1930s can only be understood in the context of Stalin's interpretations of Marxism-Leninism that claimed that socialism had in the main been built in the Soviet Union and that the struggle of its internal enemies against it would only intensify the closer socialism came to realization. As Stalin's lieutenant and Leningrad party chief, Sergei Kirov, wrote in *Pravda* (8 October 1932), "everyone can see that we were utterly correct, that the further we proceed on the path of constructing socialism, the more manifest is the counterrevolutionary character of every oppositionist tendency."[29] Alleged class enemies – like those Ukrainian "kulaks" and "Petliurist" intellectuals who led the Ukrainian countryside to resist collectivization – would raise their battle flag because of the threat to their control of agriculture. The kulaks, Stalin made clear, would be "eliminated as a class," meaning murdered or sent to the special settlements where they would also die of hunger, disease, and exposure in huge numbers. The kulak was "a bloodsucker, an oppressor, and parasite," remembered the later Soviet dissident Petro Hryhorenko (Grigorenko).[30] Many party activists in Ukraine, among them the eventual dissident and writer Lev Kopelev, convinced themselves that they must not "give in to debilitating pity" for the peasants. Despite the horrific conditions they experienced around them, they needed to be resolute in their ideologically correct tasks of fighting "kulak sabotage." "I believed," Kopelev remembered, "because I wanted to believe." [31]

The paroxysms of death and violence that shook the Ukrainian countryside at the height of the famine in 1932–33 forced a brief relaxation in Moscow's repressive policies until the assassination of Stalin favourite Sergei Kirov on 1 December 1934, which served as the pretext for a new period of terror. During the brief period of relaxation, kulaks escaped their desperately overcrowded places of exile and found ways to enter the labour-short enterprises in the cities, some 400,000 people altogether.[32] They even sometimes returned, usually illegally, to their home villages and reclaimed their confiscated property. After Kirov's assassination, Stalin personally picked up the cudgel at the beginning of 1935, when denouncing what he called the Leningrad terrorist centre of Zinovievites and the Moscow terrorist centre headed by Grigory Zinoviev and Lev Kamenev, calling them "essentially a form of White organization in disguise, making it entirely appropriate for their members to be dealt with as if they were Whites."[33] This was the beginning of widespread political purges which encompassed the entire country.

Order no. 00447, promulgated on 30 July 1937, was intended in part to destroy the kulaks once and for all. Two categories of targets were established, those to be exiled and those to be executed, and every province, territory, and republic was given quotas for each: 268,950 to be arrested, of whom 72,950 were to be executed. As we know, these quotas were, in Soviet parlance, "fulfilled and over-fulfilled" by ambitious provincial NKVD officials, who sought accolades for themselves by asking the central authorities to raise their quotas, requests that were almost always granted. Along with the elimination of kulaks, order no. 00447 envisioned the cleansing of the cities of "asocial elements," alleged criminals, prostitutes, gamblers, chronic alcoholics, street hoodlums, and so on, a process that had begun already in 1932 and continued through the middle of the 1930s. Similarly, the *byvshie liudi*, people who were earlier members of the imperial government, army, and police; former members of political parties, like the Kadets, S-Rs of various sorts, Mensheviks; and others, like the Ukrainian borot'bisty, a left Ukrainian social-revolutionary party that disbanded in 1920 in favour of joining the Bolshevik party – none would be allowed to enter the exalted stage of socialism with the rest of the population. They would be executed or isolated from the healthy body politic in the Gulag and special settlements. Order no. 00447 was extended several times and set unusually high quotas for Ukraine. By the time the operation was finished, according to NKVD statistics, 1,575,259 people were arrested, of whom 1,344,923 were convicted, and 681,692 were shot.[34] Certainly, a substantial percentage of those convicted and sent to the Gulag, probably over half, died before the decade of the thirties came to an end.

Lynne Viola emphasizes the strong continuities in the means, the methods, the organizational structure, and the personnel of the repressions in the 1930s: "The mass operations demonstrated a striking continuity with the repressive campaigns against the kulak during collectivization ... Many of the organizational structures and policies of the mass operations were derived from this first Stalinist terror and its aftermath, as were the categorization of enemies, social and ethnic, that populated both campaigns."[35] Continuities existed among the members of the troikas from the period of dekulakization and even among some of the victims. Many of the kulaks who were sent to labour camps and special settlements by the troikas in the period 1930–34 were executed by their successor troikas' orders in 1937–38.[36] The preamble to order no. 00447 characterized the action as a "*final solution to the problem of the internal enemies of the Soviet Union.*" It states: "The organs of state security face the task – of carrying out by the most merciless means the destruction of all these bands of anti-Soviet elements ... and finish at last, once and for all, with their evil underground activities."[37]

The promulgation of the new Soviet constitution forms part of the ideological backdrop to the development of the repressions in the mid-1930s. The constitution was discussed at the same party plenum in December 1936 as Yezhov's report on the crimes of the Trotskyites and Zinovievites, which set off the Great Terror.[38] At the plenum, Yezhov, it should be noted, underlined the perfidy of the alleged Trotskyite-Zinovievite conspiracy in Ukraine in particular that focused on organizing terror against the Soviet government.[39] Meanwhile, the Soviet constitution trumpeted the victory of socialism, the end of class struggle in the Soviet Union, and the creation of the new Soviet man and woman. In connection with the election campaign to the Supreme Soviet in December 1937, which was intended to ratify the constitution, Stalin and his lieutenants were determined to eliminate any possible dissonance in the country. There was no room for outliers; they would not be allowed to march into the socialist future with the "healthy" elements of Soviet society. Once considered a "class" to be eliminated, the remaining ex-kulaks were lumped together with the "socially harmful elements," who were to be cut away from society and quarantined as a lethal danger to the state.[40] The cities have been insufficiently purged, wrote Yezhov in a February/March 1938 document about the work of the NKVD in Ukraine. "The leading role of the city in our socialist state is especially great and complicated; therefore purging them of elements hostile to Soviet power has special political meaning and should be fully carried out to the end."[41]

Threat of War and Security Issues

Genocide frequently takes place in times of war and is justified in a variety of ways by security issues. According to the Young Turk government, the Armenians had to be deported (and murdered) because they connived with the Russians, who were at war with the Ottoman Turks. The Jews had to be eliminated in the rhetoric of the Nazis because they caused the approaching world war as the embodiment both of Wall Street and the Kremlin. In the case of the Soviet Union in the 1930s, the country was not at war, but was allegedly threatened by enemies all around: the Japanese, the Germans, and, especially relevant for Ukraine and the Holodomor, the Poles. This raised the stakes of any perceived opposition to government policies: dissidence could quickly be labelled traitorous behaviour in the heightened tensions associated with the threat of war.

Stalin famously expressed his worries that "we may lose Ukraine" as a result of Polish intrigues, infiltration of spies, and secret ties with the non-existent Polish underground organizations like the POV (the Polish Military Organization). "Bear in mind," he wrote to Kaganovich on 11 August 1932, "that Piłsudski is not daydreaming and his agent network in Ukraine is much stronger than Redens [Ukrainian NKVD chief] and Kosior [Ukrainian party chief] think ... Also keep in mind that the Ukrainian Communist Party (500,000 members, ha-ha) contains quite a few (yes, many!) rotten elements, conscious and unconscious Petliurites, even direct agents of Piłsudski. If things get worse, these elements will not hesitate to open a front inside (and outside) the party against the party."[42] They would make common cause with the Ukrainian peasantry, which had resisted the collectivization campaign much more than the Russians. As the Austrian specialist on Ukraine, Andreas Kappeler, argues, the Ukrainian peasants held a stronger attachment to their property than did the Russian peasants.[43] Clearly, Stalin was upset by resistance in the Ukrainian party to the continuing forced requisitioning in the face of hunger in the countryside. Ukraine was more than decimated, notes Serhii Plokhy; with 4 million dead, every eighth person succumbed to famine between 1932 and 1934.[44] When the hunger turned to famine, Stalin was also ready to eliminate the entire Ukrainian Communist leadership.

As many Ukrainian scholars have pointed out, the attack on Ukrainians in 1932–33 was not just against peasants on collective farms, but on the Ukrainian national and cultural intelligentsia. Already in 1929–30, the Yagoda-led OGPU had constructed a case against the invented SVU, the Union for the Liberation of Ukraine, arresting some 30,000 experts, artists, scientists, and others, forty-five of whom were put on trial.[45] The Ukrainian Autocephalous Orthodox Church was accused of being in partnership with the SVA in its nationalist objectives and forced to undergo "self-dissolution" as an alleged counter-revolutionary organization.[46] During the famine, the linkages between the intelligentsia and kulak resistance in the countryside were explicitly drawn. This meant that roughly 200,000 members of the Ukrainian elite – "an entire generation of educated, patriotic Ukrainians" – were arrested, while their institutions were closed down and brutally purged.[47] Engineers, teachers, agronomists, scientists, professors, priests, and officers were arrested, sent off into exile, and eliminated. "For the Ukrainians," writes Kappeler, "with their meager, and still young intelligentsia, this was particularly disastrous."[48] Despite breaking the back of the Ukrainian countryside and eliminating much of the Ukrainophile intelligentsia, Stalin was not finished with the Ukrainians. Ukrainians died in large numbers as a consequence of order no. 00447 and in the Great Terror, though at roughly the same rate as the other republics. In short, there was no let-up during the 1930s in the persecution and destruction of Ukrainians as a nation.

By the time Khrushchev arrived in Kyiv in January 1938 along with the new Ukrainian NKVD chief A.I. Uspenskii, the Ukrainian party had already been reduced by half (to 284,152 members, just 1 per cent of the population), and the Ukrainian Politburo and Central Committee had ceased to function. There were no first or second secretaries in many of the provinces. All eleven Ukrainian Politburo members would die. No one from the Ukrainian Orgburo or Party Control Commission survived.[49] As Robert Conquest writes, the purge in Ukraine "was so complete and so quick that legal authority virtually disintegrated … The Republic became little more than an NKVD fief, where even the formalities of Party and Soviet activity were barely gone through."[50] Even then, Stalin reportedly told Roosevelt at Yalta that "his position in the Ukraine was difficult and insecure."[51]

Yezhov followed Khrushchev to Kyiv in February, and apparently asked for Ukrainian speakers to accompany him in his entourage. His fellow operatives noted that there would be no need for interpreters. "Over there," stated one," there is not a single Ukrainian, just Jew after Jew." Yezhov himself noted in Ukraine that the NKVD was "not a Ukrainian apparatus, it is Birobidzhan," and began the process of purging Jews.[52] Yezhov exaggerated, of course; there were only 20 per cent Jews in the leadership of the Ukrainian NKVD in 1938, but that was radically reduced by his intervention in early 1939, when he purged close to half of the Jewish NKVD leadership. The Jewish *chekisty* were replaced not by Ukrainians, who were only 19 per cent of the NKVD in 1939, but mostly by Russians.[53] Yezhov's visit had other important implications, not just for the shift in cadres in the Ukrainian NKVD, but for the Ukrainians themselves. On 17 Feburary 1938, the Politburo raised the limit on repressions in Ukraine by 30,000, the largest increase in any of the republics.[54] These new limits were accompanied by a notable increase in the proportion of executions among those sentenced by the troikas. For example, in Vinnytsia oblast, from 26 March to 10 May, 1938, 3,427 people were "tried", of whom 3,200 were shot; in Poltava oblast, 3,100 people were processed by the troikas, *all of whom* received the "highest penalty." Supposedly, the executed were officers in the Petliura and Hetmanate armies, borot'bisty, and members of various Ukrainian nationalist organizations.[55] Khrushchev took on the task of turning the Ukrainian republic into a socialist fortress. "The next few years," writes Serhii Plokhy, would test the strength of the Ukrainian redoubt."[56]

The mania about Polish and German spies struck particularly hard at the border areas of Ukraine. Already in 1932–33, some 15,000 families (69,283 ethnic Poles and Germans) were deported from the Ukrainian borderlands to Kazakhstan and Siberia.[57] In 1935 and 1936, Balitskii continually turned up Polish and German "fascist" organizations, linked to alleged efforts to undermine the stability of the republic. This led to mass deportations of some 15,000 families (11,494 Polish and 3,506 German), primarily from Kyiv and Vinnytsia oblasts to Kazakhstan.[58] The Polish and German operations of 1937–38 were based on – and indeed fed off of – the same "arguments" that infused the anti-Ukrainian actions: that the Poles were planning to foster a Ukrainian uprising and intervene to sever Ukraine from the Soviet Union. When receiving an interim report on Yezhov's Polish operation, Stalin was pleased by the number of arrests in the country as a whole and in Ukraine. "To Yezhov," Stalin wrote, "Very good! Dig up and clean out, henceforth too, this Polish espionage filth. Eliminate it *in the interests of the Soviet Union*."[59]

Many ethnic Poles were thoroughly integrated into Ukrainian life; in many cases it would have been hard to identify who was Polish and who was Ukrainian. More than half of the Poles spoke Ukrainian as their mother language. Stanislav Kosior, who was head of the Ukrainian Communist Party from 1928 to 1938, was an ethnic Pole, and indeed was arrested in 1938 and executed in 1939 as a Polish spy and leader of an invented Polish underground group.[60] Similarly, the Soviet Germans were accused of being used by the Nazis to undermine Soviet economic and social institutions in an effort to weaken the state for the purposes of an imminent invasion. In these schemes, the Japanese, variously in cahoots with the Poles and with the Germans, were also planning to take over Siberia. This, in turn, was the reason for the deportation from the Soviet Far East to Kazakhstan and Uzbekistan of 175,000 Soviet Koreans, who were allegedly working with the Japanese in this connection.[61] Stalin is said to have expressed his regrets that the Ukrainian nation was too big to deport them all.[62]

Historians will argue about how intense the external threat was, and therefore how rational (even if perversely so) the actions were of the Soviet government to deal with the targeted groups of Ukrainians, Poles, and Germans. But, after all, there had been a comprehensive Polish-Soviet treaty of 1934 that stabilized relations between the two countries, and German-Soviet relations in the first half of the 1930s contained contradictory elements, sometimes mutually hostile but sometimes quite positive for both parties. There can be little question that the Spanish Civil War also played an important role in Stalin's thinking about potential intervention and civil war in the Soviet Union.[63] However dangerous the alleged external security threats were – and in my view they were highly exaggerated – they were exploited by Stalin and the Soviet government to eliminate opponents already targeted for their supposed treachery, which is typical for most cases of genocide.

The Dynamics of Genocide

Genocide is a process, not an event. There are many contingent factors that influence its course. Though guided by political leaders, genocide frequently assumes a dynamic of its own, usually reaching a crescendo of killing and then slowly receding, with the task – the elimination of a targeted group – accomplished in the main. This process has been labelled originally by historians of Nazi Germany "cumulative radicalization," and involves the increasing readiness of the bureaucracy to respond to signals from the top to engage in a campaign of isolating and seizing alleged enemies and eliminating them.[64]

But genocide also has after-effects, where the killing can continue, much like the aftershocks of an earthquake. The biological metaphor of an epidemic can also be applied to the process of genocide. Frequently, genocidal killing spreads from one targeted group to others, as in the case of the Nazi crimes (from handicapped Germans and Poles at the outset of the war to Jews, Sinti and Roma, and Soviet POWs), or in the Armenian genocide of 1915 (from Armenians to Syriac Christians and Pontic Greeks). In Soviet Ukraine, as we have seen, the attack on Ukrainians as a distinct people intersected with those on the Poles, Germans, and other minorities.

The case of the mass killing in the Soviet 1930s is complicated by the timing of the various campaigns. Here we might think more of periodic eruptions of violence, first of all around the dekulakization, collectivization, and hunger campaigns in 1930–33, especially in Ukraine and in the Kuban in the Northern Caucasus, but also in Kazakhstan and other areas of the country. In March 1930 Ukraine was the site of 2,945 major peasant rebellions, roughly 45 per cent of all of those that occurred in the Soviet Union as a consequence of collectivization. (Ukraine had about 20 per cent of the USSR's population.)[65] The second major explosion of violence occurred in 1937–38, as a consequence of order no. 00447 and the Great Terror. There were, of course, designated targets of this mass killing, but arrests, interrogations, torture, deportations, the "conveyor belt" rulings of troikas, executions, and beatings were infectious, encouraging denunciations, the spread of violence, and wanton killing. As the terror continued, the "biological approach," as some NKVD operatives named it, became more salient, leading to arrests of children, siblings, parents, and grandparents of alleged enemies.[66] As the campaigns against the social groups wound down, the NKVD increasingly targeted national groups, which were also swept up in the mania of eliminating alleged enemies of the people. In Ukraine, then, after the Ukrainian kulaks and intelligentsia came the Poles and Germans, then groups of "asocials" and "*byvshie*," along with various allegedly terrorist and Trotskyite political groups, whose plots and spying were as fictional as the anti-socialist activities of suspected criminals.

The extent of the purges in Ukraine surpassed the other republics. The entire party and state leadership was replaced several times. Of 102 members and candidate members of the Ukrainian Central Committee, only three were not incarcerated and maybe three more were still alive. Between summer 1937 and spring 1938 the chairman of the Ukrainian Council of Ministers and the head of the NKVD were changed three times. Members of the Ukrainian Orthodox Church were arrested, as were party members and the remaining Ukrainian intelligentsia. The Exarchate, which was founded in 1921, was eliminated and virtually all the members of the clergy were arrested and exiled to Siberia.[67]

Still, Stalin was not done with Ukraine. In February 1938, the *vozhd'* gave Yezhov permission to arrest an additional thirty thousand "kulak and miscellaneous anti-Soviet elements" in the republic, the largest increase anywhere.[68] Cumulative radicalization in the Soviet case also involved what has been called in the case of the Third Reich "working towards the Führer," meaning interpreting the signals from above, in this case from Stalin (and Molotov and Kaganovich, who sometimes delivered the messages personally), to arrest and eliminate ever-wider swaths of supposed opponents and class enemies.[69] Soviet bureaucrats, policemen, and prosecutors interpreted the leadership's vitriolic condemnation of groups as a mandate to arrest, deport, or kill.

Conclusions

It is reasonable to conclude that Ukraine was a central focus of Stalin's genocides of the 1930s. The disproportionately frequent and bitter resistance of the Ukrainian peasantry to collectivization and dekulakization only exacerbated Stalin's distrust of a nation that had already aroused his ire during the Civil War. The spread of USSR-wide famine in Ukraine in 1932–33, though in and of itself not "intentional," provided him with the opportunity to break the back of the Ukrainian peasantry in a genocidal campaign of purposely retributive, additional forced requisitioning that deprived the Ukrainian countryside of food. As Applebaum appropriately put it, in November and December 1932, Stalin "twisted the knife further in Ukraine, deliberately creating a deeper crisis," launching "a famine within a famine, a disaster specifically targeted at Ukraine and Ukrainians."[70] Stanislav Kulchytsky dates the twisting of the knife a bit later, January 1933, when, he states, a second famine was "superimposed on the Chekist special operation to confiscate produce grown on private plots. Thus, the all-Union famine caused by a dearth of grain throughout the Soviet Union morphed into the Holodomor."[71] This can certainly be thought of as a genocide.

The assault on the Ukrainian peasantry, combined with the attack on the Ukrainian intelligentsia and Ukrainian party, proved to be crucial episodes in securing Stalin's unalloyed dictatorship. The Polish and German operations, though carried out throughout the Soviet Union, were aimed primarily at securing the Ukrainian borderlands. Order no. 00447 was in part designed to ensure that Ukrainian kulaks and city dwellers would not and could not become the bases of alleged Polish intrigues. Ukraine was "among the deadliest zones of terror during the mass operations," writes Lynne Viola.[72] The devastation of Ukraine that resulted from these actions did not prevent Stalin from attacking the Ukrainian party and society during the Great Terror. Although Ukrainians did not suffer disproportionately in the Great Terror, still the republic was deprived of its political and cultural leadership.[73] It would take decades for the republic to recover. The Ukrainians, as a people, still suffer the effects.

NOTES

1 See Norman M. Naimark, "How the Holodomor Can Be Integrated into Our Understanding of Genocide," in *Contextualizing the Holodomor: The Impact of Thirty Years of Ukrainian Famine Studies*, edited by Andrij Makuch and Frank E. Sysyn, 112–26 (Edmonton and Toronto: Canadian Institute of Ukrainian Studies Press, 2015). For a world history approach that includes the Holodomor, see Norman M. Naimark, *Genocide: A World History* (New York: Oxford University Press, 2017), and Ben Kiernan, *Blood and Soil: A World History of Genocide and Extermination from Sparta to Darfur* (New Haven, CT: Yale University Press, 2007).

2 See Lucien Bianco, "Comparing the Soviet and Chinese Famines: Their Perpetrators, Actors, and Victims," *East/West – Journal of Ukrainian Studies* 3, no. 2 (2016): 51–73. For the 30 million number, see Andrew G. Walder, *China*

under Mao: A Revolution Derailed (Cambridge, MA: Harvard University Press, 2015), 364n63. Frank Dikötter has written that the Great Leap Forward cost 47 million lives: see *Mao's Great Famine: The History of China's Most Devastating Catastrophe, 1958–1962* (New York: Walker, 2002), 324–34.

3 Niccolo Panciolo states that 1.45 million Kazakhs died, or 38 per cent of the total Kazakh population. "The Collectivization Famine in Kazakhstan, 1931–1933," in *Hunger by Design: The Great Ukrainian Famine and Its Soviet Context*, edited by Halyna Hryn (Cambridge: Ukrainian Research Institute, 2008), 103. See also Panciolo's "Famine in the Steppe: The Collectivization of Agriculture and the Kazakh Herdsmen, 1928–1934," *Cahiers du Monde Russe* 45, no. 1–2 (2004): 189. See Sarah Cameron, "Questioning the Distinctiveness of the Ukrainian Famine," *Journal of Contemporary History* 27, no. 2 (August 2018): 460–4. Cameron uses the figure of 1.5 million victims; see "The Kazakh Famine of 1930–33: Current Research and New Directions," in *Communism and Hunger: The Ukrainian, Chinese, Kazakh, and Soviet Famines in Comparartive Perspective*, edited by Andrea Graziosi and Frank E. Sysyn (Toronto: Canadian Institute of Ukrainian Studies Press, 2016), 25. On the problem with the data in the Kazakh case, see Robert Kindler, *Stalins Nomaden: Herrschaft und Hunger in Kasachstan* (Hamburg: Hamburger Edition, 2014), 238.

4 This point was emphasized to me in a recent correspondence with Roman Serbyn, who has contributed a series of important essays on the Holodomor to the literature.

5 Andrea Graziosi, *The Great Soviet Peasant War: The Bolsheviks and Peasants, 1917–1933* (Cambridge, MA: Harvard University Ukrainian Research Institute, 1996).

6 Anne Applebaum, *Red Famine: Stalin's War on Ukraine* (New York: Doubleday, 2017).

7 Norman M. Naimark, *Stalin's Genocides* (Princeton, NJ: Princeton University Press, 2010).

8 Oleg Khlevniuk, *Master of the House: Stalin and His Inner Circle* (New Haven, CT: Yale University Press, 2009), 37.

9 Oleg Khlevniuk, *The History of the Gulag: From Collectivization to the Great Terror* (New Haven, CT: Yale University Press, 2007), 54.

10 Cited in George Liber, *Total Wars and the Making of Modern Ukraine, 1914–1954* (Toronto: University of Toronto Press, 2016), 166. The author cites here the words of Mendel Khataevich, the first secretary of the Dniepropetrovsk oblast party committee.

11 Getty and Naumov argue that the events from 1932–37 were less a "prelude to terror" than the result of "anxieties among the elite" and "the perceived need for iron discipline in the party." J. Arch Getty and Oleg V. Naumov, *The Road*

to Terror: Stalin and the Self-Destruction of the Bolsheviks, 1932–1939 (New Haven, CT: Yale University Press, 1999), 583.

12 Hiroaki Kuromiya, *Voices of the Dead: Stalin's Great Terror in the 1930s* (New Haven, CT: Yale University Press, 2016), 93. Nicolas Werth, *Cannibal Island: Death in a Siberian Gulag*, trans. Steven Rendall (Princeton, NJ: Princeton University Press, 2007).

13 Kuromiya, *Voices of the Dead*, 1. Kotkin suggests that 830,000 may be the correct number. Steven Kotkin, *Stalin: Waiting for Hitler, 1929–1941* (New York: Penguin, 2017), 305.

14 Robert Conquest, *The Great Terror: A Reassessment* (New York: Oxford, 2008), 485–7. Conquest's numbers are a bit difficult to sort through; this is my reading of his figures. See Getty and Naumov, *The Road to Terror*, 587–94. In their discussion of the victims of the 1930s, the authors come to a rough count of two million, which excludes victims of the famine, Ukrainian and otherwise. See Naimark, *Stalin's Genocides*, 11–12.

15 See Naimark, *Stalin's Genocides*, 11–12.

16 Alexander N. Yakovlev, *A Century of Violence in Soviet Russia*, trans. Anthony Austin (New Haven, CT: Yale University Press, 2002), 234.

17 Jörg Baberowski, *Verbrannte Erde: Stalins Herrschaft der Gewalt* (Munich: Beck, 2012), 191.

18 Khlevniuk, *Master of the House*. Kotkin, *Stalin: Waiting for Hitler*; see the useful discussion of the Stalin fond at xvi-xvii.

19 Paul Gregory, *Terror by Quota: State Security from Lenin to Stalin (An Archival Study)* (New Haven, CT: Yale University Press, 2009), 99–100.

20 All in all, Kotkin tells us, Stalin essentially supervised the trials, though "from afar." Kotkin, *Stalin: Waiting for Hitler*, 333, 371.

21 Robert Conquest, "The Speech That Shook the World," *Los Angeles Times*, 19 February 2006.

22 Iurii Shapoval, Vadim Zolotarev, *"Gil'otina Ukrainy": Narkom Vsevolod Balitskii i ego sud'ba* (Moscow: Rosspen, 2017), 198.

23 Cited in Kuromiya, *Voices of the Dead*, 15.

24 Kuromiya, *Voices of the Dead*, 16.

25 Lynne Viola, *Stalinist Perpetrators on Trial; Scenes from the Great Terror in Soviet Ukraine* (New York: Oxford University Press, 2017).

26 Cited in Viola, *Stalinist Perpetrators*, 26.

27 Khlevniuk, *History of the Gulag*, 165–6. One scholar estimates that 241,355 special settlers died in 1932 and 1933 alone. See Lynne Viola, *The Unknown Gulag: The Lost World of Stalin's Special Settlements* (New York: Oxford, 2009), 141.

28 Liber, *Total Wars*, 189.

29 Cited in Kotkin, *Stalin: Waiting for Hitler*, 107.

30 Cited in Mark Iunge and Rol'f Binner, *Kak terror stal "bol'shim": Sekretnyi prikaz No 00447: tekhnologiia ego ispolneniia* (Moscow: Airo-xx, 2003), 155.
31 Cited in Kotkin, *Stalin: Waiting for Hitler*, 123.
32 Jörg Baberowski, *Verbrannte Erde: Stalin's Herrschaft der Gewalt* (Munich: Beck, 2012), 325.
33 Khlevniuk, *Master of the House*, 116.
34 Ibid., 184.
35 Viola, *Stalinist Perpetrators*, 12.
36 Mark Iunge, Gennadii Bordiugov, and Rol'f Binner, *Vertikal' Bol'shovo Terrora: Istoriia po prikazu* NKVD *No 00447* (Moscow: Novyi Khronograf, 2008), 52.
37 Ibid., 48 (my emphasis).
38 V.N. Kolodezhnyi and L.N. Dobrokhotov, eds., *Dekabr'skii Plenum* TSK BKP*(b) 1936 goda: Dokumenty i Materialy* (Moscow: ROSSPEN, 2017). Naimark, *Stalin's Genocides*, 64–5.
39 V.N. Kolodezhnyi and L.N. Dobrokhotov, eds., *Dekabr'skii Plenum*, 213.
40 Naimark, *Stalin's Genocides*, 64–5.
41 "N.I. Ezhov o 'nedochetakh podgotovki i provedeniia massovykh operatsii' na Ukraine, konets febvralia-nachala marta 1938 g.," in *Vertikal' Bol'shovo Terrora*, edited by Mark Iunge, Gennadii Bordiugov, and Rol'f Binner, 306.
42 Cited in Kotkin, *Stalin: Waiting for Hitler*, 102.
43 Andreas Kappeler, *Ungleiche Brüder: Russen und Ukrainer vom Mittelalter bis zur Gegenwart* (Munich: C.H. Beck, 2017), 165.
44 Serhii Plokhy, *The Gates of Europe: A History of Ukraine* (New York: Basic Books, 2015), 253.
45 Applebaum, *Red Famine*, 98–9.
46 Bohdan Bociurkiw, "Ukrainianization Movements within the Russian Orthodox Church, and the Ukrainian Autocephalous Orthodox Church," *Harvard Ukrainian Studies*, 3–4 (1979), part 1: 111.
47 Ibid., 247.
48 Andreas Kappeler, *Kleine Geschichte der Ukraine* (Munich: C.H. Beck, 2000), 204.
49 Kotkin, *Stalin: Waiting for Hitler*, 520.
50 Robert Conquest, *The Great Terror: A Reassessment*, 233.
51 Ibid., 234.
52 Kotkin, *Stalin: Waiting for Hitler*, 522. Viola, *Stalin's Perpetrators*, 32.
53 Viola, *Stalin's Perpetrators*, 21, 33. The number of Jews in the all-Union NKVD leadership also declined precipitously between September 1938 and July 1939, from 21 per cent to 4 per cent, while Ukrainian participation increased from 10 per cent to 19 per cent and Russian from 57 per cent to 67 per cent. I am grateful for the research note of Olga Klymenko, "Jews in GPU-NKVD

(1929–1939): A Literature Review," Holodomor Research and Education Consortium, Canadian Institute of Ukrainian Studies, 5 July 2019, which parses the numbers from studies by N.V. Petrov and K.V. Skorkin, as well as Yu. Shapoval and V. Zolotariov. It is worth adding that there are inconsistencies surrounding the use of numbers on this question.

54 Iunge, Bordiugov, and Binner, *Vertikal' Bol'shovo Terrora*, 285.

55 Ibid., 286 (my emphasis).

56 Plokhy, *The Gates of Europe*, 256.

57 Kuromiya, *Voices of the Dead*, 237.

58 Shapoval and Zolotarev, "*Gil'otina Ukrainy*," 248–50.

59 Ibid., 238.

60 Ibid., 237.

61 Pavel Polian, *Against Their Will: The History and Geography of Forced Migration in the USSR* (Budapest: CEU Press, 2004), 100.

62 Conquest, *The Great Terror: A Reassessment*, 234.

63 Khlevniuk, *Master of the House*, 173. Kotkin, *Stalin: Waiting for Hitler*, 428–30.

64 Donald Bloxham, "The Armenian Genocide of 1915–16: Cumulative Radicalization and the Development of Destruction Policy," *Past and Present*, 18 (November 2003): 141–91. The term originated in the work of Wolfgang Mommsen; see his introduction to Gerhard Hirschfeld, ed., *The Policies of Genocide: Jews and Soviet Prisoners of War in Nazi Germany* (London: Allen and Unwin, 1986).

65 Terry Martin, *The Affirmative Action Empire: Nations and Nationalism in the Soviet Union, 1923–1939* (Ithaca, NY: Cornell University Press, 2001), 293.

66 Viola, *Stalinist Perpetrators*, 25.

67 Andreas Kappeler, *Kleine Geschichte der Ukraine* (Munich: C.H. Beck, 2000), 203–4.

68 Viola, *Stalinist Perpetrators*, 26.

69 Ian Kershaw, "'Working towards the Führer': Reflections on the Nature of the Hitler Dictatorship," *Contemporary European History*, no. 2 (July 1993): 103–18.

70 Applebaum, *Red Famine*, 218–19.

71 Stanislav Kulchytsky, *The Famine of 1932–1933 in Ukraine: An Anatomy of the Holodomor*, trans. Ali Kinsella (Edmonton and Toronto: Canadian Institute of Ukrainian Studies Press, 2018), 143.

72 Viola, *Stalinist Perpetrators*, 24

73 Kuromiya, *Voices of the Dead*, 13. At a minimum 267,579 people were arrested and 122,237 of them executed in 1937 and 1938. Viola, *Stalinist Perpetrators*, 15. Paul Gregory calculates that the number of convictions in Ukraine during the Great Terror did indeed exceed its population share. Gregory, *Terror by Quota*, 265–6.

5

The Kazakh Famine, the Holodomor, and the Soviet Famines of 1930–33: Starvation and National Un-building in the Soviet Union

Andrea Graziosi

1 Starvation, Political Famines, and Genocide

While the destruction of crops in wartime and the use of hunger to subjugate a city or a population have been common practices since time immemorial, famines and starvation in the pre-modern world often had predominantly natural components.

Since the late nineteenth century, however, the situation has radically changed: food has always been available somewhere, as have cheap and fast means to transport it to the places where it was needed. Therefore, massive international aid was always a possibility, as Herbert Hoover showed already in World War I and its aftermath.[1] It could thus be argued that all twentieth-century famines have been "political," in the sense that they somehow depended on political decisions and/or on the political situation.

This correlation between politics and hunger has been true in wartime – wars being by definition political affairs – when conditions are much more complicated; and even truer in peacetime, as students of contemporary famines have well understood. Paul Howe, who in 2004 created with Stephen Devereux the conceptual tool by which the international community measures famines, stated it clearly: starvation can be the direct result of "peacetime political decision: Governments could aim to create famine, could regard famine as the tolerable or welcome outcome of other goals, or could have conflicting demands that relegate famine prevention to a lower priority."[2] It is also worth noting that organized famine was used as a revolutionary tool since the modern era's very beginning: in his 1794 criticism of Jacobin inhumanity, Gracchus

Babeuf, the future leader of the *Conjuration des égaux*, noted that "famine too is an assassination mode." In the Vandée, Jean-Baptiste Carrier (the Jacobin envoy) "organized it" against insurgents, ordering "with *execrations nationicides* … to take away all the food, the edibles, the fodder, all in a nutshell, from this accursed country" whose peasants had dared to rebel against the revolution.[3]

As these quotations make clear, Devereux is right and not all "political famines" are equal: in some cases, hunger can be the *direct* outcome of "faminogenic" policies targeting specific populations, or parts thereof, to force their submission and alter the course of their history, by damaging or even destroying them. In a century dominated by transformative state-building attempts inspired by ethnic, ideological, national, or imperial projects, and often intricately connected with genocide and mass categorical violence – a concept that Scott Straus convincingly re-elaborated, stressing its relationship to genocide[4] – starvation at times metamorphosed into a special variety of that violence and of genocide.

Yet, as Alex de Waal has recently noted, "those who study famine tend to have a blind spot regarding political and military criminality. Those who study genocide and mass atrocity tend to have the counterpart blind spot on famine and starvation." After acknowledging the importance and the role of sexual violence, he added that students of human catastrophes should therefore do the same with starvation because, as the study of the twentieth century makes clear, to starve is both intransitive and transitive, forced mass starvation has been crucial, and starvation must be considered a method of mass killing.[5]

The fact that Africa specialists such as de Waal and Straus have made some of the sharpest contributions to our knowledge and systematization of starvation, and of its relations to genocide, should not surprise: since decolonization, Africa has perhaps become the most important locus of state- and nation-building. These phenomena, however, took on their modern guise in late eighteenth-century Europe, and it was their diffusion in continental Europe, especially but not solely in its central and eastern parts, that generated the first waves of genocide and mass categorical violence as we know them. Thus, just as we have much to learn from African specialists, so the latter can also learn from European history.[6]

In fact, in *Mass Starvation* de Waal points to the Nazi Hunger Plan as the first exemplar case of the ties between genocide, starvation, and mass categorical violence. Certainly, the use of hunger in the ghettos, and of starvation to liquidate Soviet POWs, are powerful cases.[7] Yet, I maintain that the most significant and diverse theoretical-practical case study of those ties is represented by the Soviet experience, 1918 to 1953. For thirty-five years, starting with the systemic and widespread resort to starvation to force the surrender of peasant insurgents during the Civil War (of which the repression of the *Antonovshchina* possibly provides the best illustration)[8] and up to its role in the death of 20–5 per cent of the "punished peoples" in 1941–44 and the last catastrophic Soviet famine of 1946–47, hunger was both the outcome of misguided policies and a conscious tool rationally employed to attain specific aims in an astonishing variety of cases. Within this larger context, the Soviet famines cluster of 1930–33 provides a unique basis for the study of political famines and of the use of starvation in peacetime as consequences and components of a "narrative" that justified such practices in the name of a transformative political project, a concept I utilize in the sense Straus usefully gave it.[9]

The Soviet experience, however, figures only marginally in de Waal's book, specifically devoted to famines, and it is virtually absent from Straus's contribution to and systematization of our understanding of genocides and mass categorical violence. Scholarship is thus missing the opportunity to take important strides toward increasing our understanding of these phenomena, no doubt as a result of Soviet specialists' limited capacity to speak to a wider audience, but perhaps also because of the political inconvenience and problems created when the Soviet experience is inserted into the picture. This in spite of the great progress made by Soviet studies on famines, mass categorical violence (of which the category-based Great Terror of 1937–38 is probably the twentieth century's foremost example), and genocides over the past thirty or so years, a progress that is at long last producing its first, important results.[10]

In the following pages I will thus explore what the Soviet experience in the period 1918–53 can tell us about the starvation-mass categorical violence-genocide "knot," focusing in particular, within the larger framework of 1930–34, on the Kazakh and the Ukrainian famines of 1931–33, and on the problems raised by the genocide category in dealing with them.

2 The Soviet Famines of the Early 1930s as Products of Faminogenic Behaviour

The ability to differentiate between the Soviet famines of the early 1930s without losing sight of the context of general suffering that affected the whole country and that provided the general background for each of those famines is *the* crucial factor here. I realized this in the early 2000s, thanks to the breakthrough research done in the 1990s,[11] and after reflecting upon the Holodomor and the polemics surrounding it. [12] I then saw in that differentiation the way to end most of those polemics, showing how true many of the positions of the various participants in the debate were as long as they were restricted to the specific event they were in fact addressing, rather than applied to a generic "Soviet famine." That this is in fact the case has been recently proven by the "roundtable" published in *Contemporary European History*, in which only those still confounding the Soviet general famine with, let's say, the Holodomor, kept the flame alive.[13] Today, however, I see in that ability to differentiate, and in the extremely complex picture it reveals, a tool to raise and address crucial questions.

Needless to say, among those famines, the Kazakh tragedy of 1931–33 and the November 1932–July 1933 Holodomor stand out in terms of the sheer number of their victims, reaching into millions and qualifying them both as "catastrophic" famines, according to the scale currently in use. They are not, however, the only ones. In fact, a simple chronology reveals how the 1930–33 Soviet famines include at least another five specific "great" famines (i.e., with more than 100,000 victims each), endowed with characteristics of their own.

The first was caused by dekulakization, both during the deportation of hundreds of thousands of peasant families and in the settlements that were quickly and miserably put up under OGPU supervision to house those "special settlers" (*spetspereselentsy*), as they were called. We know that over the course of three years more than 200,000 people died of starvation en route or once they arrived to their destination, a direct consequence of Moscow's political decisions, which would thus count as genocide if not for the fact that, because of the Soviet stand at the United Nations, the category excluded the targeting of social groups such as "kulaks" (the Soviet repressive policies' growing resort to "ethnic" criteria over the course of the 1930s went mostly unnoticed up until the 1990s). [14]

Then came the Kazakh famine of 1931–33, discussed more fully in the next section. Suffice it here to say that its approximately 1.5 million deaths were the result of a specific state decision to provide Slavic cities with meat rations in the aftermath of the disaster of collectivization, another state policy that was inflicted upon the Slavic countryside, whose livestock was almost wiped out. Since the Kazakhs, from whom that meat was brutally taken, were non-Slavic nomads who inhabited lands conquered by the Russian Empire, this specific famine bears the marks of the "colonial model" as clearly as is imaginable.[15]

We then have the Soviet general famine (the second of the five "great" famines), which affected the whole of the USSR after 1930.[16] It too was a direct, if undesired (but not unpredictable, given what had happened in 1920–21), consequence of state policies such as dekulakization, collectivization, and requisition-like procurements; and its victims too numbered in the hundreds of thousands. Worth noting is the Politburo's "moderate" turn in late spring 1932 that included a reduction in those requisition-like procurements and an import of grain from abroad (albeit secretive and insufficient), signals that Stalin and his comrades knew how to fight hunger when they wanted to.

This general famine hit most of the Soviet territory, but not all of it. Transcaucasia suffered comparatively less, as did sensitive border regions, thus disguising what happened inside the country and avoiding embarrassment; the regime also afforded some protection to crucial industrial areas and large cities out of political considerations (although even then, only the largest among them were spared, and only in part). As rationing was the tool used to discriminate, the Kazakh famine can be seen also as part of a hunger discrimination policy determined by state priorities. When things got really difficult in 1932, the protection of minor urban centres was for example greatly reduced, thus raising mortality rates among their "marginal" (if measured in terms of state priorities) inhabitants.

The Holodomor, which resulted in some 3.5 million deaths, peaking in the spring and early summer of 1933, was brought about through the decision, arrived at over the summer and fall of 1932, to answer the crisis by reversing the previous moderate turn and by resorting to starvation as a tool to subdue the peasantry, and in particular to tame Ukraine, its peasantry, and its national-communists. The destruction of the Ukrainian villages and the lowering of rations in minor centres had the secondary effect of ruining *shtetls* already hit by the anti-NEP and antireligious policies of the late 1920s. These *shtetls* had lived off the relations, albeit complex and difficult, with those villages, relations they lost when Moscow greatly reduced the amount of food allotted for minor, non-industrial urban centres.

The third great famine, the Northern Caucasus famine of late 1932–33, had hundreds of thousands of victims, and was very similar to the simultaneous Ukrainian one. Even though it hit the entire countryside, it too singled out specific groups that the regime had long seen as enemies, the Cossacks in general and the Kuban Ukrainians in particular, whose culture and language were also targeted. Similar mechanisms operated in the *Tsentral'no-chernozemnaia* region, the site of the fourth great famine. Its peasantry had been the protagonist of one of the Civil War's largest anti-Bolshevik uprisings (the aforementioned *Antonovshchina*), and starvation hit hardest in the Ukrainian-majority districts bordering with Ukraine.[17] The case of the Volga-German Republic is the fifth and least-studied of the great famines, but we know of the conflictual relations German colonists had with the Bolshevik regime from the Civil War up until their flight to Canada at the beginning of collectivization, as well as the extraordinary high mortality rates of 1932–33.[18]

But for the general Soviet hard times, all these specific famines targeted a specific social and national group, albeit in different ways and with different intents, and all were directly tied to a transformative project. In each, starvation was a manifestation of mass categorical violence, a set that, as these famines also show, can be constructed as a spectrum of phenomena, going from the extreme of annihilation to "milder" forms.

David Marcus's classification, based on four types and degrees of government involvement, may be applied fruitfully to better our understanding of the nature of each of these famines and its position in the set.[19] Fourth-degree faminogenic behaviour is the least deliberate: "Typically, incompetent or hopelessly corrupt governments, faced with food crises created by drought or price shocks, are unable to respond effectively to their citizens' needs. Starvation follows, although the government itself may not desire this result." Third-degree faminogenic behaviour is marked by indifference: "Authoritarian governments, impervious to the fate of their populations even though arguably possessing the means to respond to crises, turn blind eyes to mass hunger." According to Marcus, both of these behaviours, while deplorable, do not necessarily implicate a state with criminal responsibility under international criminal law.

The top two groups in Marcus's classification (second- and first-degree faminogenic behaviour) are different. The former exists when the famine is the direct consequence of policies that a government continues to follow despite knowing that they are causing mass starvation. Recklessness is therefore its *mens rea*, while intent is the *mens rea* of first-degree faminogenic behaviour. Marcus himself notes that instances of first-degree famine crimes within larger second-degree famines are common: the Soviet cases of 1930–33 confirm his point, and show how easily one could turn into the other.[20]

In this light, the kulak-special settlers hunger of 1930–33 belongs in the first degree (as was later the case with the "punished peoples" of 1941–44), while the Soviet general hunger of 1931–33 can be seen as a famine of the third degree that transformed into the second degree in 1931–32. However, the facts that Stalin and the Bolshevik leadership were told directly in 1928, and even before, of the possible outcome of the policies they had decided to pursue, and that they were aware of the consequences of the late 1920 great requisition wave (which caused large pockets of famine to appear in the spring of 1921, i.e., before the drought that sparked the great 1921–22 famine), could be used to maintain that their behaviour belonged from the beginning to the second-degree faminogenic class.

From its very inception, the political decision to seize the Kazakh herds in order to secure the meat for the rations of Slavic cities, the state apparatus, the army, and other crucial elements in Stalin's power bloc, irrespective of the consequences (which were rapidly known through officials reports that reached Moscow), unquestionably looks like a second-degree case. Moreover, it is one with clear genocidal traits, given its deadly impact upon Kazakh nomads.

The "moderate" turn in late spring 1932 is an aggravating circumstance (as noted above, it shows that Stalin and his collaborators knew what had to be done in order to stop the famine), as is the decision to deny the famine's very existence – to intimidate, slander, and/or silence those who could report about it – and the refusal to seek foreign aid. And if the hunger that hit *shtetls* and minor urban centres could be classified somewhere in between second- and third-degree faminogenic behaviour, the deadly starvation imposed on Ukraine, and especially on some of its regions, and the Northern Caucasus after the fall of 1932 clearly constitute a first-degree case, as possibly does that of the Volga German Republic, of which little is known.

3 The Kazakh Tragedy and the Holodomor as Genocidal Famines

Analysis and comparison of the two deadliest Soviet famines of the early 1930s are both revealing[21] and possible, thanks to the great strides made by demographers over the past years – owing to their efforts, for example, the Holodomor has become perhaps the best studied famine of the twentieth century. Data about Kazakhstan are not, and cannot be, as good and especially as detailed for structural reasons: the statistical apparatus was much less developed than in Ukraine, and the nomadic way of life of local inhabitants posed and still pose huge additional problems. We know, however, that in Kazakhstan approximately 1.5 million died, most of them Kazakh nomads, while in Ukraine approximately 3 million out of the 3.5 million victims died in increasingly higher numbers after the extreme requisitions following the fall of 1932 and the prohibition of peasant food-seeking migrations in January 1933.

Five million out of the approximately seven million deaths of the early 1930s Soviet famines thus took place in these two areas. The figure grows if we count as Ukrainian the Kuban and the southern fringes of the Russian oblast bordering Ukraine, which makes sense in terms of ethnic composition. The Russian Republic death toll diminishes accordingly, and even more so if one remembers that in 1930–33 Kazakhstan was still an autonomous republic of the Russian Federation, so that its victims are often counted as "Russian."

We know that in "normal" famines mortality is associated with diseases, whose diffusion hunger facilitates, so that often the majority of deaths cannot be directly imputed to hunger. However, the Ukrainian and, albeit to a lesser degree, Kazakh cases confirm de Waal's intuition that in "totalitarian famines" starvation can be the main direct killer.[22] In fact, as it was to happen again in Mao's China during the Great Leap Forward's famine of 1958–62, the public health system in both Ukraine and Kazakhstan prevented the spread of major epidemics, even though Kazakhstan's lower development and the nomadic way of life of part of its population did allow for the outbreaks of major diseases, plague included.

These outbreaks also happened because, at least at first, the flight of Kazakh nomads was not stopped; they moved in great numbers looking for food, prolonging their survival and giving epidemics the time to develop. The Kazakh famine thus had modern causes, but also features typical of older, traditional famines. In contrast, after the end of 1932, Ukrainian villagers were prevented from leaving their villages and from entering cordoned-off cities, and were deported back to the countryside when they succeeded in doing so (even those who had reached Transcaucasia were herded back to Ukraine by ship).

The sophisticated data on the demography of the Holodomor, which illuminates the enormous disparity between urban and rural deaths, confirm that this famine was in the first place a famine for peasants, a trait it shared with the general Soviet picture, with the notable exception of the Kazakhs (nomads are not peasants). To a much greater degree than in the Civil War, the regime resorted everywhere to hunger to break the peasants' hostility to collectivization or the "new serfdom" (their definition, which one finds again and again in contemporary political police reports). Bolshevik leaders, from Stalin to Stanislav Kosior, openly spoke of starvation as a tool to teach peasants what one would call a Pavlovian lesson: if you do not accept the state policies and do not comply with procurements, you shall not eat.[23] Peasants were thus thought of and treated as inferior, animal-like human beings.

In Ukraine, however, it was not only a question of grain. In fact, as demographers have demonstrated, in Ukraine the general Soviet pattern – according to which the confrontation between the state and the peasants, and thus the use of hunger by the former to break the latter, was fiercest in grain-producing areas – only holds in very general terms. Ukraine was indeed the most important grain-producing republic of the USSR, which also made it the most important locus of the "great Soviet peasant war." Yet peasant mortality (and hence requisitions and starvation) was not highest in the great grain-growing regions of the south. It was in fact much higher in the Kyiv and Kharkiv regions, where rural excess deaths averaged around 23–4 per cent of the population, and which were the republic's political hearts and the homes of its two capitals.[24]

By the way, in both regions rural excess deaths were at the end of May 1933 fourteen to fifteen times greater than in January. Given the fact that "it takes about two months for a healthy adult to die of outright starvation,"[25] the staggering growth of mortality rates after February and into June 1933 is consistent with the punitive, almost total requisitions conducted in November–January and the subsequent, rapid depletion of both the peasants' own reserves and "natural" ones (e.g., in woods, rivers, lakes, etc.). The more so since the impact of such extraordinary requisitions, which were sanctioned by the Soviet Politburo resolution of 14 December 1932, was soon aggravated by the already-recalled decision to prevent Ukrainian peasants from leaving their villages in search for food, sentencing them to death.

The very content of that Politburo resolution confirms the overtly political, anti-Ukrainian focus of the Holodomor. As its title stated, it formally concerned "Grain Procurements in Ukraine, the Northern Caucasus and the Western region." It also ordered, however, the reversal of the pro-Ukrainian national, linguistic, and educational policies in place since 1923,[26] proving once more the importance that Stalin attached to the nexus between the peasant question and the national question. In 1925, for instance, he had stated that

> The national question [is], in essence, a peasant question. Not an agrarian but a peasant question, for these are two different things. It is quite true that the national question must not be identified with the peasant question, for, in addition to peasant questions, the national question includes such questions as national culture,

> national statehood, etc. But it is also beyond doubt that, after all, the peasant question is the basis, the quintessence, of the national question. That explains the fact that the peasantry constitutes the main army of the national movement, that there is no powerful national movement without the peasant army, nor can there be. That is what is meant when it is said that, *in essence*, the national question is a peasant question.[27]

I have reconstructed elsewhere Stalin's evolution on the Ukrainian question after the launch of his Great Turning Point in 1929.[28] What happened to the leaders and cadres of Ukrainization, to Ukrainian intellectuals and teachers, and to Ukrainian national-communists in Ukrainian cities, as well as to the Ukrainian language after the end 1932, attests to Stalin's cold-blooded determination, logic, and sophistication in liquidating what he perceived after the summer of 1932 as a Ukrainian threat to his power, as well as to the state and the system he was building. On the one hand, he used hunger to break the spine of what he had called the peasant "basis" of the Ukrainian national movement, and on the other, he used repression to eliminate that movement's cultural, intellectual, and political superstructure, to use the Marxist terminology his thinking was steeped in.[29]

Soviet Ukraine thus offers us an interesting, if tragic, case of rapid, conscious, socialist-inspired, and successful *nation-building*,[30] followed by an equally conscious strategy of *nation un-building*. I prefer these to the presently more widely used "making and unmaking" because building/un-building were the terms employed by Stalin and the other Soviet leaders, and also because they imply the awareness – keenly felt by the Bolshevik leadership – that in order to successfully build or un-build, there are social materials and theoretical tools that can and must be used.

In light of this leadership's statements of the 1920s on the possible use of the countryside as a source for Marxist "primitive accumulation," and thus as a sort of internal colony, both the Soviet general famine and in particular the Holodomor can also be read as colonial famines, all the more so since the Bolshevik central leaders did see themselves, in Lenin's words, as a group of conquerors.[31] However, I don't believe such an interpretation has great interpretive potential, and there are arguments that could be used to criticize it, especially for the Soviet general case. For instance, despite the Bolsheviks' awareness of their "difference" from the population, the Civil War had given them solid if minority roots in a new country, the Soviet Union, that was of their own making.

With Ukraine, whose history can in part be read in colonial terms, things are different. Since the outbreak of the Russian-Ukrainian war at the end of 1917, the republic had been the breeding ground for transformative projects employing the conscious manipulation of language and nationality. Yet, up until 1932, these projects were far from linear, with a strong anti-Ukrainian, anti-peasant narrative coexisting with an equally strong local Bolshevik Ukrainian national-communism that gained the upper hand in 1923, and which, in spite of growing difficulties after 1926, administered the republic until the summer of 1932. And even the crushing of this national-communism in the ensuing months did not fully erase its legacy.

In Kazakhstan, however, it is impossible not to speak of a colonial famine; one, moreover, of the purest and most primitive character, in which an alien power takes away the indigenous population's resources to be consumed by others, and simply lets that population die, with no special political design in mind, a design that was present in Ukraine.[32]

As census data make clear, the 1931–33 famine uprooted Kazakhs' way of life: between the 1926 and 1937 census, Kazakhs dropped from 3.6 to 2.1 million, and in 1939 Russians, barely one third of Kazakhs in 1926, exceeded their number, becoming the top ethnic group of the Republic until the 1980s.[33] In spite of the aforementioned lack of planning or intent, therefore, the famine was a de facto powerful national un-building and therefore "genocidal" tool. As to local actors, the party and state cadres in the republic, under the guidance of Filipp Goloshchëkin, did discriminate against the Kazakhs in the distribution of the meagre available resources, favouring a Slavic population that was also repressed. Unquestionably, however, the cause of the catastrophe is found in the decision to seize local herds to serve central, Soviet aims.

In Ukraine national un-building took on more sophisticated forms, as what happened in the language field indicates (for example, dictionaries, grammars, and textbooks were withdrawn and republished with many words changed in order to make them closer to Russian ones). Ukrainian higher culture and political elites were wiped out, teachers and state employees fired or deported, the countryside broken. Ukrainian culture, language, and national ideals were relegated to an inferior position, and – at least in Stalin's hope – the ground for their regeneration was removed.[34] In a way, one could thus speak of an intentional, "scientific" attempt at nation-warping, aiming at assuring in the long run the assimilation of Ukrainians into a Soviet-Russian "higher" culture, a process that did in fact take place in the following decades, albeit incompletely.

The different "memory" of, and the names given to, the two events are also tied to the different kind of national un-building they embody, even though other factors and more recent developments may have played a major role.[35]

In Ukraine the Holodomor (as the great 1932–33 Ukrainian famine came to be known to stress its intentional nature) quickly became a crucial component of the post-1991 national revival, and was consciously used as a nation-building tool, generating strong tensions even within the country, reflecting in part the relative success of Stalin's nation-warping operation. In Kazakhstan, the Kazakh elite, though perfectly aware of the famine's crucial and crippling importance, have been much more hesitant in using it, and not just because of the problems it could create both within the country and in relations with Russia. It seems in fact possible to maintain that the famine caused an even more important and definitive break in Kazakh history, and in the Kazakh way of life, than it did in the Ukrainian case – and not just because of the much more active presence of a Ukrainian diaspora, and of Ukrainian lands such as those under Polish occupation, that were not affected by the Holodomor. While it is true that part of the Soviet Kazakh elite survived the famine because it was already urbanized, and that some nomadism did continue after 1931–33, the uprooting of Kazakh traditions and culture and the destruction of the Kazakh population in percentage terms were even more profound than the extremely violent processes that took place in Ukraine.

Perhaps because of this sharper break, the Kazakh famine did not find a proper name, and is variously remembered as "the famine" (*asharshylyk*), "the artificial famine" (*zhasandy asharshylyk*), the Holodomor (applying the Ukrainian term to Kazakh events), or the "Goloshchëkin genocide," this being a misnomer: as much as Goloshchëkin's ruthless policies contributed to the catastrophe, it was the direct result of central "economic" decisions.

Conclusions

It can be reasonably assumed that in both the Ukrainian and the Kazakh cases the intention to destroy the *entire* group (in Raphaël Lemkin's meaning of the term genocide) was missing, even though these groups' very regenerative capacities, especially in the Kazakh case, were endangered and their previous culture almost destroyed. Ukrainian development was stunted and warped, as if in a scientific experiment. Both instances, moreover, were closely tied to what Straus has called a transformative project, and an ambitious one at that. It was a project, moreover, whose initial narrative was rooted in the faith that the manipulation of history and society was indeed possible if one knew which "social" groups and categories (scare quotes are needed because, since at least 1913 but arguably even before, the adjective "social" also included national categories and groups)[36] were to be liquidated, deported, manipulated, and thus transformed (the Cossacks, the bourgeoisie, the Kulaks, Soviet citizens of suspicious national origins, etc.), or built or unbuilt (oppressed or threatening nationalities, Ukrainians, punished peoples, etc.).

Against the general background of the Soviet early 1930s, of that entire decade, and finally of the whole 1918–53 period, the Holodomor and the Kazakh tragedy thus represent extreme and special cases of the Bolshevik leaders' ideologically inspired habit of using a categorical approach to human beings, derived from the social sciences, as a tool to implement their transformative project. This project naturally evolved over time. But for a short pause during the NEP, however, for more than thirty years it continued to demonstrate and produce genocidal traits and results – intellectually sophisticated, if cold-blooded and merciless, in the Ukrainian case, brutal and simplistic in the Kazakh one.

In both these tragedies starvation organized from above played a crucial role as a genocidal tool, of which the ration-based, World War I-inspired public food distribution system, based on state political preferences and hierarchies, was the main instrument.[37] Keenly aware of this until his death, in 1952 Stalin reminded Ukrainian Communist leaders that "the history of mankind knows many tragic cases in which entire nations died because of lack of bread, and were thus cancelled from history."[38]

Finally, the multiplicity of great and catastrophic Soviet *peacetime* famines in the pre-1953 formative period, and the fact that most such famines later happened under socialist regimes at a similar stage in their development (China, Cambodia, and Ethiopia, to which North Korea could perhaps be added in spite of significant differences), raise the question of the special link between Communist-led socialist offensives (or "revolutions from above") and peacetime political famines.

The answer, of course, is not simple, but at least a partial answer may be found in socialism's anti-peasant social and economic transformative project, despite pro-peasant facades such as that devised by Lenin in 1917. Especially but not solely in moments of crisis, Marxism's category-based, friend versus enemy logic, grounded in the interpretation of history as class war (but Marx and Engels also spoke of "reactionary peoples"[39]) contained in it the potential to make things worse, as did Marx's theory of accumulation (especially in its "primitive accumulation" variant), which claimed that investment was possible only by using surplus extracted at the expenses of specific social groups. As the Holodomor suggests, the presence of "unsolved" national questions, especially if tied to peasant ones, and a willingness to "solve" these questions within the socialist, modern transformative project, can precipitate specific tragedies. Yet, as Mao's "Great Leap Forward famine" indicates, national questions are not a prerequisite for a peacetime socialist political famine – rather, it was the presence of an ambitious, ruthless, strong-willed, and possibly paranoiac political leader that proved to be the crucial, transversal factor.

NOTES

1 Frank M. Surface, *American Food in the World War and Reconstruction Period: Operations of the Organizations under the Direction of Herbert Hoover, 1914–1924* (Stanford: Stanford University Press, 1931). On ARA's Russian operations see H.H. Fisher, *The Famine in Soviet Russia, 1919–1923: The Operations of the American Relief Administration* (New York: MacMillan, 1927); Bertrand M. Patenaude, *The Big Show in Bololand: The American Relief Expedition to Soviet Russia in the Famine of 1921* (Stanford: Stanford University Press, 2002).

2 Paul Howe and Stephen Devereux, "Famine Intensity and Magnitude Scales: A Proposal for an Instrumental Definition of Famine," *Disasters* 28, no. 4 (2004): 353–72; Paul Howe, "Priority Regimes and Famines," in *The New Famines: Why Famines Persist in an Era of Globalization*, edited by Paul Howe and Stephen Devereux, 336–62 (London: Routledge, 2007).

3 Gracchus Babeuf, *Du Système de Dépopulation ou la Vie et les Crimes de Carrier* (Paris: Franklin, 1794), 84.

4 Scott Straus, *Making and Unmaking Nations: War, Leadership, and Genocide in Modern Africa* (Ithaca, NY: Cornell University Press, 2015), chapters 1 and 2.

5 Alex de Waal, *Mass Starvation: The History and Future of Famine* (Cambridge: Polity Press, 2018), 24–9.

6 From this perspective one easily discerns the intellectual *naïveté* of contrasting European and non-European history, which Lewis Namier clearly saw already decades ago. The former too had its colonial side, with both dominant and subaltern peoples, cultures, and languages; its state- and nation-building attempts inspired by a variety of political projects; and the categorical mass violence – also in the form of starvation – accompanying them. See Andrea Graziosi, "Il mondo in Europa. Namier e il 'Medio oriente europeo,' 1815–1948," *Contemporanea*, 2 (2007): 193–228.

7 Not casually, Christian Gerlach stressed the use of hunger as another technique of genocide/mass violence in his *Kalkulierte Morde. Die deutsche Wirtschafts- und Vernichtungspolitik in Weißrussland 1941 bis 1944* (Hamburg: Hamburger, 1998).

8 Andrea Graziosi, "Act I. 1918–22," in *The Great Soviet Peasant War: Bolsheviks and Peasants, 1918–1933* (Cambridge, MA: Harvard Ukrainian Research Institute, 1996); Viktor P. Danilov and Theodor Shanin, eds., *Krest'ianskoe vosstanie v Tambovskoi gubernii v 1919–1921 gg. "Antonovshchina"* (Tambov: Intertsentr, 1994) contains stunning documents on the Bolsheviks' systematic and rational use of starvation and mass categorical violence against peasant "bandits." See Jean-Louis Van Regemorter, *L'insurrection paysanne de la région de Tambov, 1919–1921. Documents* (Coeuvres–et–Valsery: Ressouvenances, 2000) for a French summary.

9 Straus, *Making and Unmaking of Nations.*

10 Robert Conquest, *The Harvest of Sorrow: Soviet Collectivization and the Terror Famine* (New York: Oxford University Press, 1986); Oleg V. Khlevniuk, *The History of the Gulag: From Collectivization to the Great Terror* (New Haven, CT: Yale University Press, 2004); Norman Naimark, *Stalin's Genocides* (Princeton, NJ: Princeton University Press, 2010); Mark Kramer, Joshua Rubenstein, Paul Hollander, Andrea Graziosi, Jeffrey S. Hardy, Michael Ellman, Roman Szporluk, Jeffrey J. Rossman, and Norman Naimark, "Reappraising Mass Terror, Repression, and Responsibility in Stalin's Regime, Perspectives on Norman Naimark's Stalin's Genocides," *Journal of Cold War Studies* 14, no. 3 (2012): 149–89; Norman Naimark, Niccolò Pianciola, Tanja Penter, J. Arch Getty, Alexander Etkind, Sarah Cameron, Stephen G. Wheatcroft, Andrea Graziosi, and Ronald Grigor Suny, "Roundtable on Soviet Famines," *Contemporary European History* 27, no. 3 (2018): 432–81.

11 The following is a list of but a few of noteworthy contributions: Conquest, *Harvest of Sorrow*; Andrea Graziosi, ed., "'Lettres de Kharkov': La famine en Ukraine et dans le Caucase du Nord à travers les rapports des diplomates italiens, 1932–1934," *Cahiers du monde russe et soviétique* 30, no. 1–2 (1989): 2–106 (later published with a wider selection of documents in Italy, Ukraine, and France); Stanislav V. Kul'chyts'kyi, ed., *Holodomor 1932–1933 rr. v Ukraïni: Prychyny i naslidky* (Kyiv: Instytut istoriï Ukraïny NAN Ukraïny, 1995); Nikolai A. Ivnitskii, *Repressivnaia politika sovetskoi vlasti v derevne (1928–1933 gg.)* (Moscow: In–t rossiiskoi istorii RAN, 2000); Viktor P. Danilov, Roberta Manning, and Lynne Viola, eds., *Tragediia sovetskoi derevni: Kollektivizatsiia i raskulachivanie*, vol. 3, *Konets 1930–1933* (Moscow: Rosspen, 2001); Terry Martin, *The Affirmative Action Empire: Nations and Nationalism in the Soviet Union, 1923–1939* (Ithaca, NY: Cornell University Press, 2001); Iurii Shapoval and Valery Vasyl'iev, *Komandyry velykoho holodu: Poïzdky V. Molotova i L.*

Kahanovycha v Ukraïnu ta na Pivnichnyi Kavkaz, 1932–1933 rr. (Kyiv: "Heneza," 2001); Viktor V. Kondrashin and D'Ann Penner, *Golod: 1932–1933 gody v sovetskoi derevne (na materiale Povolzh'ia, Dona i Kubani)* (Samara: s.n., 2002); Robert W. Davies, Oleg V. Khlevniuk, and Arfon Rees, eds., *The Stalin-Kaganovich Correspondence, 1931–36* (New Haven, CT: Yale University Press, 2003); France Meslé and Jacques Vallin, *Mortalité et causes de décès en Ukraine au XXe siècle* (Paris: INED, 2003); Robert W. Davies and Stephen G. Wheatcroft, *The Years of Hunger: Soviet Agriculture, 1931–1933* (New York: Palgrave Macmillan, 2004); Niccolò Pianciola, "Famine in the Steppe: The Collectivization of Agriculture and the Kazak Herdsmen, 1928–1934," *Cahiers du monde russe* 45, no. 1–2 (2004): 137–92, and *Stalinismo di frontiera. Colonizzazione agricola, sterminio dei nomadi e costruzione statale in Asia centrale (1905–1936)* (Roma: Viella, 2009).

12 Andrea Graziosi, "The Soviet 1931–33 Famines and the Ukrainian Holodomor: Is a New Interpretation Possible, and What Would Its Consequences Be?," in *Hunger by Design: The Great Ukrainian Famine and Its Soviet Context*, edited by Halyna Hryn, 1–19 (Cambridge, MA: Harvard Ukrainian Research Institute, 2009). Originally published in *Ukraïns'kyi Istorychnyj Zhurnal*, 3 (2005): 120–31.

13 See for instance John Arch Getty, "New Sourced and Old Narratives," in "Roundtable on Soviet Famines": 450–5.

14 Viktor N. Zemskov, "Spetsposelentsy," *Sotsiologicheskie issledovaniia*, 11 (1990): 3–17; "Zakliuchennye, spetsposelentsy, ssyl'noposelentsy, ssyl'nye i vyslannye," *Istoriia SSSR*, 5 (1991): 151–62, and "Kulatskaia ssyl'ka v 30e gody," *Sotsiologicheskie issledovaniia*, 10 (1991): 2–21; Lynne Viola, *The Unknown Gulag: The Lost World of Stalin's Special Settlements* (New York: Oxford University Press, 2007); Terry Martin, "The Origins of Soviet Ethnic Cleansing," *The Journal of Modern History* 70, no. 4 (1998): 813–61; Eric D. Weitz, et al., "Racial Politics without the Concept of Race: Reevaluating Soviet Ethnic and National Purges," *Slavic Review* 61, no. 1 (2002): 1–65.

15 Niccolò Pianciola, "Famine in the Steppe," *Stalinismo di frontiera*, and "Sacrificing the Kazakhs: The Stalinist Hierarchy of Consumption and the Great Famine in Kazakhstan of 1931–33," in *Thirty Years of Crisis: Empire, Violence, and Ideology in Eurasia from the First to the Second World War*, edited by Tomohiko Uyama (Sapporo: Slavic–Eurasian Research Center, forthcoming); Robert Kindler, *Stalins Nomaden: Herrschaft und Hunger in Kasachstan* (Hamburg: Hamburger Edition, 1914); Sarah Cameron, *The Hungry Steppe: Famine, Violence, and the Making of Soviet Kazakhstan* (Ithaca, NY: Cornell University Press, 2018), and the book forum in the *Journal of Genocide Research* 22, no. 4 (2020) devoted to Cameron's book, with the

participation of Igor Çasu, Shoshona Keller, Niccolò Pianciola, Irena Vladimirsky, and Stephen Wheatcroft.

16 Viktor V. Kondrashin, *Golod 1932–1933 godov: Tragediia rossiiskoi derevni* (Moscow: Rosspen, 2008).

17 Kondrashin and Penner, *Golod: 1932–1933 gody v sovetskoi derevne*; Milana Esikova, "Hunger in the *Tsentral'no–chernozemnaia* region, 1932–33," unpublished paper.

18 Samuel D. Sinner, *The Open Wound: The Genocide of German Ethnic Minorities in Russia and the Soviet Union, 1915–1949 and Beyond (Der Genozid an Russlanddeutschen 1915–1949)* (Fargo: North Dakota State University Libraries, 2000); Ronald J. Vossler, *We'll Meet Again in Heaven: Germans in the Soviet Union Write Their American Relatives* (Fargo: North Dakota State University Libraries, 2001); Eric J. Schmaltz and Samuel D. Sinner, "'You Will Die under Ruins and Snow': The Soviet Repression of Russian Germans as a Case Study of Successful Genocide," *Journal of Genocide Research* 4, no. 3 (2002): 327–56.

19 David Marcus, "Famine Crimes in International Law," *The American Journal of International Law* 97, no. 2 (2003): 245–81.

20 de Waal, *Mass Starvation*: 106–8.

21 This I learned studying comparisons of the Soviet and the Chinese cases, such as Lucien Bianco, *La Récidive. Révolution russe, Révolution chinoise* (Paris: Gallimard, 2014); Felix Wemheuer, *Famine Politics in Maoist China and in the Soviet Union* (New Haven, CT: Yale University Press, 2014); Andrea Graziosi and Frank E. Sysyn, eds., *Communism and Hunger: The Soviet, Kazakh, Ukrainian and Chinese Famines in Comparative Perspective* (Edmonton: CIUS, 2016). See also Andrea Graziosi, "Political Famines in the USSR and China: A Comparative Analysis," *Journal of Cold War Studies* 19, no. 3 (2017): 42–103.

22 de Waal, *Mass Starvation*, 92.

23 Stanislav Kosior, the secretary of the Ukrainian Communist Party, explicitly said so on 15 March 1933 (in Ruslan Pyrih, ed., *Holodomor 1932–33 rokiv v Ukraïni* [Kyiv: Instytut istoriï Ukraïny NAN Ukraïny, 2007], 771), and Stalin clearly alluded to such lesson in his famous 1933 reply to Mikhail A. Sholokhov (in Yurii G. Murin, *Pisatel' i vozhd': Perepiska M.A. Sholokhova s I.V. Stalinym, 1931–1950 gody* [Moscow: Raritet, 1997]).

24 Oleh Wolowyna, Nataliia Levchuk, and Alla Kovbasiuk, "Monthly Distribution of 1933 Famine Losses in Ukraine and Russia at the Regional Level," in Andrea Graziosi, ed., "Special Issue on the Soviet Famines of 1930–1933," *Nationality Papers* 48, 3 (2020): 530–48. A mortality comparable to that of the Kyiv and Kharviv regions is to be found only in the German Volga Republic.

25 de Waal, *Mass Starvation*, 21.

26 Martin, *Affirmative Action Empire*; Liudmila S. Gatagova et al., eds., *TSK RKP(b)–VKP(b) i natsional'nyi vopros*, kniga 1, *1918–1933* (Moscow: Rosspen, 2005), 696–8.

27 Iosif V. Stalin, "Concerning the National Question in Yugoslavia," *Bol'shevik*, no. 7 (15 April 1925), in *Works*, vol. 7, *1925*, 69–76. Bohdan Klid was kind enough to send me excerpts from two interventions (M. Demchenko and F. Holub) at the 1934 CP(b)U Congress, held on the eve of the 17th All-Union Party Congress. Both speakers clearly linked the national with the peasant (kulak) problem, and they were not the only ones (*Stenographic report*: 370–3 and 437–9).

28 Andrea Graziosi, "The Uses of Hunger: Stalin's Solution of the Peasant and National Questions in Soviet Ukraine, 1932–1933," in *Famines in European Economic History: The Last Great European Famines Reconsidered*, edited by Declan Curran, Lubomyr Luciuk, and Andrew G. Newby (London: Routledge, 2015), 225.

29 Anne Applebaum, *Red Famine: Stalin's War on Ukraine* (New York: Doubleday, 2017). On the post-1933 attack on Ukrainization see Hennadii Efimenko, "The Kremlin Nationality Policy in Ukraine after the Holodomor," in *After the Holodomor: The Enduring Impact of the Great Famine in Ukraine*, edited by Andrea Graziosi, Lubomyr Hajda, and Halyna Hryn (Cambridge, MA: Harvard Ukrainian Research Institute, 2013), 69–98; Hennadii Efimenko, "Bolshevik Language Policy as a Reflection of the Ideas and Practice of Communist Construction, 1919–1933," in *The Battle for Ukrainian: A Comparative Perspective*, edited by Michael S. Flier and Andrea Graziosi (Cambridge, MA: Harvard Ukrainian Research Institute, 2017), 167–94; and Yuri Shapoval, "The Ukrainian Language under Totalitarianism and Total War," in *The Battle for Ukrainian*, edited by Michael S. Flier and Andrea Graziosi, 215–46.

30 Andrea Graziosi, "Communism, Nations, and Nationalism," in *The Cambridge History of Communism*, vol. 1, edited by Silvio Pons and Stephen Smith (Cambridge: Cambridge University Press, 2017), 449–74.

31 As Nikolai I. Bukharin told Lev B. Kamenev in July 1928, Stalin was then repeating the Trotskyite Evgenii A. Preobrazhenky's 1924 thesis about the need to use the countryside as an internal colony out of which the resources needed for industrialization were to be extracted (in Yurii G. Fel'shtinsky, "Konfidentsial'nye besedy Bukharina," *Voprosy istorii*, 2–3 [1991]: 182–203). In 1920–23 Lenin at times compared Bolsheviks to conquerors of an alien, vanquished nation (see for instance *Collected Works*, Moscow: Progress Publishers, vol. 31, 401, and vol. 33, 288), while Stalin called them "a sort of *Order of Knights of the Sword*," that is, a Teutonic conquering order (as the Livonian Brothers of the Sword), in "The Political Strategy and

Tactics of the Russian Communists," July 1921, available at https://www.marxists.org/reference/archive/stalin/works/1921/07/x01.htm.

32 We are thus dealing with a particularly merciless case of alien rule, the very opposite of the one envisioned by Michael Hecther in *Alien Rule* (Cambridge: Cambridge University Press, 2013).

33 A graphic illustration of the demographic changes can be seen in "Major Ethnic Groups in Kazakhstan, 1897–1970," Wikimedia Commons, https://commons.wikimedia.org/wiki/File:Kazakhstan_demographics_1897-1970_en.png.

34 Graziosi, Hajda, and Hryn, eds., *After the Holodomor*; Graziosi and Flier, eds., *The Battle for Ukrainian*.

35 James Richter, "Famine, Memory and Politics in the Post-Soviet Space: Contrasting Echoes of Collectivization in Ukraine and Kazakhstan," in "Special Issue on the Soviet Famines," *Nationality Papers*: 476–91. The following discussion owes much to Niccolò Pianciola's criticism of a previous version, for which I am grateful.

36 Graziosi, "Communism, Nations, and Nationalism."

37 de Waal, *Mass Starvation*, 106; Elena A. Osokina, *Our Daily Bread: Socialist Distribution and the Art of Survival in Stalin's Russia, 1927–1941* (Armonk, NY: Sharpe, 2001).

38 Quoted in Valery Vasyl'iev, ed., *Politicheskoe rukovodstvo Ukrainy, 1938–1989* (Moscow: Rosspen, 2006), 168.

39 Roman Rosdolsky, *Engels and the 'Nonhistoric' Peoples: The National Question in the Revolution of 1848* (Glasgow: Critique Books, [1948] 1987); Graziosi, "Communism, Nations, and Nationalism."

6

The "Lemkin Turn" in Ukrainian Studies: Genocide, Peoples, Nations, and Empire

Douglas Irvin-Erickson

Raphaël Lemkin coined the word *genocide* and inspired a movement at the United Nations between 1946 and 1948 to outlaw the crime.[1] An increasingly important figure in the field of comparative genocide studies, peace and conflict studies, and a number of fields studying specific conflicts and cases of genocide, the body of Lemkin scholarship has grown over the last decade.[2] My own journey in studying Lemkin's body of written works, as I researched and wrote my book on Lemkin, led me to understand Lemkin's legal and social thought in very different terms than how he is presented in received scholarship. Without recounting my entire book in this chapter, there are three lessons I want to highlight that are important for scholars to remember when using Lemkin's social scientific theories of genocide in their own work. These lessons strike at the core of the tension, the problem, this book has taken up, between the legal understandings of genocide on the one hand, and the ethical-political understandings of genocide on the other.

Given that this book has been commissioned by two of the world's leading historians of Ukraine, and was the outcome of a major international conference convened by a leading scholarly society dedicated to the study of the Holodomor, I will attempt to illustrate how these three lessons have played out in academic debates in Ukrainian studies over interpretations of the Holodomor, the great famine in Soviet Ukraine between 1932–33. Indeed, in the last decade, Lemkin has increasingly become a figure of interest to those who study the famine.[3] This interest stems from Lemkin's 1953 speech on the Ukrainian genocide, which he intended to publish in his unfinished three-volume world history of genocide.[4] What was important, conceptually, in Ukrainian studies was that Lemkin viewed the Great Famine of 1932 to 1933 not as a genocide but, rather, as one part of a longer-running genocide against a distinct Ukrainian social identity that was committed through violent and non-violent forms of repression and oppression within the context of Soviet empire-building.

The discovery of Lemkin's 1953 speech and unpublished essay on the Ukrainian genocide did spark something of a "Lemkin turn" in Holodomor studies, which raised the question of whether we should limit the Holodomor term to the Great Famine (and call the famine the genocide) or adopt Lemkin's view that the Great Famine was only one episode of a larger genocide against the Ukrainian social group. For other scholars of the Holodomor, it is Lemkin's notion of peoplehood – and the destruction and construction of nations through cultural, social, and physical violence – that makes his writings particularly compelling. I would contend that it was more than a coincidence that the "Lemkin turn" in Holodomor studies occurred at the same time that scholars began asking whether the concepts of empire and colony were useful concepts for understanding Ukrainian history. Lemkin believed genocide was a "colonial crime" that entailed the "destruction of the national pattern of the oppressed" and the "imposition of the national patterns of the oppressors," all of which makes Lemkin's concept of genocide useful for analyzing the problems of empire and colonialism in Ukrainian studies.[5]

While this chapter will present an overview of what has proven to be a "Lemkin turn" in Ukrainian studies, especially with regard to interpretations of the Holodomor through the conceptual lens of genocide, there are parallel developments afoot, with "Lemkin turns" emerging in the literature of a number of cases. My broader lessons about Lemkin's thought should be applicable across the board. In her important chapter in this volume, Michelle Tusan notes that scholars today "continue to reconcile themselves to Lemkin's concept, whether it is to reject or accept his formulation," while reminding us that: "This definition came out of a historical context – the lead-up to World War II – and had its own politics. But to reject or embrace it on the grounds of this particularity does little good. Rather, defining an act as genocide must be followed by a reconciliation of the event and its definition as the experience of a people. The study of genocide, then, becomes a study of the materiality, ideas, and events of genocide that moves beyond the act itself."[6] I find Tusan's reflections instructive and, as I hope this essay can show, there is a way to use Lemkin's theory and definition of genocide that can bring scholarship on the Ukrainian genocide to this point.

Three Lessons on Lemkin and Lemkin's Conception of Genocide

The first quotation below presents the legal definition of genocide as codified in the 1948 UN Genocide Convention. The second quotation is Lemkin's definition of genocide from his 1944 book, *Axis Rule in Occupied Europe*. Only four years separates these texts, but the definitions of genocide are radically different. How did the definition change? Notice that the legal definition specifies the kinds of acts that constitute genocide, whereas Lemkin's definition of genocide does not. And, notice that the legal definition restricts genocide to the destruction of very specific kinds of groups, while there is no such restriction of groups in Lemkin's definition.

> Article I The Contracting Parties confirm that genocide, whether committed in time of peace or in time of war, is a crime under international law which they undertake to prevent and to punish.
>
> Article II In the present Convention, genocide means any of the following acts committed with intent to destroy, in whole or in part, a national, ethnical, racial or religious group, as such:
>
> (a) Killing members of the group;
> (b) Causing serious bodily or mental harm to members of the group;
> (c) Deliberately inflicting on the group conditions of life calculated to bring about its physical destruction in whole or in part;
> (d) Imposing measures intended to prevent births within the group; [and]
> (e) Forcibly transferring children of the group to another group.
>
> Article III The following acts shall be punishable:
>
> (a) Genocide;
> (b) Conspiracy to commit genocide;
> (c) Direct and public incitement to commit genocide;
> (d) Attempt to commit genocide; [and]
> (e) Complicity in genocide.

> Article IV Persons committing genocide or any of the other acts enumerated in article III shall be punished, whether they are constitutionally responsible rulers, public officials or private individuals.[7]

> This new word, coined by the author to denote an old practice in its modern development, is made from the ancient Greek word *genos* (race, tribe) and the Latin *cide* (killing), thus corresponding in its formation to such words as tyrannicide, homicide, infanticide, etc. Generally speaking, genocide does not necessarily mean the immediate destruction of a nation, except when accomplished by mass killings of all members of a nation. It is intended rather to signify a coordinated plan of different actions aiming at the destruction of essential foundations of the life of national groups, with the aim of annihilating the groups themselves … Genocide is directed against the national group as an entity, and the actions involved are directed against individuals, not in their individual capacity, but as members of the national group.

> … Genocide has two pages: one, the destruction of the national pattern of the oppressed group; the other, the imposition of the national pattern of the oppressor. This imposition, in turn, may be made upon the oppressed population which is allowed to remain, or upon the territory alone, after removal of the population and the colonization of the area by the oppressor's own nationals.[8]

Why did the definition of genocide change? Why does this matter?

My first lesson on Lemkin is that Lemkin was not the author of the United Nations Convention on the Prevention and Punishment of Genocide of 1948 (Genocide Convention). He coined the word genocide in his famous study of the Second World War, *Axis Rule in Occupied Europe*, which was published in 1944 (we can date the time he coined the term to the winter of 1941–42 based on annotations in his notebooks). He authored the first draft of the treaty presented to the UN and, wielding a new type of power that prefigured the human rights social movements later in the twentieth century, he was able to keep himself involved in the political deliberations over the treaty's text by strategically directing a significant amount of international public pressure on the governments of UN member states, while maintaining authentic if calculated friendships with a number of individual delegates from across the Middle East and Asian (the Egyptian, Pakistani, and Filipino delegations were the ones that most closely coordinated their strategies with

Lemkin, and Gabriela Mistral and Pearl Buck were vital for marshalling the support of Latin American member states and China). Even this brief glimpse into the history of the concept of genocide demonstrates that the Genocide Convention's definition of genocide was a fundamentally political definition.

The primary goal of the delegations representing major world powers at the UN, as I argue in my book, and as my colleague Anton Weiss-Wendt has also documented in his scholarship and outlined in this volume, was to narrow the definition of genocide as much as possible, and to ensure the passage of an international law that could not be applied to them but could still be applied to their geopolitical opponents. While many scholars of genocide and anti-genocide activists uphold the Genocide Convention as a kind of moral document, Weiss-Wendt's scholarship and my research has attempted to show just how much the Genocide Convention was a product of post-World War II geopolitics, starting as an explicitly anti-colonial document and being transformed into something that colonial powers could tolerate. I would agree with Weiss-Wendt's argument in this volume, that the implication for scholars – and all sorts of genocide-prevention practitioners – is that if you adopt the legal definition of genocide as your working definition of the concept, or even if you take the legal definition as an ethical or moral concept, you implicitly align your work with a concept that was designed to erase from its boundaries the vast majority of the kinds of repression and oppression being committed by the major powers at the time. As I tell my students, Weiss-Wendt has found drafts of the UN treaty heavily annotated by Soviet prosecutor general Andrei Vyshinsky and Joseph Stalin, indicating that they poured over the text line by line. So, we must understand that the legal definition of genocide was co-authored by Vyshinsky and Stalin – and their peers at the UN who knew their governments were committing atrocities that would have been genocide according to Lemkin's first definition.

It is worth considering why Lemkin's initial ideas about how to define genocide would be rejected by the major powers at the UN. My second lesson on Lemkin, therefore, is that Lemkin framed his concept of genocide in 1944 as an explicitly *colonial* crime. In *Axis Rule*, he called the German occupation of Europe an act of colonialism, framing the destruction of the groups targeted by the Germans for physical extermination as part of a larger colonial program of group destruction that included a wide spectrum of repressive and oppressive acts. Later in his unpublished writings Lemkin set out to study the genocides of European colonialism, framing both Nazi and Soviet genocides as part of this history of European colonial empires using genocide as a technique of governance, and charting the direct and structural violence that these genocides entailed. In 1946, when Lemkin brought his ideas to the United Nations, he wrote that his strategy was to gain the support of the North African delegations first, since they represented peoples against whom genocide had been committed, and to assemble a coalition of small states and former colonies to force the major powers to the bargaining table. Then he would step back and let the US, UK, and USSR take all the public credit for working so hard to outlaw genocide after the recent experience of World War II. And that is precisely what happened, except the major powers opposed the Genocide Convention more than he had anticipated. The Canadian and Swedish delegations were instructed by their governments not to sign a treaty that could be applied to indigenous peoples; the South African delegation warned the convention was "dangerous" where backwards people were concerned, stating their position that genocide against Black Africans was progress; the Brazilian delegation mused that outlawing genocide would be a genocide against Latin America since it was their cultural tradition to exterminate political opponents; the UK and French observers wanted a treaty that could not apply to the colonies; and Washington instructed the US delegation to make sure the treaty couldn't be applied to American Indians or government-sanctioned racial segregation and lynching.

Not surprisingly, during the diplomatic negotiations at the UN over how genocide would be defined in the international treaty, the definition of "genocide" changed dramatically, narrowing to such a degree that Lemkin no longer recognized his own concept, as delegates from UN member states carefully negotiated each word of the treaty. As I show in my book by looking at Lemkin's personal correspondences and personal writings, Lemkin left the UN in 1948 believing that his time at the UN was a failure – even though he publicly celebrated the passing of the Genocide Convention in newspaper editorials and scholarly journal articles. The law against genocide after 1948, Lemkin wrote in his memoirs, was now in the hands of statesmen "who lived in perpetual sin with history" and "treated human life like currency in a bank."

Thirdly, and perhaps most importantly for scholars looking to use Lemkin's definition, Lemkin did not define genocide as a type of violence. Instead, he defined genocide as a type of conflict that involved a spectrum of coercive actions that ranged from repression and marginalization to acts of oppression and sometimes (but not always) violence – acts we would call "structural violence" or "cultural violence" in today's parlance.[9] Importantly, Lemkin had worked out his definition of genocide before the onset of the Final Solution, which is widely recognized as the moment the Nazi party settled on a policy of physically exterminating the Jewish people. And, interestingly, the earliest iterations of the concept Lemkin called genocide in the early 1940s can be traced to his writings in the late 1920s on the Soviet penal code, where he was primarily worried about the way the Soviets used the law to direct the force and violence of the state towards the elimination of "enemy nations" and forms of social consciousness the Bolshevik party deemed antithetical to the revolution. (For this, Lemkin was denounced by Andrei Vyshinsky as an enemy of the revolution).[10]

To return to the tension highlighted in this volume's title, between the legal and the ethical-political conceptions of genocide, I would suggest that the legal definition is highly political as well. Thus, scholars who employ an ethical-political understanding of the genocide concept, and follow the broader writings of Lemkin, will necessarily position the Holodomor in a wider context of Soviet empire-building, "internal" colonialism, nationalities conflicts, and identity group-based repression and oppression – all of which Lemkin would have viewed as structurally and historically connected. Using this broader definition of genocide means, however, that the concept of genocide loses its reference point in international law. Yet, this is not *a priori* a bad thing. Because the legal definition was the product of a high-stakes political drafting process, and the explicit goal of many UN member states was to remove the actions of their governments from the purview of this treaty, the Genocide Convention gives us a very poor scholarly definition of genocide (unless of course the scholar is specifically concerned with legal history or the law), as it is designed to conceal far more about human history and social behaviour than it reveals. We thus find ourselves in the dilemma announced in the very title of the book. An ethical-political definition of genocide, such as Lemkin's, lacks a grounding in international law, and is thus unsatisfactory for many scholars and activists.[11] The legal (or legal-political) definition of genocide, on the other hand, fails to encompass many of the very acts we find so morally abhorrent, such as the Soviet Union's attempt to intentionally starve to death millions upon millions of human beings.[12]

As Tusan reminds us, it does little good to reject or embrace the concept of genocide on the grounds that the concept is a product of post-World War II politics; it is more fruitful to define an act as genocide by reconciling the event and its definition to the experience of a people, specifically the experience of being subjected to an attempted destruction.[13] What I would like to remind the reader is that Lemkin himself did not use the legal definition of genocide in his historical and social scientific scholarship (of course, he used the legal definition in his legal work). When he returned to the classroom at Yale University, his lectures went right back to his broad, experience-of-the-victim-centred understanding of the concept. He defined genocide simply as "the destruction of nations and peoples," Lemkin told his student, because the specific act of how such destruction was carried out would always change through history. Much like Tusan's argument that the study of genocide necessarily moves beyond the study of the materiality of the act itself, Lemkin's unfinished three-volume *World History of Genocide*, and his unfinished manuscript *Introduction to the Study of Genocide in the Social Sciences*, shows us that Lemkin was utterly unconcerned with the legal definition when it came to writing history and social science. Over and again in these unpublished works, Lemkin proves more concerned with defining the crime based on the subjective experience of the victim, rather than on objective criteria preferred by international lawyers. In his proposal for *World History of Genocide*, he even stated that his goal was to write a "victim-centered history."

In the context of the current state of Ukrainian studies, which has become highly politicized in the context of the conflict between Ukraine and Russia from 2013 to the present, it is important to consider the definitions of genocide that scholars use, and my three lessons on Lemkin. It is clear to any observer of the conflict that scholarship is being picked up in the national media of Ukraine and Russia, and academic research is filtering into the narratives of the conflict from parties on all sides.[14] There is a certain fixation on the concept of genocide, as activists and partisans seek to use scholarship on "the Ukrainian genocide" during the Soviet era to delegitimize the current Russian involvement in Ukrainian.[15] Putting aside these questions of contemporary politics, however, my three lessons on Lemkin can help clarify certain points in this "Lemkin turn" in Ukrainian studies.

For one, Lemkin's definition of genocide (not the legal definition of genocide) would force us to separate conceptually the famine and the genocide. The famine can be seen as part of a genocide, but the famine was not the genocide. This means that, analytically, the killing of at least 3.5 million peasants is no longer presented as the primary objective of the man-made famine, but rather a means to a larger end. In the Lemkin frame, the starvation of people is not genocide; the people were starved *as a way of committing* genocide. This is why Lemkin argued, in his famous speech in 1953, that the Soviet regime orchestrated mass starvation as part of a larger effort to stamp out a distinct Ukrainian social identity. What is more, Lemkin's analysis of the famine not as the genocide, but the most violent manifestation of the genocide, connects the famine to a larger pattern of social, political, economic, and cultural conflict within the Soviet Union – between the regime in Moscow and those who suffered from the regime's genocide in Ukraine. As such, for Lemkin, it becomes irrelevant (both legally and theoretically) whether Stalin and Soviet administrators actually gave explicit orders to orchestrate a famine, because the famine emerged from a larger program of conflict that was already an explicit expression of Soviet empire-building and thus was state policy.[16]

These theoretical implications of Lemkin's writings for Ukrainian studies have deepened and helped legitimize two existing threads in the field. The first thread is characterized by scholars of Ukraine studying what we now call "structural violence" and "cultural violence." The second thread would be scholars studying the Ukrainian case through the lenses of empire and colony. I will analyze both at the conclusion of this chapter, while arguing that Lemkin's theory of genocide is useful for the intellectual project of both threads. The chapter also underscores what these two threads have in common: a conceptual and moral focus on the processes, consequences, and costs (in economic and human terms) of group destruction in the Soviet Union. Before proceeding to this analysis of the "Lemkin turn" in Ukrainian studies, however, it is necessary to briefly outline the contours of Lemkin's thinking on genocide, empire, and the destruction of peoples and nations.

Lemkin's Theory: A Quick Sketch

The twentieth-century "history of genocide" is very much a history of the creation of the concept of genocide: how the idea emerged historically in Lemkin's thinking, in relationship to the ideas and concerns of his Jewish, Polish, and professional legal milieu in the 1920s and 1930s;[17] how the drafting process at the United Nations transformed the concept to emphasize that genocide was a physical act rather than a complex sociological process related to other forms of conflict;[18] and how the concept again was transformed through geopolitical pressure during and after the Cold War.[19] Lemkin's understanding of the core concepts that underpinned his constantly evolving definition of genocide also changed with the times.[20] But, as I have argued in my book on Lemkin, some things remained consistent in Lemkin's thought from the 1920s to his final works in the 1950s.

Genocide, Violence, and Conflict

The first consistency in Lemkin's thought was his notion that the roots of armed conflict, war, and genocide were not found in the balance of power politics or the calculations of interests of abstract social groups, such as states or religions, but rather in the sentiments, values, demands, and interests of domestic social and political movements and specific groups in a society in conflict. For Lemkin, genocide was the result of decisions made by individuals whose immediate interests led them to commit these acts or lend their support to these acts, and genocide was conditioned and legitimized through social norms and values. But groups themselves were not responsible for genocide. Individuals were. Genocide was, therefore, both a complex social process involving many small actions that, in isolation, would not amount to genocide; and, simultaneously, a choice made by people across a society who decided to participate in the program in one way or another.

Genocide as a Social Process

Second, Lemkin believed the destruction of human groups was a sociological process. Genocide was, therefore, a type of conflict and not a type of violence. This remained consistent throughout his writings in the 1920s on the Soviet penal codes (before he coined the word genocide) through his work in the 1950s, including his sociological and historical studies of genocide and his legal advocacy work. To be sure, Lemkin was most concerned with, and saved his strongest moral condemnation for, genocides committed through terror, torture, and death. However, for genocide to have taken place did not necessarily require physical violence in Lemkin's definition of the term; genocide could be committed without killing a single individual. In fact, when Lemkin wrote about physical killings as a technique of genocide, he often discussed this violence in terms of the sociological consequences of violence – in terms of the collective trauma that violence inflicts upon survivors across a society, the weakening of the bonds of social solidarity and group cohesion that often accompanies horrific forms of violence such as hunger and rape, and the particular kinds of terror and loss that occur across a society when cultural figures such as poets and civil leaders are killed. For Lemkin, killing was not necessary for genocide, and when genocide involves killing, the killing part was not the genocide, per se.

Genocide versus Social Change

Third, turning to the thought of Giuseppe Mazzini, Lemkin believed national groups were the basic components of world civilization, and that national diversity is what animated the world and served as the engine of human creativity, progress, beauty, and peace. Lemkin departed from Mazzini in important ways, most notably in his belief that it was not the objective qualities of nations that animated world civilization like a "subtle concerto," but rather the changing of national groups' objective and imaginative characteristics. The ability for groups to change, Lemkin believed, is what is generated by the interactions between ideas, values, and beliefs that occur when people meet those from other nations, become part of other nations, and move between nations.

Cultural assimilation via cultural hegemony, a constant in human history, was not necessarily a bad thing for Lemkin, who was not opposed to old "groups" disappearing and new groups emerging. In fact, Lemkin positions the slow disappearance of groups and nations as a healthy occurrence for human societies, because it means that cultures and groups were changing and such change was a fundamental good. There is an implicit contradiction in Lemkin's thinking here about where to draw the line between group diffusion versus group destruction (i.e., genocide). Yet, for Lemkin, the boundary rested between the ability of individuals to freely choose to abandon or adopt identities – which could result in the disappearance of a group – and purposeful attempts to destroy a group as a sociological entity, which is what he called genocide. The disappearance of a group or a culture, even through cultural assimilation, was not genocide in Lemkin's formulation.

In fact, Lemkin believed that cultural diffusion and assimilation could enrich the human experience because social change is what allowed human societies to adapt to constantly changing historical conditions. What was to be condemned, he believed, was forced cultural destruction, or forced cultural assimilation. This he called genocide. Genocide deprived the world of cultural diversity, and cultural diversity was necessary for cultural change to occur. Thus, Lemkin argued that genocide prevented social groups from changing and evolving, because it depleted the kinds of cultural diversity in "world civilization" that drove social innovation and constructive social change. Genocide was a "crime against humanity," he wrote, precisely because it deprived individuals of the ability to experience the fruits of diversity, and as a consequence it deprived people from the positive benefits of social change that diversity inspired. The ultimate consequence of genocide was a world that lacked diversity and thereby lacked the mechanism that made progress, creativity, and beauty possible. The law against genocide, in Lemkin's thinking, was a way to safeguard a diverse world to preserve the mechanism that allowed for change in national groups. Genocide was to be outlawed because the purposeful destruction of national groups would lead to a "world civilization" that lacked diversity and was therefore static and unable to change, which would lead to the impoverishment and destitution of all.

Nations, Peoples, New Words, and New Ideas

As we noted above, the word genocide first appeared in print in Lemkin's 1944 magnum opus, *Axis Rule in Occupied Europe: Laws of Occupation, Analysis of Government, Proposals for Redress.* Lemkin derived "genocide" from the Greek word *genos* (race, family, tribe) and the Latin *cide* (to kill). In a footnote, he added that genocide could equally be termed "ethnocide," with the Greek *ethno* meaning "nation." Genocide signified the attempt to destroy a national group, but "it did not necessarily mean the immediate destruction of a nation, except when accomplished by mass killings of all members of a nation."[21] Rather, for Lemkin, genocide signified "a coordinated plan of different actions aiming at the destruction of essential foundations of the life of national groups, with the aim of annihilating the groups themselves." In *Axis Rule*, Lemkin further defined genocide as a colonial process of destroying the national patterns of the oppressed and imposing upon the victims the national patterns of the oppressor. The objective of such a plan, Lemkin added, was the "disintegration of the political and social institutions, of culture, language, national feelings, religion, and the economic existence of national groups, and the destruction of the personal security, liberty, health, dignity, and even the lives of the individuals belonging to such groups."[22]

As a new word, Lemkin felt that "genocide" would also be free of the connotations carried by similar existing words, such as the German word *Völkermord*, meaning "murder of nations." *Völkermord* appeared in reports about the German colonial war against the Herero and Nama peoples, to describe the Ottoman campaign against Armenians, and in reference to Russian politics.[23] Lemkin was fluent in German and had used the term, but decided against it – perhaps because the root *Volk* was too close to the German Romantics' use of *Volk* to describe an organic nation, a concept that Lemkin believed was an important structuring aspect of the Nazi genocide.[24] Similarly, *nationicides* was first used by François-Noël Babeuf in his 1794 book, *Du Système de Dépopulation ou la Vie et les Crimes de Carrier*, to describe and condemn the conduct of Jean-Baptiste Carrier in the war of the Vendée, when troops sent from Paris started a project of depopulation to destroy the "nations" living in the territory.[25] Regarding the English word "denationalization," Lemkin explained that the word denoted the deprivation of citizenship or the removal of national groups from geographical territories, not the destruction of a national pattern as a sociological entity, nor the attempt to replace a given national pattern with national patterns of the oppressor.[26] "Genocide" would be the neologism Lemkin had been searching for, "coined by the author to denote an old practice in its modern development," in order to mobilize efforts around the world to denounce the practice and remove it from the repertoire of human actions.[27]

Scholars have been quick to notice that Lemkin's idea of peoples, culture, and the destruction of peoples resembles the writings of German Romantic philosopher Johann Gottfried Herder.[28] I have also heard scholars at various Ukrainian studies conferences sharing this interpretation of Lemkin, regarding discussions of a primordial Ukrainian nation. This is a misreading of Lemkin. Herder first developed the notion of culture and cultural relativism, and he inspired movements that called for compassion for those suffering because of colonial attempts to destroy culture in the name of civilization. While the Romantic nationalism of Herder generated an appreciation for cultural diversity, Lemkin wrote, there was a downside to this movement, which exalted "peoples" and "cultures" as primordial entities that transcended history. This notion of peoples and cultures as organic and primordial was grounded in a form of nationalism, Lemkin wrote, that would later be used by antisemitic and militarist thinkers who set the stage for the rise of Nazi nation-race ideologies.[29] While Lemkin borrowed much from Herder's writings on culture and his critique of colonial processes of cultural destruction, Lemkin ultimately rejected Romantic conceptions of nationhood. The "Herderian Romantic approach," he wrote, "became culturally atavistic in the nineteenth century and politically aggressive in the late nineteenth and the first half of the twentieth centuries," when it "coupled with the strive for power, aggrandizement, internal anxieties, and disrespect for minorities [to] create a climate … for the perpetration of genocide."[30] A Lemkin-inspired reading of Ukrainian history, therefore, would not uphold "Ukraine" or the "Ukrainian nation" as a primordial people that exists transhistorically, but rather affirm that a Ukrainian national identity is a historical, political, and sociological project – as was the Soviets' efforts to destroy this social identity group.

Lemkin's definition of peoples and nations was derived most directly from national cultural autonomy theorists – not organic or Romantic nationalists – precisely because Lemkin rejected atavistic theories of the nation and was resolute in his opposition to a relativistic form of nationhood. As A. Dirk Moses has written, Lemkin did not structure identity like a zero-sum game, and never believed that any individual had to express any one identity or be reduced to just one national identity.[31] In Lemkin's understanding, all individuals held multiple forms of what we now would call "social identity," and it was this ability of individuals to belong to many "nations" at once that enriched the human experience. "Cultural relativity," if it were freed from the xenophobic strictures of the Herderian Romantic approach, "can be a doctrine of hope rather than despair."[32] In the endeavour "at unifying the world for peace," Lemkin continues: "This doctrine [of cultural relativity] has a two-fold significance. It means that we must respect every culture for its own sake. It also means that we must probe beyond specific cultural differences in our search for a unified conception of human values and human rights. We know that this can be done."[33]

In his unfinished manuscript *Introduction to the Social Scientific Study of Genocide*, Lemkin turns to the Italian Romantic thinker Giuseppe Mazzini for an understanding of how national diversity could ground a universal form of world citizenship, made concrete by an international law prohibiting the destruction of nations.[34] Lemkin writes that Mazzini, "the prophet of the 19th century idea of nationality in a humanist, democratic form with a strong admixture of romanticism," posited a belief that nationality, not state citizenship, is what provides people with "citizenship in the world."[35] Lemkin borrowed Mazzini's metaphor of the symphony of nations,[36] explaining that nations were like musical instruments in the "subtle concerto" of world civilizations, which was "nourished and gets life from the tone of every instrument."[37] Yet, Lemkin still did not define nations in Mazzini's exact terms. When Lemkin told the *Christian Century* in a 1956 interview that he did "not belong exclusively to one race or one religion," he was acknowledging that he held a personal sense of belonging to Polish, Jewish, and American national groups, and was implicitly rejecting a strict nationalist worldview without giving up his sentiments that national groups and identities were the most basic foundation of the human experience.[38]

While Lemkin held on to Mazzini's ethical defense of nations as the source of all creativity in world civilization, and of cultural diversity as the key to a peaceful and humane world order, Lemkin offered a different definition of nations. Quoting the French Romantic philosopher of art history Henri Focillon, Lemkin wrote that "nations are families of mind," not transhistorical and primordial entities.[39] Focillon had used medieval and Mesopotamian art history to theorize that nations were constituted by a shared belief among individuals that they were unified, which manifested itself through patterns of aesthetic taste, reoccurring tropes, and shared understandings of symbols.[40] Above all, a nation, according to Lemkin, was a group of people who thought of themselves as belonging to the same group. Shared languages, arts, mythologies, folklores, collective histories, traditions, religions, and even shared ancestry or shared geographical location were important only because people *believed* that these things mattered. This meant an individual could belong to more than one nation at the same time, since the criteria for establishing nations were not mutually exclusive. Individuals could enter into and out of certain "families of mind," expressing one identity now and another one later, or several at once. Within this conception, no individual could ever be fully representative of a nation; nor could any individual be reduced to a nation.

Lemkin thus considered many different kinds of groups to be "nations," believed that nations were constituted by people's recognition that they were part of a nation, argued that nations were always changing their national character and that this dynamism enriched the lives of individuals, and felt that each individual could hold many different national identities throughout his or her life – often several simultaneously. His definition of a nation was so broad that it could include groups as small as "those who play at cards" or groups as large as Jews, Armenians, and Poles. Lemkin's goal with this definition was to outlaw a broad range of attempts to destroy a wide range of human groups by various means, from cultural, sociological, political, or economic repression, or even physical attacks against individuals intended to harm the collectivity.

In further developing his theory of nations as mental processes and acts of imagination, Lemkin borrowed heavily from the Austro-Hungarian Marxist and social democratic theorists and political figures Karl Renner and Otto Bauer. Indeed, he told Renner this much in his personal correspondences.[41] Bauer had argued that modern nations were "communities of character" that developed out of "communities of fate."[42] For Bauer, nations were not territorially derived, as liberal nationalism professed, and nor were they the closed-off and organic entities that conservatives (and German Romantic theorists) believed them to be. For Bauer, national consciousness was "by no means synonymous with the love of one's own nation or the will for the political unity of the nation." Instead, "national consciousness is to be understood as the simple recognition of membership in the nation."[43] This also meant that the content of national identity was always changing, because both nationality and nations as social groups were historical products of the consciousness of individuals.[44] Thus for Bauer, nations were neither transhistorical nor primordial entities, but constantly changing as individuals themselves changed and as new "communities of fate" formed and developed into new "communities of character." Consequently, national identities were not mutually exclusive. Lemkin would borrow these ideas explicitly in his late, unfinished writings on genocide, and quietly announced this position in a footnote in *Axis Rule*.[45]

As Lemkin taught his students at Yale Law School in 1948 after returning to the classroom, nations were the primary object of protection of the law against genocide, but nations were aspects of human consciousness.[46] Lemkin taught his class at Yale that a nation was a mental process that took on objective characteristics, sociologically, and therefore a nation was just as much an act of imagination as it was a historical object. Because of this, nations could come into and out of existence, and they could change. Lemkin told his students that he settled on the term "genocide" because the Greek and Sanskrit connotations of the root word "genos" signified a human group that was constituted through a shared way of thinking, not objective relations. The concept of the "genos," Lemkin said, "was originally conceived as an enlarged family unit having the conscience of a common ancestor – first real, later imagined."[47] It was in this imagined connection between people, he observed, where "the forces of cohesion and solidarity were born." The same forces for group cohesion could also serve as "the nursery of group pride and group hate" that is "sometimes subconscious, sometimes conscious, but always dangerous, because it creates a pragmatism that justifies cold destruction of the other group when it appears necessary or useful."[48]

The "Lemkin Turn" in Holodomor Studies

As I discussed in the introduction to this chapter, Lemkin has become an increasing figure of interest to those who study the Holodomor in the last decade.[49] Roman Serbyn and Lubomyr Luciuk may have been at the forefront of this movement in Ukrainian studies, applying Lemkin's theory to the field through their individual readings of Lemkin's 1953 speech on the Ukrainian genocide.[50] Crucially, for both scholars, the importance of Lemkin's thinking is that it positioned the Great Famine of 1932–33 as the most violent chapter of a decades-long genocide against the Ukrainian social group or Ukrainian national identity. Also important to both theorists is that, through this framing, an explicit order by Stalin or Soviet elites was irrelevant legally and theoretically, because legal and theoretical "intent" was constituted by the act, which was an explicit expression of state policy.[51] This broad application of Lemkin's thinking to interpretations and analyses of Ukrainian history and society has helped deepen two distinct areas of focus with Ukrainian studies, beyond the study of famine or political violence, to consider questions of "structural violence" or "cultural violence," as opposed to direct violence. The second area of Ukrainian studies that Lemkin's thinking has deepened and enriched is the analysis of Ukrainian history, society, politics, and economics through the concepts of empire and colony. The "structural/cultural violence" thread and the "empire/colony" thread of Ukrainian studies have clear overlaps, as empire-building and colonialism both involve systems of direct, structural, and cultural violence, but this "Lemkin turn" has helped unite both threads by focusing on the way each entails processes of group destruction and group construction, nation-building and national destruction, in other words: genocide.

Structural Violence, Cultural Violence, and the Destruction of Peoples

For Lubomyr Luciuk, Lemkin's significance rests in the fact that this "father of the UN Genocide Convention" recognized the horror and criminal nature of the Holodomor during a time when many notable public intellectuals and leaders in the 1950s either denied the atrocities or ignored them out of geopolitical expediency.[52] It was not only Lemkin's views on Communist crimes against humanity that were overlooked by scholars and the global public, Luciuk writes. Also ignored was Lemkin's assessment that "the 'destruction of the Ukrainian nation' [was a] 'classic example of Soviet genocide'" and "'not simply a case of mass murder'" because it involved "'the destruction, not of individuals only, but of a culture and a nation.'"[53] Lemkin's ideas, for Luciuk, had political implications in the 1950s and in the present day. The famine in Ukraine from 1932 to 1933 received little official recognition then and now because the structural relationship between Ukraine and the Soviet Union, and later the Russian Federation, has led foreign governments, global interest groups, and "Moscow's handmaidens" to recognize the famine as a tragedy but refuse to acknowledge that the famine was part of a wider identity-based conflict waged with the intention of destroying a Ukrainian social group.

For peace and conflict scholars more generally, Lemkin's emphasis on the cultural and social aspects of group destruction resembles the field of peace studies' focus on the symbolic aspects of group destruction in conflict. Through Lemkin's writings we can "understand genocide as more than mass murder or extensive and extreme violence," Jonathan Hobson writes, but as a social assault on a "group in its entirety, so that group, its history, and its social constructs no longer exist."[54] From this basis, Hobson argues that Lemkin's theory of genocide spans political, social, cultural, economic, biological, physical, religious, and moral spheres, and has much in common with the work of the seminal peace studies theorist Johan Galtung, "who offers a way to articulate the encompassing destructive processes genocide entails, and in doing so helps to better understand what it is that makes something a genocidal event."[55] Within Galtung's phenomenology of violence, Hobson continues, the concepts of "direct, structural and cultural violence" are used to "explain how different societal processes might exclude and victimize certain groups in society."[56] What comes to the fore of Luciuk's reading of Lemkin's analysis of the Ukrainian genocide is this exact sense that the conflict involved a total sociological and cultural assault on a marginalized victim group, the Ukrainian nation; that part of this social and cultural assault entailed an attempt by elites in Moscow to erase the distinct ethnic character of Ukrainian identity; and finally, that those Soviet elites denied the genocide and set the terms by which the international community perceived and interpreted the conflict.

In Lemkin's thought, the institutionalization and normalization of repression and violence against a group, with the goal of destroying the group as a social unit, meant that the cultural, social, and structural dynamics of genocide went hand-in-hand. The process of selecting a group as victims of genocide required that the perpetrators of genocide arbitrarily define human beings into categories, and deny the possibility that individuals could belong to many different social groups at once.[57] Lemkin's extremely broad definition of a nation meant that, in his thinking, any individual would belong to a seemingly infinite number of "nations." In this regard, his ideas again intersect with some of the foundational literature in peace and conflict studies, because, as Hobson notes, Lemkin's notion of genocide is by definition "an act of cultural violence in the sense that it is a crime committed by one group identifying as against another."[58] Individuals may commit the individual acts of violence in genocide, but

> genocide as a crime involves significant organization and, frequently, the convincing of a population, force, or army that this form of violence is the solution. In this sense, genocide needs to exist as a cultural concept before it can exist as a physical act. Using Galtung's words, we can see how it is "Cultural violence [that] makes direct and structural violence look and feel right." Genocide involves embedding ideas of superiority and legitimate violence into cultural discourse, and for Galtung it is "the study of cultural violence [that] highlights the ways in which the acts of direct and structural violence are legitimized, internalized, and thus rendered acceptable in society.[59]

And, indeed, when Luciuk uses Lemkin's ideas to analyze the Holodomor as genocide, he argues that the cultural and social aspects of the attempted destruction of a Ukrainian social group implies the presence of a structural conflict between the political regime centred in Moscow and the Ukrainian national group, while the structural conflict and structural violence implies cultural violence and social conflict that predates the violence of the Holodomor and continues long after the famine formally ended.

The structural aspects of Lemkin's genocide concept are even more pronounced in Roman Serbyn's use of Lemkin to analyze the Holodomor, especially because Serbyn follows Lemkin exactly and argues that the events that led up to the famine qualify as genocide. In Serbyn's writings on Lemkin, the conceptual significance of Lemkin's emphasis on the identity or group-based nature of the Soviet conflict in Ukraine in the 1930s cannot be understated.[60] What is especially important for Serbyn is that Lemkin connected the famine to a larger social, economic, and political program of destroying the Ukrainian nation. Therefore, the physical violence of the Holodomor, in Serbyn's analysis, emerged historically as an extension of the structural and cultural violence applied by the Soviet state with the intention of destroying a distinct Ukrainian social identity. For Serbyn, like Lemkin, the famine is only one part of the Soviet genocide against Ukraine. In fact, in Lemkin's analysis, what made the famine genocidal was not that Stalin's regime killed so many people by orchestrating grain shortages, but that people were killed with the purpose of destroying a distinctly Ukrainian "national pattern" or "family of mind." More importantly, for Serbyn, Lemkin demonstrated that the goal of the famine was not just to prevent the people living in Ukraine from resisting integration into the Soviet political system and economy; the famine was furthermore structurally connected to a wider system of Soviet repression against a Ukrainian national identity. Thus the famine was, in Lemkin's words, one "prong" in a multi-pronged attack upon the foundation of the Ukrainian nation. For Serbyn, the analytical power of Lemkin's concept of genocide, as applied to the Ukrainian case, is that it provides a coherent frame for understanding just what the destruction of a people entailed. The assault on religious traditions of the Ukrainian Church, the songs and folk traditions of the peasantry, the art and literature of the urban elite, the economic debasement of the rural economies, and mass violence were all aspects of a coherent political and social program to "solve" different "nationalities problems" faced by state-building programs – in this case, the Soviet Union's "Ukrainian problem."

Empire, Colony, and the Destruction and Construction of Nations

Ukrainian history provides an interesting laboratory, writes Andrea Graziosi, "in which to study the language-people-state nexus that was at the center of post-1848 European history" of state-building, nationalism, and nationalities violence.[61] The Russification of the Donbas during tsarist modernization and the Ukrainization program in the prewar Soviet experience "are there to remind us that 'nations' can indeed be built" and "for precisely the same reasons and employing similar tools, they can also be at least partially dismantled and disabled."[62] For Graziosi, however, the Ukrainian genocide is not sui generis, but part of the history of this "borderlands" region, the site of twentieth-century Europe's most brutal nation-building and nation-destroying population transfers and annihilation projects, from the anti-Jewish pogroms of 1919, Red and White terror in the Civil War, anti-Mennonite persecutions, dekulakization, the national terror of 1933–34, the Great Terror of 1937–38, the Nazi extermination of Soviet prisoners of war and Slavic populations, the Shoah, and the Holodomor – conflicts that all played a role in shaping Lemkin's conception of genocide.[63]

In borderlands regions, twentieth-century state-building or rebuilding "fed other conflicts that were intensified by insecure and poorly demarcated borders, which often had to be drawn in formerly unified imperial territories and did not possess the stability they had attained slowly – mostly thanks to repeated conflicts – in Western Europe."[64] In the theory of nation-state building that defined post-French Revolution political projects, it was whole and unified "peoples" that were supposed to legitimize state construction.[65] The supposed need to base the state-building project on "peoples" or "nations" gave rise to efforts to reshape the demographics of territories, and the social content of the people living there, as imperial and postimperial elites "engaged in both 'constructive' efforts" to create new peoples for the coherence of the region "generally based on cultural projects that included language building and reform as well as the mass alphabetization of peasant populations," and "'deconstructive' projects which, in times of conflict or even in peacetimes, could take the form of expulsions, forced deportations, and even genocidal or quasi-genocidal operations."[66] These dynamics of conflict were crucial to Lemkin's theory of genocide, which presented genocide as an act of group creation as much as it was an act of group destruction.[67] It was also the impetus for Lemkin's insistence in the 1940s that outlawing genocide under international law was necessary for preventing states from using national identity as a criteria of belonging, and using "peoples" as the basis of political unity.[68]

Within this context it is also possible, Graziosi writes, to speak of a Ukrainian history of Soviet colonization and an anti-imperial sentiment among the peasanty, for surely in 1918 and 1919 Ukrainian Communist leaders "understood the revolutionary potential and danger of the peasant-based national and social liberation movements."[69] Here again, Lemkin has much to say on Ukrainian history. Lemkin saw genocide as an explicitly colonial practice.[70] Genocide had two phases, he wrote: "One, the destruction of the national pattern of the oppressed group; the other, the imposition of the national pattern of the oppressor."[71] "Directed against the national group as an entity," he wrote, "the actions involved" in committing genocide "are directed against individuals, not in their individual capacity, but as members of the national group." Lemkin thus interpreted the genocide perpetrated by Nazi Germany as a colonial project of transforming the demographics of Germany and the newly conquered regions of occupied Europe. "In line with this policy of imposing the German national pattern, particularly in the incorporated territories, the occupant has organized a system of colonization of these areas," he wrote.[72] As a consequence of this German colonization of the occupied territories, he concluded, "participation in economic life is thus dependent upon one's being German or being devoted to the cause of Germanism. Consequently, promoting a national ideology other than German is made difficult and dangerous."[73] Lemkin saw Soviet rule in Ukraine in similar terms, as an empire exerting colonial control over a territory and attempting to forcibly and purposefully change the "national patterns" of the people living there for strategic ends. "If it were possible to do this even without suffering we would still be driven to condemn it," he wrote about Stalinist policies aimed at extinguishing a distinct Ukrainian national identity, because it is

> the family of minds, the unity of ideas, of language and of customs that form what we call a nation that constitutes one of the most important of all our means of civilization and progress. It is true that nations blend together and form new nations – we have an example of this process in our own country – but this blending consists in the pooling of benefits of superiorities that each culture possesses. What then, apart from the very important question of human suffering and human rights that we find wrong with Soviet plans is the criminal waste of civilization and of culture. For the Soviet national unity is being created, not by any union of ideas and of cultures, but by the complete destruction of all cultures and of all ideas save one – the Soviet.[74]

In this view, the destruction of a people, the Ukrainian nation, was also an attempt to build a new people, the Soviet nation. To borrow Graziosi's terms, the constructive and destructive aspects of this conflict were intertwined in Lemkin's final analysis; as were the cultural, social, symbolic, and direct forms of violence entailed in the destruction and creation of nations in the Ukrainian genocide in the Soviet empire.

For as violent as nationalist state-building efforts were, Lemkin believed that twentieth-century state-building and nationalist movements were not the first to commit genocide or use genocide as a technique of governance. Lemkin sought a definition of genocide that would therefore capture what genocide was as a type of conflict, and not limit the concept of genocide to a particular type of violence in the twentieth century. For much of history before the rise of the nation-state, he wrote, the "fury or calculated hatred" of genocide was directed "against specific groups which did not fit into the pattern of the state [or] religious community or even in the social pattern" of the oppressors. The victims of genocide were any nation "selected for destruction according to the criterion of their affiliation with a group which is considered extraneous and dangerous for various reasons," he wrote. He included under the rubric of nations groups as large as Jews and Ukrainians, as well as groups as narrow as the aforementioned card-players "or those who engage in unlawful trade practices or in breaking up unions."[75] Genocide, Lemkin reasoned, could even be conducted against criminals because states often criminalized certain types of subjectivities and identities. Lemkin derived this point from his study of the Soviet penal codes that criminalized forms of "enemy consciousness," and the Soviet policies aimed at transforming the population into a nation of "new Soviet men."

Towards this point, Mark von Hagen has drawn a lesson from his reading of Lemkin – who, he writes playfully, "knew all of this long before most of us did."[76] Divided between two empires that would fall during World War I, Ukraine saw "the emergence of a transnational movement for national liberation" with "strong roots in those two empires," which faced repartition after the war "between an already imperialist Soviet Russia and a nationalizing Second Polish Republic whose practices also closely resembled imperial rule."[77] Stalinist Ukraine, von Hagen writes, "was the site of another excess of colonial rule, the man-made famine and terror, the Holodomor" and "counterinsurgency warfare against local nationalist insurgents."[78] Echoing Lemkin's notion that genocide was a peacetime crime because the conflict could be waged without direct violence, von Hagen writes that for most of the twentieth century, "Ukraine's history combined wartime occupations and periods of 'peacetime' colonialism."[79] Through the concept of empire, and by positioning the Holodomor within the context of Soviet empire-building, von Hagen's analysis of the famine brings together the threads of Lemkin's analysis that presents genocide as a synthesis of cultural, structural, and direct physical violence.

From this perspective, "genocide requires a form of structural violence against the target group," either "as a tool to manage resources or as a broader structure of social power," that has been "accepted and normalized by a population through cultural violence."[80] As Lemkin explained in his unfinished manuscript *Introduction to the Study of Genocide in the Social Sciences*, "like all social phenomena, [genocide] represents a complex synthesis of a diversity of factors; but its nature is primarily sociological, since it means the destruction of certain social groups by other social groups or the individual representatives."[81] Any analysis must, therefore, recognize that "genocide is a gradual process and may begin with political disenfranchisement, economic displacement, cultural undermining and control, the destruction of leadership, the break-up of families and the prevention of propagation. Each of these methods is a more or less effective means of destroying a group. Actual physical destruction is the last and most effective phase of genocide."[82] The violence of genocide in Lemkin's, Luciuk's, Serbyn's, and von Hagen's analyses of the Holodomor, therefore, presents the direct violence of the famine as a physical manifestation of a larger system of repression, marginalization, and group destruction and group creation in the service of Soviet empire-building in Ukraine.[83]

NOTES

1 William Korey, *An Epitaph for Raphael Lemkin* (New York: Jacob Blaustein Institute for the Advancement of Human Rights, 2001); John Cooper, *Raphael Lemkin and the Struggle for the Genocide Convention* (New York: Palgrave Macmillan, 2008); Raphael Lemkin, *Totally Unofficial: The Autobiography of Raphael Lemkin*, edited by Donna-Lee Frieze (New Haven, CT: Yale University Press, 2013); Philippe Sands, *East West Street: On the Origins of Genocide and Crimes against Humanity* (New York: Knopf, 2016); Douglas Irvin-Erickson, *Raphaël Lemkin and the Concept of Genocide* (Philadelphia: University of Pennsylvania Press, 2017); Anton Weiss-Wendt, *The Soviet Union and the Gutting of the UN Genocide Convention* (Madison: University of Wisconsin Press, 2017).

2 Agnieszka Bienczyk-Missala and Slawomir Debski, eds., *Rafał Lemkin: A Hero of Humankind* (Warsaw: Polish Institute of International Affairs, 2010); and Dominik Shaller and Jürgen Zimmerer, eds., *The Origins of Genocide: Raphael Lemkin as a Historian of Mass Violence* (New York: Routledge, 2009). See three special issues on Lemkin in the *Journal of Genocide Research* 15, no. 3 (2013), *Journal of Genocide Research* 7, no. 4 (2005); and *Genocide Studies and Prevention* 13, no. 1 (2019).

3 Andrea Graziosi, "Viewing the Twentieth Century through the Prism of Ukraine: Reflections on the Heuristic Potential of Ukrainian History," *Harvard Ukrainian Studies* 34, nos. 1–4 (2015–16): 107–28.

4 It is not necessary to cite the speech at length here because it has been published in journals and presses relevant to Ukrainian studies that are likely familiar to readers of this chapter. See Roman Serbyn, "Lemkin on Genocide of Nations," *Journal of International Criminal Justice* 7, no. 1 (2009): 123–30; and see Raphael Lemkin, *Soviet Genocide in the Ukraine*, edited by L.Y. Luciuk (Kingston, ON: Kashtan Press, 2014).

5 Raphael Lemkin, *Axis Rule in Occupied Europe: Laws of Occupation, Analysis of Government, Proposals for Redress* (New York: Carnegie Endowment for International Peace, 1944), 79.

6 Michelle Tusan, this volume.

7 Convention on the Prevention and Punishment of the Crime of Genocide approved and proposed for signature and ratification or accession by General Assembly resolution 260 A (III) of 9 December 1948. Entry into force: 12 January 1951, in accordance with article 13.

8 Raphaël Lemkin, *Axis Rule in Occupied Europe: Laws of Occupation, Analysis of Government, Proposals for Redress* (New York: Carnegie Endowment for International Peace, 1944), 79.

9 For an important new consideration on cultural violence and genocide, see Fatma Müge Göçek and Fiona Greenland, eds., *Cultural Violence and the Destruction of Human Communities: New Theoretical Perspectives* (United Kingdom: Taylor and Francis, 2020).

10 Douglas Irvin-Erickson, "From Geneva to Nuremberg to New York: Andrei Vyshinsky, Raphaël Lemkin, and the Struggle to Outlaw Revolutionary Violence, State Terror, and Genocide," in *Stalin's Soviet Justice: Show Trials, War Crimes, and Nuremberg*, edited by David Crowe (Bloomsbury, 2019), 217–32.

11 See for example, Douglas Irvin-Erickson, "Genocide Discourses: American and Russian Strategic Narratives of Conflict in Iraq and Ukraine," *Politics and Governance* 5, no. 3 (2017): 130–45.

12 Norman Naimark has made the strongest case possible that the Holodomor and other aspects of Soviet oppression and repression constitute genocide under the UN legal definition. See Naimark, *Stalin's Genocides* (Princeton, NJ: Princeton University Press, 2010). Naimark's scholarship is persuasive. Between 1946 and 48, however, Vyshinsky was heading the Soviet delegation's legal team at the UN, and had squared off with Lemkin a number of times. It is clear that, by the final draft of the treaty in 1948, Vyshinsky and Stalin were satisfied that the version of the treaty the USSR would sign would not include these acts as acts of genocide. The great historian Naimark may have proved the case, but Stalin's lawyers believed they had succeeded in sufficiently constricting the definition and crippling the treaty.

13 Michelle Tusan, this volume.

14 Douglas Irvin-Erickson, "Genocide Discourses."

15 Nicolas Dreyer, "Genocide, *Holodomor*, and Holocaust Discourse as Echo of Historical Injury and as Rhetorical Radicalization in the Russian-Ukrainian Conflict of 2013–2018," in *The Holocaust/Genocide Template in Eastern Europe*, edited by Ljiljana Radonić (London: Routledge, 2020), 63–82.

16 I have written about Lemkin's conceptions of state policy and responsibility, both in a legalistic context and a social scientific context, elsewhere. See Douglas Irvin-Erickson, "Prosecuting Sexual Violence at the Cambodian War Crimes Tribunal: Challenges, Limitations, and Implications," *Human Rights Quarterly* 40, no. 3 (2018): 570–90.

17 Irvin-Erickson, *Raphaël Lemkin and the Concept of Genocide*; and see James Loeffler, "Becoming Cleopatra: the Forgotten Zionism of Raphael Lemkin," *Journal of Genocide Research* 19, no. 3 (2017), 340–60.

18 Irvin-Erickson, *Raphaël Lemkin and the Concept of Genocide*; Cooper, *Raphael Lemkin and the Struggle for the Genocide Convention*; Anton Weiss-Wendt, *The Soviet Union and the Gutting of the UN Genocide Convention.*

19 Irvin-Erickson, *Raphaël Lemkin and the Concept of Genocide*; Lawrence J. LeBlanc, *The United States and the Genocide Convention* (Durham, NC: Duke University Press, 1991); Anton Weiss-Wendt, *A Rhetorical Crime: Genocide in the Geopolitical Discourse of the Cold War* (New Brunswick, NJ: Rutgers University Press, 2018).

20 The subject that has been studied extensively. For instance, see A. Dirk Moses, "Raphael Lemkin, Culture, and the Concept of Genocide"; Cooper, *Raphael Lemkin and the Struggle for the Genocide Convention*; Irvin-Erickson, *Raphaël Lemkin and the Concept of Genocide*; Martin Shaw, *What is Genocide? 2nd Edition* (London: Polity, 2015); Martin Crook, Damien Short, and Nigel South, "Ecocide, Genocide, Capitalism and Colonialism: Consequences for Indigenous Peoples and Glocal Ecosystems Environments," *Theoretical Criminology* 22, no. 3 (2018): 298–317.

21 Lemkin, *Axis Rule*, 79.

22 Ibid.

23 Henry R. Huttenbach, "From the Editor: Lemkin Redux; In Quest of a Word," *Journal of Genocide Research* 7, no. 4 (2005): 443–5.

24 Irvin-Erickson, *Raphaël Lemkin and the Concept of Genocide*, 6. But see Claudia Kraft, "Völkermord Als Delictum Iuris Gentium: Raphaël Lemkin's Vorarbeiten Füreine Genozidkonvention," *Simon Dubnow Institute Yearbook* 4 (2005): 79–98.

25 Carmelo Domenico Leotta, *Il Genocidio Nel Diritto Penale Internationale: Dagli Scritti di Raphael Lemkin allo Statuto di Roma* (Torino: G. Giappichelli Editore, 2013), 72–6.

26 Lemkin, *Axis Rule*, 79–80.

27 Ibid., 79.

28 See Daniel Marc Segesser and Myriam Gessler, "Raphael Lemkin and the International Debate on the Punishment of War Crimes (1919–1948)," *Journal of Genocide Research* 7, no. 4 (2005): 453–68; Thomas M. Butcher, "A 'Synchronized Attack': On Raphael Lemkin's Holistic Conception of Genocide," *Journal of Genocide Research* 15, no. 3 (2013): 253–71. On this debate, see A. Dirk Moses, "Moving the Genocide Debate beyond the History Wars," *Australian Journal of Politics and History* 54, no. 2 (2008): 267. Seyla Benhabib has defended Lemkin against charges that he advocated a relativist nationalism of vulnerable peoples in *Dignity in Adversity: Human Rights in Trouble* (Cambridge: Polity Press, 2011), 51, 220n24.

29 Raphaël Lemkin, "Introduction: The New Word and the New Idea," New York Public Library (hereafter NYPL), n.d., Reel 3, Box 2, Folder 2, p. 8.

30 Raphaël Lemkin, "Collective Frustrations as a Prelude to Genocide," NYPL, n.d., Reel 3, Box 2, Folder 4.

31 Moses, "Raphael Lemkin, Culture, and the Concept of Genocide," 24.

32 Raphael Lemkin, "Diffusion versus Cultural Genocide," Raphael Lemkin Papers, Manuscript Collection 1730, Manuscript and Archives Division, NYPL, Reel 3, Box 2, Folder 3. See Irvin-Erickson, *Raphaël Lemkin and the Concept of Genocide*, 224.
33 Lemkin, "Diffusion versus Cultural Genocide."
34 Lemkin, "Introduction: The New Word and the New Idea," Raphael Lemkin Papers, Reel 3, Box 2, Folder 2, p. 8. For a communitarian analysis of Mazzini and Herder, see Michael Walzer and David Miller, *Thinking Politically: Essays in Political Theory* (New Haven, CT: Yale University Press, 2007), 212.
35 Raphael Lemkin, "Introduction: The New Word and the New Idea," 8.
36 A. Dirk Moses raises this point in "Raphael Lemkin, Culture, and the Concept of Genocide."
37 Raphael Lemkin, "Draft Supplemental Remarks by Dr. Lemkin," Raphael Lemkin Papers, NYPL, Reel 2, Box 1, Folder 34.
38 Robert Merrill Bartlett, "By the Way: Pioneer vs. an Ancient Crime," *Christian Century,* 16 July 1956.
39 Raphael Lemkin, "Genocide," Raphael Lemkin Papers, NYPL, Reel 4, Box 3, Folder 1–2.
40 Henri Focillon, *Vie des Formes* (Paris: Librairie Ernest Leroux, 1934). Indeed, Lemkin admired Henri Focillon, a public intellectual of note. On Focillon, see George Kubler's essay commemorating the lifetime achievement of the scholar upon his death: "Henri Focillon, 1881–1943," *College Art Journal* 4, no. 2 (1945): 71–4.
41 See Karl Renner, "State and Nation," in *National Cultural Autonomy and Its Contemporary Critics*, edited by Ephraim Nimni, 15–48, esp. 30, 39 (New York: Routledge, 2005). Compare this to Lemkin's correspondences with Renner. Raphael Lemkin to Karl Renner, 29 March 1950, Raphael Lemkin Papers, American Jewish Association, Cincinnati, Ohio, United States, box 1, folder 15.
42 Otto Bauer, *The Question of Nationalities and Social Democracy*, trans. Joseph O'Donnell, edited by Ephraim J. Nimni (Minneapolis: University of Minnesota Press, 2000), 7.
43 Ibid., 120.
44 Ibid., 21.
45 Lemkin, *Axis Rule*, 91n5.
46 See Irvin-Erickson, *Raphaël Lemkin*, chapter 7.
47 Lemkin, *Totally Unofficial*, 181–2.
48 Ibid.
49 Graziosi, "Viewing the Twentieth Century through the Prism of Ukraine."
50 See Roman Serbyn, "Lemkin on Genocide of Nations," and see Luciuk's edition of Lemkin's *Soviet Genocide in the Ukraine*.

51 I have written about Lemkin's conceptions of state policy and responsibility, both in a legalistic context and a social scientific context, elsewhere. See Irvin-Erickson, "Prosecuting Sexual Violence at the Cambodian War Crimes Tribunal."

52 Lubomyr Luciuk, "Remembering the Man Who Told the Truth of Stalin's Assault on Ukraine," *National Post*, 24 September 2018, https://nationalpost.com/opinion/remembering–the–man–who–told–the–truth–of–stalins–assault–on–ukraine.

53 Lubomyr Luciuk, "Lemkin: Holodomor 'Classic' Genocide," *Kyiv Post*, 19 November 2009, https://www.kyivpost.com/article/opinion/op–ed/lemkin–holodomor–classic–genocide–53243.html. The quotes from Lemkin are taken from Luciuk to show the ideas Luciuk finds instructive.

54 Hobson, "Three Theoretical Approaches to Lemkin's Definition of Genocide," *Genocide Studies and Prevention: An International Journal* 13, no. 1 (2019): 14.

55 Ibid.

56 Ibid.

57 A. Dirk Moses, "Raphael Lemkin, Culture, and the Concept of Genocide," 24.

58 Hobson, "Three Theoretical Approaches to Lemkin's Definition of Genocide," 14.

59 Ibid.

60 Roman Serbyn, "The Ukrainian Famine of 1932–1933 as Genocide in the Light of the UN Convention of 1948," *The Ukrainian Quarterly* 62, no. 2 (2006): 181–94.

61 Graziosi, "Viewing the Twentieth Century through the Prism of Ukraine," 123.

62 Ibid.

63 Ibid.

64 Ibid., 116.

65 Ibid.

66 Ibid.

67 Irvin-Erickson, *Raphaël Lemkin*, 39, 220.

68 Ibid., 220, 246.

69 Graziosi, "Viewing the Twentieth Century through the Prism of Ukraine," 119.

70 Lemkin, *Axis Rule*, 79.

71 Ibid. See generally A. Dirk Moses, ed., *Empire, Colony, Genocide: Conquest, Occupation, and Subaltern Resistance in World History* (London: Berghahn Books, 2008).

72 Lemkin, *Axis Rule*, 83.

73 Ibid., 86.

74 Raphael Lemkin, "Soviet Genocide in the Ukraine." NYPL, Reel 3, Box 2, Folder 16, pp. 1–8.

75 Raphaël Lemkin, "The Nature of Genocide," n.d., Raphaël Lemkin Collection, P–154, American Jewish Historical Society, New York, New York, United States, Box 2, Folder 2, p. 14.

76 Mark von Hagen, "Wartime Occupation and Peacetime Alien Rule: 'Notes and Materials' toward a(n) (Anti-) (Post-) Colonial History of Ukraine," *Harvard Ukrainian Studies* 34, nos. 1–4 (2015–16): 183n8.

77 Ibid., 154.

78 Ibid.

79 Ibid.

80 Hobson, "Three Theoretical Approaches to Lemkin's Definition of Genocide," 14.

81 Raphael Lemkin, "The Concept of Genocide in Sociology," in Raphaël Lemkin, *Introduction to the Study of Genocide*, n.d., NYPL, Reel 3, Box 2, Folders 1–4.

82 Lemkin, "The Concept of Genocide in Sociology."

83 This chapter was originally delivered as a lecture at the "Genocide in Twentieth Century History" conference at the University of Toronto's Munk School of Global Affairs in October 2018. Earlier versions of the lecture were delivered at the University of Stockholm, Georgetown University, American University, and Harvard University between 2018 and 2019. Some parts of this chapter appeared in Douglas Irvin-Erickson, *Raphaël Lemkin and the Concept of Genocide* (Philadelphia: University of Pennsylvania Press, 2017). Thank you to Penn Press for permission to reproduce portions of the book. Thank you to Scott Howard, Marta Baziuk, Frank E. Sysyn, and Andrea Graziosi for their thoughtful comments and suggestions, which improved this manuscript considerably.

7

The Orchestrated Inapplicability of the Law of Crimes against Humanity and Genocide – *une exception française*?

Caroline Fournet

Just like most states at some point in their history, France has, in the relatively recent past, been related in one way or another, and at various degrees, to contemporary genocides. If this is arguably not peculiar to France, what might be more intriguing is the French attitude towards the very concept of genocide, be it at the legal, judicial, or political level. If opacity in politics is to be expected, the French law and prosecution of genocide are themselves – perhaps more surprisingly – not deprived of ambiguity and strategic twists. What is particularly striking is the divergence between a progressive law and a disinclined practice, perhaps encouraged by obscure and ambivalent political discourses.

The French definition of the crime of genocide dates from the 1994 New Penal Code and draws upon the definition enshrined in article II of the 1948 United Nations Convention on the Prevention and Punishment of the Crime of Genocide.[1] However, it also significantly departs from it in two important – and admittedly progressive – ways, which, from a theoretical viewpoint, could and probably should have allowed for a more enhanced judicial use of the concept. Yet French practice has failed to adequately follow the theory, and the crime of genocide has more often than not remained totally and inexplicably absent from the courtroom.[2] It is only very recently that "genocide" as a legal qualification has been used by French courts, and only in a few cases related to the Rwandan genocide. This chapter explores this belated and sporadic use of the legal qualification of genocide by French courts by first addressing whether it was indeed applicable in the trials of the Second World War that preceded the New Penal Code's entry into force. This initial absence of the "genocide" characterization had a double impact: it generated a confusion between crimes against humanity and genocide based on an unconvincing and varying definition of the former, which in turn created a time gap during which no accusation of either genocide or crimes against humanity could be validly invoked before French courts, including against the French state. These two consequences are analyzed successively in the second and third sections. The entry into force of the New Penal Code only timidly brought to an end decades of judicial reluctance and avoidance, to the point that, as the fourth section exposes, France's concern during the drafting of the Genocide Convention that any domestic prosecution of the crime would be "inconceivable" seems to have materialized.[3]

1 The Crime of Genocide: An Applicable Legal Qualification under French Law before the Entry into Force of the New Penal Code

France signed the Genocide Convention on 11 December 1948, only two days after its adoption by the General Assembly of the United Nations on 9 December 1948. France subsequently ratified the Genocide Convention on 14 October 1950, thus showing its attachment to the prevention and punishment of the crime of genocide rather early on.[4] Interestingly, and as noted by Karen Smith,

> one issue that, somewhat curiously, did not really arise during the negotiations or ratification process is *concern that European colonial powers could be accused of genocide themselves*. Several countries still had colonies after the Second World War, including Belgium, France, the Netherlands, Portugal and the UK. Those countries might thus have reason not to accede or ratify the Convention, not because they were intent on committing genocide but because they feared being accused of having committed genocide in their colonies. Yet, two colonial powers, Belgium and France ratified the Convention almost immediately; the Netherlands, Portugal and the UK did not.[5]

Relying on national archives, Smith further details the position of the UK, which initially refused to accede to the convention, calling it a "miserable" document particularly for its implications regarding extradition.[6] There seemed however to have been no concern "in the Foreign Office arguments … that the UK could be held in breach of the Convention because of its colonial policies. There is no indication that this was ever a worry."[7]

It seems fair to assert that France also had no such concerns when it ratified the convention, which entered into force on 12 January 1951. Whether such worries arose afterwards is unclear, but it is striking that the crime of genocide only made its "formal entrance" in French legislation on 1 March 1994 – that is to say, forty-three years later – with the entry into force of the New Penal Code, which defines genocide in its article 211–1:

> Genocide occurs where, in the enforcement of a *concerted plan* aimed at the partial or total destruction of a national, ethnic, racial or religious group, or of *a group determined by any other arbitrary criterion*, one of the following actions are committed or caused to be committed against members of that group:
>
> - wilful attack on life;
> - serious attack on psychic or physical integrity;
> - subjection to living conditions likely to entail the partial or total destruction of that group;
> - measures aimed at preventing births; [and]
> - enforced child transfers.[8]

Although this definition was clearly influenced by the Genocide Convention, it also deviates from it in two important aspects. First, while the conventional definition defines the crime of genocide by the *intent* to destroy a group, the French definition puts the emphasis on the planned and systematic feature of the crime and, to this end, adopts a more objective criterion, that of the existence of a *concerted plan*.[9] Second, the scope of application of the definition of genocide is significantly enlarged. In addition to the conventionally protected groups – namely, "national, ethnic, racial or religious groups as such" – the French disposition also grants protection to "group[s] determined by any other arbitrary criterion." The Genocide Convention's narrow sphere of application and its selective protection of groups is an ongoing point of contention in genocide studies,[10] and it thus seems that France, by recognizing that genocide could be committed against other groups than the ones expressly listed in the convention, has adopted a more progressive approach. In this French proactive legislative context, it is intriguing that the concept of genocide has remained largely absent from prosecutions, and the question arises as to whether legal obstacles could have impeded its application in such prosecutions.

1.1 The Direct Applicability of the Genocide Convention under French Law

The first potential legal obstacle to the application of the Genocide Convention to acts perpetrated before the entry into force of the French New Penal Code relates to the applicability of the convention in French law. France is a country of monist tradition, where ratified treaties have a force superior to that of national laws. In his *Commentary of the Genocide Convention*, Robinson expressly cited France as one of the states where "an international agreement becomes domestic law by ratification."[11] When France ratified the convention in 1950, this principle was unequivocally stated in article 26 of the 1946 Constitution.[12] It was subsequently reiterated in article 55 of the 1958 French Constitution, which is still in force today.[13] Thus, although the qualification of genocide only entered the French Penal Code in 1994, the convention should have been of immediate application in France as soon as it had entered into force in January 1951.

Yet, it is correct that the Genocide Convention does not provide for any penalties and is thus not a self-executing instrument. Rather, under its article V, "the Contracting Parties undertake to enact, in accordance with their respective Constitutions, the necessary legislation to give effect to the provisions of the present Convention, and, in particular, to provide effective penalties for persons guilty of genocide or any of the other acts enumerated in article III." It could thus be convincingly argued that, even in monist states, the enforcement of the prohibition of genocide before domestic courts requires an express domestic statute of implementation, which France only adopted in 1994 by virtue of its New Penal Code. In other words, it took France forty-three years to finally comply with its obligations under article V of the Genocide Convention; a timeframe which seems to indicate a certain unwillingness to effectively prosecute the crime of genocide. Further, and even if the argument based on the conventional lack of penalties is valid, it does not appear to have prevented the prosecution and punishment of crimes against humanity before French courts, despite the fact that – under French law – such crimes were equally deprived of any domestic statute of implementation, with French courts exercising their jurisdiction based on the law of Nuremberg, which did not provide for any specific penalties.[14]

1.2 *The Non-applicability of Statutory Limitations to the Crime of Genocide*

The second possible impediment to the qualification of a crime as genocide under French law before the entry into force of the New Penal Code could be statutory limitations. The Genocide Convention was totally silent on this matter. The first international instrument to explicitly prohibit the application of statutory limitations to the crime of genocide was the 1968 UN Convention on the Non-Applicability of Statutory Limitations to War Crimes and Crimes against Humanity,[15] which, while ratified by only a small number of states, entered into force in 1970. Although France was among those states that did not ratify this convention, the then-French Foreign Affairs Ministry still unequivocally held that "le droit international ignore en général la prescription extinctive. Pour lui, celle-ci ne se présume pas, et à défaut d'une mention explicite, elle ne s'applique pas" ("international law generally ignores extinctive prescription. According to international law, extinctive prescription cannot be presumed and therefore applies only if expressly mentioned").[16] It can thus be inferred that the French Foreign Affairs Ministry interpreted the silence of the Genocide Convention as confirmation that the crime of genocide was not subjected to statutory limitations.

If France failed to ratify the 1968 convention, it is most probably due to its refusal to recognize the non-applicability of statutory limitations to war crimes. In 1964, the French legislature had indeed unanimously adopted a law exclusively recognizing the non-applicability of statutory limitations to crimes against humanity,[17] which, as the *travaux préparatoires* indicate, included genocide[18] as a form of crime against humanity.[19] The non-applicability of statutory limitations to genocide was later confirmed in article 213-5 of the New Penal Code, which states that "the public action relating to the crimes envisaged by this title [genocide and crimes against humanity], as well as the sentences passed, are imprescriptible."

1.3 *The Applicability of Retroactive Criminal Norms*

A third possible obstacle to the application of the Genocide Convention to acts committed prior to the entry into force of the New Penal Code could be derived from the prohibition of retroactive criminal norms. Yet, and although the Genocide Convention is silent on the issue, international law recognizes certain exceptions to this prohibition. Article 15 of the International Covenant on Civil and Political Rights (ICCPR) reads:

> No one shall be held guilty of any criminal offence on account of any act or omission which did not constitute a criminal offence, under national or international law, at the time when it was committed. Nor shall a heavier penalty be imposed than the one that was applicable at the time when the criminal offence was committed. If, subsequent to the commission of the offence, provision is made by law for the imposition of a lighter penalty, the offender shall benefit thereby.
>
> Nothing in this article shall prejudice the trial and punishment of any person for any act or omission which, at the time when it was committed, was criminal according to the general principles of law recognized by the community of nations.

It does not seem too far-fetched to suggest that the "general principles of law recognized by the community of nations" encompass the prohibition of genocide,[20] although it may also be argued that this prohibition stems from the rules of international customary law and is therefore covered by the reference to "international law" in article 15 (1) rather than by article 15 (2).[21] Interestingly, this "reference to international law in article 15 (1) is attributable to proposals by Uruguay *and France*," who argued that it would prevent persons responsible for the commission of international crimes to evade punishment by simply pleading that their offenses were not punishable under the domestic law of their state(s).[22] France is also a party to the European Convention on Human Rights (ECHR)[23] which almost identically replicates article 15 of the ICCPR in its article 7:

> 1. No one shall be held guilty of any criminal offence on account of any act or omission which did not constitute a criminal offence under national or international law at the time when it was committed. Nor shall a heavier penalty be imposed than the one that was applicable at the time the criminal offence was committed.
>
> This Article shall not prejudice the trial and punishment of any person for any act or omission which, at the time when it was committed, was criminal according to the general principles of law recognised by civilised nations.

In fact, the French Cour de cassation expressly recognized the applicability of both article 15 (2) of the ICCPR and article 7 (2) of the ECHR to crimes perpetrated during the Second World War.[24] These crimes were, however, qualified as crimes against humanity, not as genocide.

2 A Confusing Legacy: The Judicial Preference for the Qualification of Crimes against Humanity

The first French trial related to the Shoah was that of Klaus Barbie,[25] followed by those of Paul Touvier, active member of the French *Milice*; Maurice Papon, former high civil servant; and Aloïs Brunner, Adolf Eichmann's assistant in the implementation of the Nazi genocidal plan.[26] These defendants, who stood accused for their participation in the Shoah, were not charged with genocide but with crimes against humanity. If, in theory, one could argue that crimes against humanity and genocide do cover the same reality, genocide being an aggravated form of crimes against humanity, the consequences of this amalgam in practice were far more important as it generated a problematic equalization of intrinsically distinct crimes.

The trial of Klaus Barbie may be seen as symptomatic of the reluctance of French courts to apply the Genocide Convention. The chief of the Gestapo in Lyon owed his reputation of "the butcher of Lyon" to his fierce and relentless struggle against Resistance fighters, but he was also responsible for the deportation of Jews and his active participation in the Shoah.[27] Barbie was nonetheless exclusively charged with crimes against humanity and not with genocide.

As the Court of Appeal of Lyon acknowledged the clear differences between crimes committed against Resistance fighters and crimes committed against Jews, it established two distinct qualifications for these two distinct types of crimes, characterizing crimes against Resistance fighters as war crimes and crimes against Jews as crimes against humanity. Due to the applicability of statutory limitations to war crimes under French law, Barbie's crimes against Resistance fighters would go unpunished. Faced with the question of the qualification of the crimes perpetrated against Jewish Resistance fighters, which arose with respect to one of Barbie's victims, Professor Gompel, the court unconvincingly explained that "Barbie could have thought that he was a Resistance fighter and, therefore, the presumption of innocence must apply here. We must consider, by presumption, that he was a non-innocent Jew and that the tortures Gompel had to endure fell within the statutory limitations applicable to war crimes."[28]

Pushing its distinction to the extremes, the court, in order to exclude all Resistance fighters from the scope of application of crimes against humanity, defined Jews who were also members of the *Résistance* as "non-innocent" Jews – a very unfortunate choice of terminology, to say the very least. In the eyes of the court, it could not be ascertained that

Barbie knew that these fighters were Jews, and so their role as Resistance fighters had to prevail. The crimes perpetrated against these victims were thus war crimes subjected to statutory limitations under French law.

On 20 December 1985, the Cour de cassation quashed the decision of the Court of Appeal and found that:

> According to Article 6 (c) of the Charter of the International Military Tribunal at Nuremberg, appended to the London Charter of 8 August 1945, inhumane acts and persecutions which have been systematically committed in the name of a state practising a policy of ideological supremacy against individuals by reason of their belonging to a racial or religious community as well as against the opponents to this policy, whatever the form of their opposition – whether armed or not – constitute imprescriptible crimes against humanity, and this even if they also qualify as war crimes by virtue of Article 6 (b) of the Charter of the International Military Tribunal at Nuremberg.[29]

Legally speaking, this meant that crimes against humanity were no longer defined by the identity of the victims, but rather by the acts committed and the ideology of the perpetrators.[30] Crimes against Resistance fighters were thus qualified as imprescriptible crimes against humanity, just like the crimes perpetrated against Jews. The problem with the different decisions in the *Barbie* case lies in the starting point itself. If the Court of Appeal was initially correct in distinguishing between crimes perpetrated against Resistance fighters and crimes perpetrated against Jews, it nonetheless erred in the legal qualification of these crimes. Subsequently, in order not to let some crimes go unpunished, the Cour de cassation included crimes perpetrated against Resistance fighters within the ambit of crimes against humanity. Far from artificially extending this notion, the court merely applied article 6 (c) of the Charter of the Nuremberg Tribunal,[31] according to which crimes against humanity are: "murder, extermination, enslavement, deportation, and other inhumane acts committed against any civilian population, before or during the war, or persecutions on *political*, racial or religious grounds in execution of or in connection with any crime within the jurisdiction of the Tribunal, whether or not in violation of the domestic law of the country where perpetrated."[32]

In other words, right from the beginning of the legal proceedings, crimes against Resistance fighters should have been qualified as crimes against humanity, by direct application of article 6 (c) of the Nuremberg Charter. On the other hand, French courts should have distinguished between the crimes committed against Resistance fighters – crimes against humanity – and crimes perpetrated against Jews, which should have been recognized as genocide. By qualifying all Nazi crimes as crimes against humanity, the Cour de cassation proceeded to an equalization of the crimes and of the victims and thus failed to acknowledge the crucial differences between them. It is indeed a different crime to target political opponents, who had chosen to become opponents, than to target whole families, men, women, children, for the only reason that they were Jewish, and for whom no choice was ever possible.[33]

The *Barbie* case, which received intense media coverage, could have been a major opportunity for the Cour de cassation to ascertain the specificity of the crime of genocide, and most particularly of the Shoah. This missed opportunity was to be repeated in subsequent cases.

3 A Judicial Black Hole: The Inapplicability of the Qualifications of Genocide and Crimes against Humanity, 1945–94

With its decision of 20 December 1985, the Cour de cassation made a strict and restrictive reading of article 6 (c) of the Nuremberg Charter and interpreted the Nuremberg definition as requiring, for a crime against humanity to be qualified as such, that it be committed "in the name of a state practising a policy of ideological supremacy."[34] In other words, the *Barbie* definition turned what was merely a jurisdictional limitation at Nuremberg into a definitional requirement of crimes against humanity, unduly linking the latter to a particular state policy: Nazism. Practically speaking, there could be no crimes against humanity outside the very specific context of the Second World War.

This inherently flawed definition rapidly showed its limits in the *Touvier* case as it allowed the Paris Court of Appeal to dismiss the charges against the accused, a member of the Milice, Vichy France's own police. The court found that the expression "state practising a policy of ideological supremacy" could only apply to Hitler's Reich and reached the aberrant conclusion that no precise ideology reigned in Vichy, "a constellation of 'good intention and political animosities.'"[35] This infamous finding – in which, incidentally, judges did not hesitate to enter into the expert domain of historians – was fiercely criticized. As Conan and Rousso observed: "While this ruling is enough to make one shudder with its pseudo-historical reasoning, which would have caused any university student to fail on a history exam, it nevertheless came off as highly clever on a legal level, in that it slipped through the loopholes that had been left open by the contradictions, incertitudes, and variations of the jurisprudence on crimes against humanity."[36]

On 27 November 1992, the Cour de cassation partially overturned this ruling and gave a new – and artificial – reading of the law of Nuremberg, which only added further confusion and complexity to the case. The court found that, according to article 6 of the Nuremberg Charter, "the authors or accomplices of crimes against humanity are punished only if they acted for the sake of a European country of the Axis[;] the Court of Appeals could not without contradicting itself, declare that the murders being prosecuted did not constitute crimes against humanity while at the same time pointing out that they had been perpetrated at the instigation of an official of the Gestapo, an organization that has been declared to be criminal in that it belonged to a country which had practised a policy of ideological hegemony."[37]

If this finding clearly established that the crimes which Touvier stood accused of qualified as crimes against humanity, it still insisted on a necessary link between the authors and accomplices of crimes against humanity and a state practising a policy of ideological supremacy, or, put differently, one of the Axis Powers.[38] Vichy France's ideology was thus safe from scrutiny: to convict Touvier of crimes against humanity, it had to be proven that he had acted pursuant to the orders of the Nazi occupier.[39] When the case was referred back to the criminal court in Versailles, the court unequivocally excluded Vichy France from any possible judicial enquiry: the "responsibility [of Paul Touvier] is engaged by the simple fact of his personal dealings, even though he was not himself a national of a European Axis country. It is therefore not necessary to follow the private parties in their argumentation, which attempts to prove that the Milice and the government of the French State, which Touvier served, had themselves been accomplices of the Nazi state in its policies of ideological hegemony."[40]

On 21 October 1993, the Cour de cassation further stated that "it makes no difference whether or not the deeds prosecuted may have been committed following the assassination of a member of the Vichy government who also belonged to the Milice[:] as long as these deeds were carried out at the instigation of an official of a Nazi criminal organization and involved victims chosen exclusively because they belonged to the Jewish community, the deeds were therefore an integral part of a concerted plan of extermination and systematic persecution of this community that was put into action by the German National-Socialist government."[41]

In a rather clever twist, the Cour de cassation managed to shield Vichy France and its antisemitic policy from judicial scrutiny[42] while still finding Touvier himself guilty of complicity of crimes against humanity for having murdered pursuant to the orders of the Gestapo, an organization belonging to a state practising a policy of ideological hegemony. In defiance of the historical truth and of the findings of the investigation in this case, Paul Touvier, the main author of a French crime and a member of a French organization who had pledged allegiance to the Vichy government, was judicially found to be an agent of the Nazi policy of exterminating Jews, and was sentenced to life imprisonment for having been the accomplice of the Gestapo.[43]

The subsequent *Papon* case gave yet another opportunity to French courts to alter and modify their approach to crimes against humanity. In its decision of 23 January 1997, the Cour de cassation directly contradicted the *Touvier* precedent and held, without any further explanation or reasoning, that article 6 of the Nuremberg Charter did not require an accomplice in crimes against humanity to have adhered to the policy of ideological supremacy of the main authors of the crime.[44] As a result, the court condemned Maurice Papon, general secretary of Gironde in charge of the "Jewish section" of the prefecture, while still maintaining that he was unaware of the Nazi extermination plan. This judicial conclusion amounts to affirming that Vichy high civil servants were not aware of the Nazi genocidal enterprise; an assertion that shines by its historical incoherence, if not obvious bad faith, but which also enabled French courts to once again preserve Vichy France from any accusation of active participation in the Nazi destruction enterprise. Following the *Papon* verdict, Vichy France could only be deemed responsible for complicity in illegal arrests and arbitrary confinements.

Was this judicially created requirement that the crime be committed "in the name of a state practising a policy of ideological supremacy" an incorrect reading of the Nuremberg Charter, or a very "clever" interpretation? One can of course not answer this question with absolute certainty. What is certain, though, is that French courts, which on other aspects of the law of crimes against humanity have shown expert accuracy, here made a mistake which (conveniently?) impeded both the consideration of Vichy France as "a state practising a policy of ideological supremacy," and also the possible characterization as crimes against humanity of any act perpetrated after the end of the Second World War, particularly during the decolonization process. This major shortcoming of the French definition was actually upheld by the Cour de cassation in the *Boudarel* case, in which Georges Boudarel faced charges of crimes against humanity for acts perpetrated during the Vietnam War,[45] and in which the court unequivocally held that crimes against humanity "concern exclusively acts committed on behalf of the European Axis Powers ... the qualification of crimes against humanity can therefore not apply to the acts alleged by the civil parties, which occurred after the Second World War."[46]

Such "lamentable"[47] judgements should not happen again, however. With the entry into force of the New Penal Code, French law now encapsulates a more general definition of crimes against humanity, deprived of any nexus requirement to the European Axis Powers or to the Second World War. Article 212-1 reads as follows: "Deportation, enslavement or the massive and systematic practice of summary executions, abduction of persons followed by their disappearance, of torture or inhuman acts, inspired by political, philosophical, racial or religious motives, and organised in pursuit of a concerted plan against a section of a civil population are punished by criminal imprisonment for life."[48]

With the entry into force of the Rome Statute of the International Criminal Court, the French legislature further modified the definition of crimes against humanity so that it now encompasses a much wider range of criminal acts, still without any linkage to the Second World War:

> Also constituting a crime against humanity punished by criminal imprisonment for life are any of the following acts perpetrated in pursuit of a concerted plan against a section of a civil population within the context of a widespread or systematic attack:
>
> 1 Murder;
> 2 Extermination;
> 3 Enslavement;
> 4 Deportation or forcible transfer of population;
> 5 Imprisonment or other severe deprivation of physical liberty in violation of fundamental rules of international law;
> 6 Torture;
> 7 Rape, sexual slavery, enforced prostitution, forced pregnancy, enforced sterilization, or any other form of sexual violence of comparable gravity;
> 8 Persecution against any identifiable group or collectivity on political, racial, national, ethnic, cultural, religious, gender, or other grounds that are universally recognized as impermissible under international law;
> 9 Arrest, detention or abduction of persons, followed by their disappearance and the refusal to acknowledge that deprivation of freedom or to give information on the fate or whereabouts of those persons, with the intention of

removing them from the protection of the law for a prolonged period of time;

10 Acts of segregation committed in the context of an institutionalized regime of systematic oppression and domination by one racial group over any other racial group or groups and committed with the intention of maintaining that regime; [and]

11 Other inhumane acts of a similar character intentionally causing great suffering, or serious injury to the body or to mental or physical health.[49]

This contemporary definition notwithstanding, the qualification of crimes against humanity remains inapplicable under French law to acts perpetrated in the period between 1945 and 1994, the date of entry into force of the New Penal Code. Crimes committed during the decolonization process are thus immune from any prosecution. Symptomatically, French courts have consistently refused to exercise their jurisdiction over crimes perpetrated by French nationals during the Algerian war, hiding behind the principle of legality, an unduly restrictive understanding of crimes against humanity, *and* the dispositions of the 1968 amnesty law over all crimes committed during the war in Algeria.[50] This was the reasoning adopted in the case of General Paul Aussaresses, accused of atrocities in Algeria. The Paris Court of Appeal unequivocally rejected all possibility of adjudicating these crimes[51] and the Cour de cassation expressly upheld the French amnesty law for crimes perpetrated in Algeria.[52]

The *Aussaresses* case marked a shift in the attitude of French courts, which – until then – had avoided directly and explicitly applying the amnesty law, preferring to rely on other legal arguments to dismiss the cases. Lelieur-Fischer highlights the "Court of Cassation's discomfort in applying an amnesty law to acts which may be characterized as crimes against humanity."[53] She recalls that, in the 1998 *Lakdhar-Toumi* and *Yacoub* cases, "concerning acts of torture followed by disappearances during the Algerian war, the High court, in rejecting the appeals by the civil petitioners (partie civile) against the investigating judge's refusal to proceed, did not rely upon amnesty laws adopted after the acts were committed. It relied instead on arguments concerning the inadmissibility of the civil action and the authority of *res judicata*."[54] In the case of Aussaresses, however, the Cour de cassation explicitly applied the amnesty law and refused to categorize the acts as crimes against humanity. In 2000, it "upheld the investigating judge's refusal to investigate acts committed in the context of the Algerian war, on the basis that such acts did not amount to crimes against humanity," and argued that "the only prohibitions in ordinary criminal law which these acts could fall under, arise necessarily from the scope of application of the law no. 68–697 of 31 July 1968, providing for the amnesty of crimes committed in relation to the events in Algeria."[55]

The 2003 decision is remarkable in its insistence that the acts for which amnesty was granted were not crimes against humanity. This deplorable finding perpetuates a situation of crime minimization and crime denial in which the war is qualified as "events,"[56] and the systematic enforced disappearances, torture, and summary executions are denied the qualification of crimes against humanity. Not content with shielding France from any responsibility for international crimes committed in the course of decolonization, French courts also seem to have used questionable strategies to uphold French interests.

4 The "Inconceivable" Domestic Prosecution of Genocide

The entry into force of the New Penal Code also marked the express entry into the code of the crime of genocide with a disposition which expressly provides for life imprisonment as the sentence to be attached to this crime.[57] If one could have legitimately thought that French judges would thus have to apply the law of genocide, such hopes proved to be illusory. In the *Javor* case, both the court of appeals[58] and the Cour de cassation[59] asserted that they had no jurisdiction over the crime of genocide. If they could no longer found their incompetence on the lack of a domestic statute of implementation, this time they based it on the unavailability of universal jurisdiction. For the French courts, the failure of the Genocide Convention to expressly provide for universal jurisdiction purely and simply impeded its use with respect to the crimes perpetrated in Bosnia-Herzegovina, regardless of the fact that the crimes the accused were indicted for were crimes under French law.

The first cases regarding the Rwandan genocide were no more successful than the Bosnian complaints.[60] When M. Munyeshyaka, a Hutu priest suspected of having actively participated in the Rwandan genocide, was found to be in France, a joint complaint was filed for both acts of genocide and torture, leading to the suspect's arrest. While the court of first instance found that it had jurisdiction only over the acts of torture and cruel and inhuman treatment as defined by the Torture Convention,[61] the Court of Appeal of Nîmes subsequently reversed this decision on the grounds that jurisdiction could only be established on the basis of the "highest criminal qualification namely, genocide."[62] Insofar as the Genocide Convention fails to provide for universal jurisdiction, the finding of the Court of Appeal amounted to dismissing the case by excluding any possibility of French courts exercising their jurisdiction. Where the Court of Appeal found this principle of the "highest criminal qualification" remains a mystery. Its ruling was reversed by a subsequent decision of the Cour de cassation, which emphasized that it was sufficient for the acts to qualify as offences over which French courts could have jurisdiction for them to be able to exercise it,[63] thus referring the case back to the Paris Court of Appeal.[64] In 2015, the case was dismissed for lack of evidence. To date, very few trials related to the Rwandan genocide have occurred in France, the first condemnation having been that of Pascal Simbikangwa in December 2016.[65]

Several other cases were brought to an abrupt end with the Cour de cassation consistently refusing to accede to extradition requests by Rwanda. The constant reasoning of the court responded to a very rigorous reading of the principle of non-retroactivity, the court recalling in all its decisions that the Rwandan law establishing the penalty for genocide was only introduced on 19 June 1994,[66] while overlooking the fact that Rwanda had ratified the 1948 Convention on the Prevention and Punishment of Genocide back in 1975. If the position of the Cour de cassation can be open to criticism, what is also questionable is the fact that these refusals to extradite were seldom followed by investigation and prosecution under French law, thereby undermining the universal jurisdiction principle *aut dedere aut judicare*. Yet, recent developments might be indicating a certain relaxing of this judicial rigidity. In July 2020, the Paris tribunal opened a preliminary investigation for crimes against humanity in the case of Aloys Ntiwiragabo, Rwandan colonel and former head of Rwanda's military intelligence, against whom Rwanda has issued an arrest warrant and who allegedly resides on French territory.[67] Concurrently, the French authorities have shown their willingness to work in close cooperation with the Office of the Prosecutor of the International Residual Mechanism for Criminal Tribunals (IRMCT). In Paris on 16 May 2020, they indeed arrested – in collaboration with the Office of the Prosecutor of the IRMCT – Félicien Kabuga, who, as president of the *Comité Provisoire* of the *Fonds de défense nationale* and president of the *Comité d'Initiative of Radio Télévision Libre des Milles Collines* during the period of the genocide, is suspected of having financed the Rwandan genocide.[68] He has now been transferred to the IRMCT's custody.[69]

There is little doubt that the Rwandan genocide represents a dark page of French history, and one that French courts have proved reluctant to open and judicially read. Reasons for this reluctance are kept unknown and it is out of the scope of this chapter to speculate on them. Yet, it is worth recalling here that the French official position during the genocide was the theory of the "double genocide" defended by both former president Mitterrand and former prime minister de Villepin;[70] a position that might find its roots in a form of "colonizing reasoning." As trivial as it may seem, it does indeed appear that in Rwanda, a concern for the protection of francophonie, or in other words the French language, might have driven France's support for the genocidal regime. As Gérard Prunier explained, "the French political thinking was that the RPF came from Uganda (a former British colony, and perceived as falling under American influence, therefore in the 'Anglo-Saxon orbit') to destabilise a Francophone country; France therefore had to support one of its own":[71] "This is how Paris found itself backing an ailing dictatorship … This blind commitment was to have catastrophic consequences because, as the situation radicalised, the Rwandese leadership kept believing that *no matter what it did*, French support would always be forthcoming. And it had no valid reasons for believing otherwise."[72]

Beyond the defense of francophonie, the French government might also have chosen to defend legality by supporting the government in place in Rwanda; two arguments which, if anything, might well be the perpetuation of a radically colonial mindset: "[The French] trained Rwandan police and army officers, trained the Presidential Guard (which played a crucial role in the later genocide), advised the government on how to fight the RPF, checked IDs at checkpoints (since Tutsis were suspected of supporting the RPF) and supplied equipment to the Rwandan army. The French government justified this as defending the 'legal government, which represented 80% of the population', against 'external aggression', which threatened the privileged position of France in Rwanda. It never wavered in this support of the Rwandan government."[73]

While turning to postcolonialism to view the French position in and towards Rwanda might be useful, this explanation is less convincing when it comes to Bosnia-Herzegovina. Yet, France showed the exact same reluctance to unequivocally use the term "genocide" without attaching to it a double genocide theory, and the exact same tendency to side with the legal government in place.[74] At the same time, France, as a permanent member of the Security Council, did support the creation of the two ad hoc international criminal tribunals for the former Yugoslavia and for Rwanda respectively – a support which can only be condoned but which admittedly adds another layer of opacity to the French attitude. Interestingly, already during the drafting of the

Genocide Convention, "France was … firmly in favour of the setting up of an international criminal court,"[75] and Smith specified that "France's insistence on including a reference to an international criminal tribunal stemmed from its belief that genocide was a crime perpetrated by states or government officials, and therefore prosecution by national courts would be inconceivable."[76] This belief, in the light of French judicial history with respect to genocide and crimes against humanity, proved to be solidly grounded.

5 Concluding Remarks

The reluctance of French courts to adjudicate international crimes affects both the implementation of the law of genocide and that of crimes against humanity. In a sense this is not that surprising, since French law has traditionally understood genocide as a crime against humanity. If France was ultimately among the states supporting the adoption of the Genocide Convention, it is worth recalling that this had not always been the case. As Smith has explained, France "*had initially described the term 'genocide' as a 'useless and even dangerous neologism.'* Instead, it persistently argued that the issue of genocide should be considered as one aspect of crimes against humanity, and therefore initially rejected the idea that genocide was a crime of war and of peacetime. For example, it wanted the preamble to describe genocide as a crime against humanity. But other states successfully argued that the two concepts were distinct and separate."[77]

In preparation for the debate on the Secretariat's draft of a convention on the crime of genocide, France had circulated a memorandum "on the subject of genocide and crimes against humanity" which challenged the use of the term 'genocide' to the benefit of the notion of 'crimes against humanity.'"[78] During the second session of the General Assembly, the heart of the issue was whether to consider genocide as one variety of crime against humanity, or to treat it as a distinct crime. During the debates in the ad hoc committee, France was the most insistent about the linkage between genocide and crimes against humanity, while others firmly believed that the concepts had to be separate. In particular, France urged that the preamble of the convention describe genocide as "a crime against humanity,"[79] but this was rejected by the ad hoc committee, which chose instead to characterize it as "a crime against mankind."[80] The committee's preference for the term "mankind" can probably be explained by the fact that it was devoid of any legal or judicial connotation. This seems to be confirmed by the final report of the committee, whose members "categorically opposed the expression 'crimes against humanity' because, in their opinion, it had acquired a well-defined legal meaning in the Charter of the Nuremberg Tribunal."[81]

As further noted by William Schabas,

> France, on the other hand, regarded the draft [of the Genocide Convention] as too preoccupied with domestic prosecution for genocide: 'The utility of such provisions would appear to be relative since the crime can only take place with the complicity of the government.'[82] According to France, the convention should affirm its relationship with the principles of the Nuremberg Tribunal, and explained that genocide was merely one aspect of crimes against humanity. It believed that genocide ought to relate directly to State action and punishment, on an international basis, and should be restricted to rulers who would otherwise enjoy impunity within their own States.[83]

The French New Penal Code now expressly includes a section entitled "crimes against humanity and against persons" ("des crimes contre l'humanité et contre l'espèce humaine"),[84] whose first article defines genocide;[85] "other crimes against humanity" ("des autres crimes contre l'humanité") are defined in the following disposition. The inclusion of genocide within crimes against humanity in the text of the law might have incited and encouraged French courts to favour the legal qualification of crimes against humanity over that of genocide. In a way, it might have fostered their reluctance to use the qualification of genocide even in cases of genocide. Yet, as shown in the above discussion, the judicial reluctance is not confined solely to the crime of genocide and the different judgements related to international crimes issued by French courts show an equal disinclination towards crimes against humanity.

NOTES

1 Convention on the Prevention and Punishment of the Crime of Genocide, approved and proposed for signature and ratification or accession by General Assembly resolution 260 A (III) of 9 December 1948, entry into force 12 January 1951, in accordance with article XIII. Hereafter referred to as the Genocide Convention.

2 This stands in stark contrast with the fact recalled by Stiller that, at Nuremberg, "the French prosecution also used the concept of 'genocide.'" See

Alexa Stiller, "The Mass Murder of the European Jews and the Concept of 'Genocide' in the Nuremberg Trials: Reassessing Raphaël Lemkin's Impact," *Genocide Studies and Prevention: An International Journal* 13 (2019): 157. Intriguingly, she also points out that the term "genocide" "already existed in other languages: in French *nationicides*" (146).

3 Cited in Karen Smith, *Genocide and the Europeans* (Cambridge: Cambridge University Press 2010), 39–40. Footnote omitted.

4 It can be noted here that, upon ratification, France made no declaration, no reservation, and no objection.

5 Smith, *Genocide and the Europeans*, 43 (emphasis added).

6 Ibid., 46.

7 Ibid., 48

8 Emphasis added.

9 "Plan concerté." On this particular point, the French law deviated from the position taken by its prosecutors at Nuremberg, whose view, as Stiller recounts, "both on the functioning of the Nazi regime and on the division of labor in implementing the extermination policy, can be seen as the most complex and elaborate interpretation on the mass violence of the Nazi regime put forward during the IMT trial. *This interpretation was not intentionalist, for it neither needed a 'plan' conceived* at an early stage, nor a fanatical anti-Semitism, an order by Hitler (*Führerbefehl*) to murder the Jews, or the construction of a 'main perpetrator' such as Eichmann." Stiller, "The Mass Murder of the European Jews and the Concept of 'Genocide' in the Nuremberg Trials," 158 (emphasis added).

10 As noted by Markusen, definitions by scholars encompass "a wider array of targeted groups, destructive actions and actual cases." Eric Markusen, "Genocide, Total War, and Nuclear Omnicide," in *Genocide: A Critical Bibliographic Review, Volume Two*, edited by Israel W. Charny (London: Mansell 1991), 232. For scholarly definitions, see, e.g., Henry R. Huttenbach, "Locating the Holocaust on the Genocide Spectrum: Towards a Methodology of Definition and Categorization," *Holocaust and Genocide Studies* 3 (1988): 289–303.

11 Nehemiah Robinson, *The Genocide Convention: A Commentary* (New York: Institute of Jewish Affairs – World Jewish Congress 1960), 34–5.

12 "Les traités diplomatiques régulièrement ratifiés et publiés ont force de loi dans le cas même où ils seraient contraires à des lois françaises, sans qu'il soit besoin pour en assurer l'application d'autres dispositions législatives que celles qui auraient été nécessaires pour assurer leur ratification." Constitution of France, 27 October 1946.

13 "Les traités ou accords régulièrement ratifiés ou approuvés ont, dès leur publication, une autorité supérieure à celle des lois, sous réserve, pour chaque

accord ou traité, de son application par l'autre partie." Constitution of France, 4 October 1958.

14 Article 24(k) of the Nuremberg Charter merely states that "the Tribunal shall deliver judgment and pronounce sentence." Charter of the International Military Tribunal, Annex to Agreement for the Prosecution and Punishment of Major War Criminals of the European Axis, London, 8 August 1945, 82 UNTS 279. Reprinted in *AJIL* 39 (supp. 1945): 257. The rules of procedure of the tribunal are equally silent on the issue of penalties. See *Nuremberg Trial Proceedings Vol. I, Rules of Procedure*: https://avalon.law.yale.edu/imt/imtrules.asp, accessed 13 October 2020.

15 New York, 26 November 1968, entry into force 11 November 1970. Article I (b).

16 15 June 1979. See de Bernard Bigault du Granrut, "Le Crime Contre l'Humanité," in *Le Crime Contre l'Humanité, mesure de la responsabilité? Actes du cycle des conférences « Droit, Liberté et Foi », Juin 1997*, Ecole Cathédrale – Institut de Formation Continue du Barreau de Paris (Paris: CERP 1998), 97. Translation by the author.

17 See Law n° 64-1326 of 26 December 1964 and article 213–5 of the New Penal Code (France).

18 See Journal officiel, Document de l'Assemblée Nationale, annexes aux procès-verbaux des séances, 2e session ordinaire de 1963–64, n°46, 11 mai 1965, Annexe n°1026, 806–7. Cited in Pierre Mertens, *L'imprescriptibilité des crimes de guerre et contre l'humanité* (Bruxelles: Editions de l'Université de Bruxelles 1974), 51.

19 Journal officiel du 18 décembre 1964, Débats parlementaires, Sénat, première session ordinaire de 1954–65, compte rendu intégral de la séance du 17 décembre 1964, 2.429. Cited in Mertens, *L'imprescriptibilité*, 53–4.

20 See Manfred Nowak, *U.N. Covenant on Civil and Political Rights: CCPR Commentary* (Kehl am rhein: N.P. Engel Publishers, 1993), 276.

21 See Antonio Cassese, "Balancing the Prosecution of Crimes against Humanity and Non-Retroactivity of Criminal Law: The *Kolk and Kislyiy v. Estonia* Case before the ECHR," *Journal of International Criminal Justice* 4 (2006): 414–15.

22 Manfred Nowak, *U.N. Covenant on Civil and Political Rights: CCPR Commentary* (Kehl am rhein: N.P. Engel Publishers, 1993), 276. Referring to E/CN.4/SR.112, 5 ff.; A/2929, 45 (§94) (emphasis added).

23 France signed the ECHR on 4 November 1950 and subsequently ratified it on 3 May 1974.

24 *Barbie* case, Cass. crim., 6 October 1983.

25 If numerous trials were held in the aftermath of the Second World War, they were based on article 75 of the French Penal Code, which dealt with the crimes of treason and of intelligence with the enemy.

26 Aloïs Brunner was tried *in absentia* by the Cour d'assises of Paris on 2 March 2001. He was charged with, and found guilty of, crimes against humanity for the following acts committed between 21 July 1944 and 4 August 1944: illegal arrests and confinements of 352 children, 345 of whom were deported; complicity of murders and/or attempted murders against 284 children, all of whom were murdered in Auschwitz-Birkenau and Bergen-Belsen. The youngest, Alain Blumberg, was fifteen days old, and the oldest was eighteen years old. Brunner was sentenced to life imprisonment, although nobody knows whether he is still alive.

27 Klaus Barbie had already been tried by French courts *in absentia*. He was tried in 1952 and again in 1954 and sentenced to death for his participation in more than 4,000 killings and in the deportation of more than 7,000 Jews to concentration camps. Barbie managed to evade justice for nearly forty years, and was supposedly supported by American intelligence officers who sought his assistance in anti-Soviet intelligence. In 1951, he emigrated to Bolivia and, under the name Klaus Altmann, acquired Bolivian citizenship in 1957. After being discovered by Serge and Beate Klarsfeld in 1971, Barbie was extradited to France. His trial lasted from 11 May 1987 to 4 July 1987. He was sentenced to life imprisonment and died in prison on 25 September 1991.

28 Translation by the author. The original version reads as follows: "Barbie a pu penser qu'il était résistant, par conséquent la présomption d'innocence qui joue en sa faveur doit jouer là, et l'on doit considérer, par présomption, que c'était un *juif non-innocent* et que les tortures qu'on a fait subir à ce malheureux Gompel étaient couvertes par la prescription des crimes de guerre." See Antoine Lyon-Caen, A., "De Nuremberg au Procès Barbie," in *Le Procès de Nuremberg – Conséquences et actualisation, Actes du Colloque international, Université Libre de Bruxelles, Bruxelles, le 27 mars 1987*, Centre de droit international de l'Institut de Sociologie de l'Université Libre de Bruxelles (Centre Henri Rolin), Fondation Auschwitz-Stichting (Centre d'Etudes et de Documentation) (Bruxelles: Editions Bruylant, Editions de l'Université de Bruxelles 1988), 55.

29 Translation by the author. The original version reads as follows: "Attendu que constituent des crimes imprescriptibles contre l'humanité, au sens de l'article 6 (c) du Statut du Tribunal militaire international de Nuremberg annexé à l'accord de Londres du 8 août 1945, alors même qu'ils seraient également qualifiables de crimes de guerre, selon l'article 6 (b) de ce texte, les actes inhumains et persécutions qui, au nom d'un Etat pratiquant une politique d'hégémonie idéologique, ont été commis de façon systématique, non seulement contre des personnes en raison de leur appartenance à une collectivité raciale ou religieuse, mais aussi contre les adversaires de cette politique quelle que soit la forme de leur opposition – autrement dit forme armée ou forme non-armée." See Lyon-Caen, "De Nuremberg au Procès Barbie," 56.

30 See Jean-Pierre Delmas Saint-Hilaire, "La définition juridique de la complicité de crime contre l'humanité au lendemain de l'arrêt de la Chambre criminelle du 23 janvier 1997 (affaire *Maurice Papon*)," *Recueil Dalloz* (1997): 249.

31 Charter of the International Military Tribunal. The Nuremberg Tribunal was established by a treaty, originally signed by the four major Allies, and thus by France.

32 Emphasis added.

33 See the poignant words of André Frossard in *Le crime contre l'humanité* (Paris: Editions Robert Laffont 1987), 68–9.

34 *Barbie* case: *Fédération Nationale des Déportés et Internés Résistants et Patriotes et Autres* v. *Barbie*, cass. crim., 20 December 1985, in (1986) RGDIP 90, 1024.

35 Court of Appeal, Paris, 13 April 1992. Translation by the author. The original reads as follows: "à Vichy ne régnait pas une idéologie précise," Vichy was "une constellation de 'bonnes intentions' et d'animosités politiques." See Arno Klarsfeld, *Touvier, Un crime français* (Paris: Librairie Arthème Fayard 1994), 31.

36 Eric Conan and Henri Rousso, *Vichy – An Ever–Present Past* (Hanover: University Press of New England 1998), 91.

37 Cass. crim., 27 November 1992. Translated in Conan and Rousso, *Vichy – An Ever–Present Past,* 91.

38 See Arno Klarsfeld, *La Cour, Les Nains et Le Bouffon* (Paris : Editions Robert Laffont 1998), 32: "L'arrêt modifiait encore une fois le crime contre l'humanité tel que défini à Nüremberg. Il exigeait que la personne poursuivie eût agi pour le compte d'une puissance européenne de l'Axe, c'est-à-dire l'Allemagne ou l'Italie. Aboutissement cocasse d'un point de vue historique, quand on sait que les Italiens arrêtaient parfois les fonctionnaires de Vichy qui tentaient de procéder à des rafles de Juifs! Mais résultat tout aussi cocasse au niveau du droit, quand l'on se donnait la peine d'étudier les textes sur lesquels se basait la décision de la Chambre d'Accusation."

39 See ibid., 33.

40 Arrêt de la chambre d'accusation de Versailles, 2 June 1993. Translated in Conan and Rousso, *Vichy – An Ever-Present Past*, 93. The original version reads: "La responsabilité [Paul Touvier] est engagée du seul fait de ses agissements personnels, bien qu'il n'ait pas été lui–même ressortissant d'un pays européen de l'Axe. Il n'est donc pas nécessaire de suivre les parties civiles dans leur argumentation tendant à établir que la Milice et le gouvernement de l'État français, dont Touvier était le serviteur, auraient été eux–mêmes complices de l'État nazi dans sa politique d'hégémonie idéologique."

41 Cass. crim., 21 October 1993. Translated in Conan and Rousso, *Vichy – An Ever-Present Past*, 93. The original version reads as follows: "Attendu … qu'il

n'importe que les faits poursuivis aient pu être commis à l'occasion de l'assassinat d'un membre du gouvernement de Vichy appartenant à la Milice, dès lors qu'exécutés à l'instigation d'un responsable d'une organisation criminelle nazie et concernant des victimes exclusivement choisies en raison de leur appartenance à la communauté juive, ils s'intégraient au plan concerté d'extermination et de persécution systématiques de cette communauté, mis en œuvre par le gouvernement national-socialiste allemand."

42 See Conan and Rousso, *Vichy – An Ever-Present Past*, 93–5.

43 Cour d'assises, Yvelines, 20 April 1994.

44 See Jean-Pierre Delmas Saint-Hilaire, "La définition juridique de la complicité de crime contre l'humanité," 251–2.

45 Georges Boudarel had allegedly deserted the French army to serve the Viet-Minh and act, from 1952 to 1954, as assistant supervisor in a prisoner of war camp where he was accused of having committed atrocities against his fellow countrymen. Even though France had issued a general amnesty concerning crimes committed in connection with the Vietnamese war of independence in 1966, the investigating judge had nonetheless brought charges against Boudarel, on the grounds that crimes against humanity, not being subject to statutory limitations, were not covered by amnesties. Although the court of first instance upheld the qualification of crimes against humanity, it found that they did benefit from the general amnesty. The qualification of crimes against humanity was to be quashed by the Cour de cassation.

46 *Affaire Georges Boudarel*, Cass. crim. (1 April 1993) *Bull. Crim.* 143, and also reprinted in Denis Alland, "Jurisprudence Française en Matière de Droit International public," RGDIP 98 (1994): 474. Translation by the author. The original version reads as follows: "ne concernent que les faits commis pour le compte des pays européens de l'Axe … ainsi, les faits dénoncés par les parties civiles, postérieurs à la seconde guerre mondiale, n'étaient pas susceptibles de recevoir la qualification de crimes contre l'humanité aux sens des textes précités."

47 The expression is of Axel Marschik. See "The Politics of Prosecution: European National Approaches to War Crimes," in Timothy L.M. McCormack and Gerry J. Simpson, *The Law of War Crimes: National and International Approaches* (The Hague: Kluwer Law International 1997), 86.

48 Article 212–1 of the New Penal Code (France). Translation available at legislationline.org/documents/section/criminal-codes (accessed 13 October 2020).

49 Article 212–1 of the New Penal Code (France) modifié par la loi n° 2010–930 du 9 août 2010 portant adaptation du droit pénal à l'institution de la Cour pénale internationale. Translation by the author.

50 Loi n°68-697 du 31 juillet 1968 portant amnistie, *Journal Officiel* (2 August 1968): 7521.

51 Cour d'appel, Paris, 14 December 2001.

52 Cass. crim., 17 June 2003, *Bulletin des arrêts de la Chambre criminelle de la Cour de cassation – Chambre criminelle (Bull.Crim.)* (2003): 465–9, and RGDIP (2003): 754. See Ward N. Ferdinandusse, *Direct Application of International Criminal Law in National Courts* (The Hague: T.M.C. Asser Press 2006), 66.

53 Lelieur-Fischer, J. (2004) "Prosecuting the Crimes against Humanity Committed during the Algerian War: An Impossible Endeavour? The 2003 Decision of the French Court of Cassation in *Aussaresses,*" *Journal of International Criminal Justice* 2 (2004): 241.

54 Cass. crim. 29 November 1988, unpublished s, see *Recueil Dalloz* (1991), 231. Cited in Juliette Lelieur–Fischer, "Prosecuting the Crimes against Humanity," 241.

55 Cass. crim. 30 May 2000, *Bull. Crim.* (2000): 603. Quote, including the translation, in: Juliette Lelieur–Fischer, "Prosecuting the Crimes against Humanity," 242. Article 1 of the amnesty law reads: "Sont amnistiées de plein droit toutes infractions commises en relation avec *les évènements* d'Algérie" ("all offences perpetrated in relation to the Algerian *events* are amnestied by law"; translation by the author, emphasis added).

56 Yves Beigbeder also uses the qualification "dirty war." See *Judging War Crimes and Torture: French Justice and International Criminal Tribunals and Commissions (1940–2005)* (Leiden: Martinus Niijhoff Publishers 2006), 26–7, 93–129, 354–7.

57 Article 211–1 of the New Penal Code (France).

58 CA Paris, 24 October 1994. See Brigitte Stern, "*In re* Javor ... *In re* Munyeshyaka," AJIL 93 (1999): 527.

59 *Javor*, Cass. crim., 26 March 1996, *Bull. Crim.* (1996): 379.

60 See *Kalinda et al.*, Tribunal de grande instance de Paris, complaint filed on 4 July 1994; *Dupaquier et al.*, Tribunal de grande instance de Paris, complaint filed on 19 July 1994; Ordonnance, Tribunal de grande instance de Paris (23 February 1995). See Brigitte Stern, "Universal Jurisdiction over Crimes against humanity under French Law," AJIL 93 (1999): 527n15.

61 *Dupaquier, Kalinda et al.*, Ordonnance, Tribunal de grande instance de Privas (9 January 1996). See Stern, "Universal jurisdiction over crimes against humanity under French law," 528.

62 Cour d'appel de Nîmes (20 March 1996). See Stern, "Universal Jurisdiction over Crimes against Humanity under French Law," 528. Translation by the author. The original version reads as follows: "la compétence du juge doit s'apprécier uniquement au regard de la plus haute acception pénale qui est le génocide."

63 Cass. crim. (6 January 1998). Reprinted in Denis Alland and François Ferrand, "Jurisprudence Française en matière de Droit International Public," RGDIP 102 (1998): 825–32.

64 See ibid., 829–30. Following an arrest warrant issued by the ICTR on 21 June 2007, the *Munyeshyaka* case underwent a series of judicial events. See Stéphanie Maupas, "Le TPIR demande à la France d'arrêter et de juger deux Rwandais, un prêtre et un ex–préfet, accusés de génocide," *Le Monde*, 4 July 2007; Stéphanie Maupas, "Deux Rwandais accusés de génocide ont été arrêtés en France," *Le Monde,* 21 July 2007; "La justice française libère deux Rwandais accusés de génocide," *Le Monde,* 1 August 2007; "Deux Rwandais inculpés pour génocide ont été à nouveau interpellés en France', *Le Monde*, 8 September 2007; "La cour d'appel reporte sa décision sur les deux Rwandais réclamés par le TPIR," *Le Monde*, 26 September 2007; "Le TPIR se dessaisit au profit de la France pour juger deux Rwandais," *Le Monde,* 21 November 2007. In November 2007, the ICTR ultimately decided to defer the case to French courts. See *Munyeshyaka*, Décision relative à la requête du procureur aux fins de renvoi de l'acte d'accusation contre Wenceslas Munyeshyaka aux autorités françaises, Chambre de première instance, 20 November 2007.

65 Simbikangwa case, Cour d'assises, Bobigny, 3 December 2016; *Ngenzi and Barahira* case, Cour d'assises, Paris, 6 July 2018.

66 See, e.g., the case of Innocent Musabyimana, against whom Rwanda had issued an extradition request for genocide and crimes against humanity. Following his arrest by the French authorities, the Dijon Court of Appeal granted his extradition in January 2013. On 25 April 2013, the Cour de cassation quashed this and referred the case to the Paris Court of Appeal which, on 29 January 2014, acceded to the extradition request. On 26 February 2014, the Cour de cassation once again refused the extradition. See https://trialinternational.org/latest-post/innocent-musabyimana/#section-2 (accessed 13 October 2020). In the case of Claude Muhayimana, the Cour de cassation had similarly refused to accede to Rwanda's extradition request. Following a complaint lodged by the Collectif des Parties Civiles pour le Rwanda, Muhayimana was indicted for complicity in genocide and crimes against humanity and the investigative judge referred the case to the Cour d'assises; the referral was confirmed on appeal by the Paris Court of Appeal on 4 April 2019. The accused has, however, announced that he will appeal to the Cour de cassation. See https://trialinternational.org/latest-post/claude-muhayimana/#section-2 (accessed 13 October 2020).

67 See "Le Rwanda a émis un mandat d'arrêt international contre Aloys Ntiwiragabo, accusé de génocide," *Le Monde,* 26 August 2020, https://www.lemonde.fr/afrique/article/2020/08/26/le-rwanda-a-emis-un-mandat-d-arret-international-contre-aloys-ntiwiragabo-accuse-de-genocide_6049987_3212.html (accessed 13 October 2020). Back in 1998, Ntiwiragabo was mentioned in some of the indictments before the International Criminal Tribunal for

Rwanda. Ibid. See also "Un ex-haut responsable rwandais visé par une enquête en France pour 'crimes contre l'humanité,'" *Le Monde*, 25 July 2020, https://www.lemonde.fr/afrique/article/2020/07/25/un-ex-haut-responsable-rwandais-vise-par-une-enquete-en-france-pour-crimes-contre-l-humanite_6047288_3212.html (accessed 13 October 2020).

68 See IRMCT, Office of the Prosecutor, "Mechanism Fugitive Félicien Kabuga arrested today," 16 May 2020, https://www.irmct.org/en/news/20-05-22-mechanism-fugitive-f%C3%A9licien-kabuga-arrested-today (accessed 13 October 2020).

69 See https://www.irmct.org/en/cases/mict-13-38 (accessed 4 June 2021).

70 See Smith, *Genocide and the Europeans*, 167.

71 Ibid., 146.

72 Gérard Prunier, *The Rwanda Crisis: History of a Genocide* (London: C. Hurst and Co., 1998), 107 (emphasis in original). Cited in Smith, *Genocide and the Europeans*, 146.

73 Smith, *Genocide and the Europeans*, 145. Citing Daniela Kroslak, *The Role of France in the Rwandan Genocide* (London: C. Hurst and Co. 2007), 105, 130, 144.

74 On the apathy of the French government and the political non-use of the word "genocide," see Smith, *Genocide and the Europeans*, 132.

75 Ibid., 39.

76 Ibid., 39–40 (footnote omitted).

77 Ibid., 40 (footnote omitted; emphasis added).

78 UN Doc A/AC.20/29. Cited in William A. Schabas, *Genocide in International Law – The Crime of Crimes*, 2nd ed. (Cambridge: Cambridge University Press 2009), 63.

79 UN Doc E/AC 25/SR 20, 7. Cited in William A. Schabas, *Genocide in International Law – The Crime of Crimes*, 1st ed. (Cambridge: Cambridge University Press 2000), 64.

80 UN Doc E/794/, 2. Cited in Schabas, *Genocide in International Law*, 1st ed., 64.

81 UN Doc E/794/, 3. Cited in Schabas, *Genocide in International Law*, 1st ed., 64.

82 UN Doc A/401 (reference for this quote in the original).

83 Schabas, *Genocide in International Law*, 2nd ed., 65.

84 Articles 211–1 to 215–4 of the New Penal Code (France). Translation available at legislationline.org/documents/section/criminal-codes (accessed 13 October 2020).

85 Article 211–1 of the New Penal Code (France).

8

Is It Time to Forget Genocide? Conceptual Problems and New Directions

Michelle Tusan

How scholars think about genocide is changing. Some see it as a concept that has lost its analytical power due to its too-widespread application, while others want to use it to expand the study of the number of cases that can be counted as genocide.[1] These approaches have led to a deeper engagement with the problems addressed and methods used to study acts of mass atrocity that result in the extermination of a people. A clearer understanding of genocide and its consequences has come into focus, drawing on interdisciplinary methods and theory from across the social sciences and humanities including both new and familiar voices.[2] But as genocide studies expands in breadth and finds new application across disciplines, it faces inevitable questions about the usefulness of the concept as a tool to explain and understand the inhumanity of humankind.[3] A too-sharp focus on the anatomy of genocide – what qualifies and what does not, who is to blame for committing the act or failing to prosecute it – risks painting the scholarship into a corner by positing the study of genocide as a moral and political act. It certainly is both of those things, but as this chapter argues, it is also something else. Genocide as act and consequence is the story of a particular and shared historical experience.

Raphaël Lemkin gave us a valuable working definition of genocide, which, as those engaged in this work know, remains problematic. Today, scholars continue to reconcile themselves to Lemkin's concept, whether it is to reject or accept his formulation.[4] His definition came out of a historical context – the lead-up to World War II – and had its own politics.[5] But to reject or embrace it on the grounds of this particularity does little good. Rather, defining an act as genocide must be followed by a reconciliation of the event and its definition as the experience of a people. The study of genocide, then, becomes a study of the materiality, ideas, and events of genocide that moves beyond the act itself. In practical terms, it means reading the archive differently. Material artifacts of genocide, what people left behind, what they took with them, where they ended up, are read against official orders to remove subject populations. Popular media accounts are read alongside autobiography, and even, controversially, fictional accounts of survivors and their children attempting to reconcile the event in the collective memory.[6] This methodology that reads such texts against the grain and in intimate connection with one another and in changing interpretive contexts has the potential to make the response to genocide both more particular in its very materiality and universal in its humanity.

During the first half of the twentieth century it became axiomatic that genocide happened under the cover of war. The two world wars both witnessed genocides and offered ways of seeing and knowing the act in its modern form. Though the study of genocide has moved beyond these confines to include crimes committed by the state in peacetime and times of civil unrest, the context of the two great wars of the first half of the twentieth century remains important for understanding the act as experience. The wave of scholarship on World War I which uses social and cultural history methods to understand how people experienced war, and the ways in which this experience transformed postwar society, provides a useful model to begin writing a history of the experience of genocide.[7] The purpose of this methodology is to show the consequences on individuals and society of Total War, understood as a large-scale conflict that effectively blurs the lines between home front and battleground. This chapter inserts genocide into the temporal and cultural narrative of the Great War by mapping the stories of survivors of the 1915 Armenian genocide in a broad human and historical context.

World War I and Genocide

The commemoration of the hundred-year anniversary of World War I has revealed how much more work needs to be done to understand its human costs. Though the war was over for those living in Western Europe in 1918, it continued for another five years in the east until the signing of the Treaty of Lausanne in 1923. This makes the end of the conflict seem less than certain.[8] Can we consider the Armenian genocide in the same way? When it ended is more than a chronological question, just as it is for World War I. Genocide as lived experience continues well into the 1920s and 1930s, as most clearly manifested in the refugee crisis and resettlement schemes taken on by the Great Powers and humanitarian organizations. This crisis falls outside of the traditional definitional boundaries of the Armenian genocide. Tracing where survivors ended up as part of a growing diaspora has been studied separately from the events of the genocide itself.[9] Survival, however, remains part of the shared experience of genocide, not only for the Armenian, Assyrian, and Greek victims, but for those who attempt to mitigate its effects – humanitarian aid workers, international institutions, and individual actors – and for minority and majority populations who had to deal with a massive influx of refugees. These included Arabs who faced the disruptive effects of mass migration to the Middle East and Russians in the Caucasus.

The Armenian massacres offer an important case study of genocide as lived experience. Under the cover of world war, the Ottoman Empire committed the first widely reported and widescale incident of what would later be recognized as genocide.[10] The genocide affected other Ottoman Christian minorities, primarily Assyrian and Greek populations, forced to flee the killing fields of Anatolia during World War I.[11] Victims have had their stories used as evidence to prove that the killings met the condition of genocide. Similarly, scholars have used the diplomatic and humanitarian response largely to confirm that the wartime massacres constituted "crimes against humanity" that violated emerging human rights standards. But what if these testimonies and responses were read from the inside out – read for what they say, rather than what they prove? Undoing the logic of genocide that relies on the dehumanization of the other requires a reanimation of the contexts, stories, and people who bore witness and the assessment of the range of contexts in which these representations are read.

My attempt to map these experiences began with the stories left by those who were sent, by the decree of the Ottoman government, on the deportation routes starting in the spring of 1915. Collecting, reading, and cataloguing these narratives also revealed clear patterns of experiences of displacement and survival; where people were sent and where they eventually ended up. More than a repetitive catalogue of atrocity and human loss, they proved important sources of information in making the case for genocide. In his masterful history of the Armenian genocide Raymond Kevorkian effectively used these testimonies alongside official documents and correspondence to show the Ottoman government's intent to eliminate and exterminate the Armenian population. His pinpointing of concentration camp locations in southern Anatolia and northern Syria relied on a combination of sources that included survivor accounts.[12] This work has opened the door to consider other ways to read the experience of deportation. Broadening the category of those caught up in the genocide to aid workers, perpetrators, and the military, as well as the timeline of the experience of genocide, allows for a much more diverse and wide-ranging understanding of the event. Over the map of the World War I Ottoman concentration camps plotted by Kevorkian where so many perished can now be laid the map of refugee camps, clinics, hospitals, food distribution centres, and orphanages that would later assist deportees.[13]

Understanding the experience of displacement in and around the Ottoman Empire after the war, both internal and external, was part of a longer story of genocide. Not just in terms of cause and effect, but in terms of the materiality of loss, a sense of longing for home and renewal. Mapping the hundreds of refugee camps and auxiliary aid institutions associated with relief work is key to such an investigation in the case of the Armenian genocide. During World War I, the British, with the cooperation of the international community, set up refugee camps to deal with the crisis of mass displacement. Never had temporary camps been used in this way. Refugee camps for displaced persons were created by international and state actors to move people across and within borders according to normative ideals of national identity. In this way, genocide was generative of a novel set of practices that shaped modern humanitarianism and internationalism. The inhabitants of these camps, once targeted for elimination, were now part of new project of rescue and resettlement in and around the post-Ottoman Middle East.

Reading Survivor Testimony

Once dismissed as the hazy and unreliable reflections of traumatized victims, researchers now see eyewitness accounts as a window into a world of human experience inaccessible through other forms of documentation and expression.[14] Whether written down by the victim or delivered as oral testimony, the political motivations and context in which the stories are told matter, and no longer constitute a contested form of historical evidence and witness. From the very beginning, genocide survivor testimony was used to prove that the event happened and establish a pattern to determine guilt. James Bryce's British parliamentary Blue Book, *The Treatment of the Armenians in the Ottoman Empire* (1916), collected hundreds of testimonies in nearly a thousand pages with the purpose of proving to the British government and international community that the massacre of Armenians starting in 1915 was a premeditated attempt to destroy the entire community.[15] Victim testimonies in the Blue Book – so called because of the report's blue cover – were used to prove the extent and scope of the massacres, both during the war and after. A similar thing took place after World War II. The collection of victim testimony was valued initially because it showed a pattern and offered evidence of the attempt to annihilate the Jewish people.[16]

New methodologies and scholarly priorities have made it possible to consider survivor testimony in much broader terms that can ultimately narrate the experience of genocide.[17] Archives dedicated to collecting victim testimony continue to provide valuable access to these experiences to reveal patterns within and across genocidal events. The Shoah Foundation at the University of Southern California, for example, collects victim testimony from not only the Holocaust but also the Armenian genocide, Rwanda, and other genocides to further its project of disseminating knowledge about crimes against humanity and genocide prevention. This work has been crucial in helping to counter challenges levelled by denialists as well as those who question labelling an event as genocide. Eyewitness testimonies thus form a pattern of knowing that, when considered in total, offers a particular kind of tangible, quantifiable narrative, gives proof of a shared experience, and counters claims by those who deny continuities between genocidal events.

Beyond providing the human face to challenge denialist accounts of genocide, survivor testimony also and importantly reconstructs emotional and psychological worlds left out of other forms of data and evidence.[18] Primo Levi's eyewitness narrative *Survival at Auschwitz*, for example, remains a powerful testament of human brutality. We now recognize that his individual experience of genocide shows something more. What happened after he left Auschwitz, recounted in his book *The Reawakening*, tells us much about the postwar world in which the trauma of genocide continued to affect his choices and movement in and across Europe. His long, arduous physical journey back to Italy, and mapping that return, remains as much a part of the experience of genocide as does his time in the camp.

Reading survivor testimonies as more than courtroom evidence against the crime of genocide has placed a new burden on historians. The question of whether an event counts as genocide, while still important, has given way to broader concerns about the long term and lasting effects of genocidal acts and *how* they destroy communities and what is created in their wake. Mass murder is the most obvious way, but the destruction of communal, religious, and gendered identities and a sense of belonging also matter. In the case of the Armenian genocide, testimonies by those who experienced and witnessed the deportations have proved valuable in demonstrating patterns that prove the intent to eliminate the minority Christian population.

In short, mapping the journey taken by individuals on these routes reveals more complex patterns that intersect with larger geopolitical realities and the destruction of social practices caused by genocide. It can render less opaque the way individuals deal with trauma and find ways to negotiate privation. Although these remain distinctive experiences for victims and those who bear witness, deportation narratives follow decipherable patterns that remain valuable beyond the purpose of proving that genocide happened. These testimonies show the long-term effects of displacement on individuals, towns, and communities, as the following sampling of experiences from survivors and eyewitnesses of the Armenian genocide collectively illustrates.

On the Deportation Route

Astrid Aghajanian was a genocide survivor who remembered her family's experience of exile years later in a recorded interview. Her journey along the Euphrates with her mother and brother on the deportation route from central Anatolia continued her family's ongoing experience of exile. Her grandfather, a businessman from Guren, was killed during a previous wave of massacres; her mother left the town, now an orphan, and later married her father, a Protestant. Before leaving on the deportation route on foot, her father was taken away and later shot. She witnessed atrocities including the throwing of young women in the Euphrates who were shot if they tried to swim and the death of her brother. Along the route, the Quakers and the Red Cross aided refugees. Aghajanian's mother joined the knitting and sewing group of the aid workers. Her mother's second marriage to an Armenian Orthodox man in the employ of the British took them from Aleppo to Haifa. There they lived on army rations and income from her mother's work as a seamstress. She married Gaspar Aghajanian and moved to Jerusalem in the 1940s, and eventually to Britain in the mid-1970s. "We have lost our homes," she concluded, but added her own understanding of what exile meant to her family. Armenians were like spiders; they build webs and when they are destroyed they build again.

The women and children who left behind deportation stories reveal important patterns that depict the experience of exile as one of survival and accommodation. What Aghajanian remembered most vividly was her own gendered experience of a child surviving genocide. While distinctive as her own individual remembrance, this history of herself as a child speaks to the helpless condition of someone whose fate was determined both by the conditions of deportation and the actions of the adults around her.[19] Her mother had tried to protect her children by painting their faces with mud, hoping it would keep them from being taken away and forced to become brides or servants. She believed her mother brave for doing this and recalled feeling proud of her when she told her, "if you aren't afraid of death you aren't afraid of anything."[20] As I listened to this story in the Imperial War Museum archives in London last summer, a cold chill went down my spine as I thought of my own grandmother's story. Mary Thomassian, too, had been deported along the Euphrates route with her mother during the genocide. Her father previously had emigrated to the United States, and she recalled her mother lying to a family that wanted to take her away that her child was deaf and mute. Other Christian minorities shared the fate of exile and tell similar stories of childhood exile. For Sano Halo, a Pontic Greek who survived deportation from northern Anatolia when she was ten years old, the route to exile also led south in 1920. After the breakup of her family along the deportation route after the war, her fate was tied to the Armenians who took her in and led her to Aleppo, where at the age of fifteen she married an Assyrian man who took her to the US.[21]

For single men, deportation was a very different experience. Yervant Odian was one of the approximately two hundred intellectuals rounded up at the beginning of the Armenian genocide in April 1915. His personal account of exile from Constantinople to Der al Zor and back again shows how he used his contacts and status to slip between the worlds of Ottoman dictates which forced him to keep on the move. He started his journey with some money in his pocket, knowledge of the terrain, and people he could contact along the way. He lacked the encumbrance of family which helped him avoid the convoys and concentration camps that swallowed up the women, children, and elderly deportees also heading south. Odian also managed to avoid the fate of so many able-bodied young men who were either killed or sent to forced labour camps.

Writing his story years later, he recalled how he watched and waited as the war changed course during his exile. When Baghdad fell to the British in 1917, he believed that "after getting to Der Zor we might be able to escape and, by reaching Baghdad, free ourselves from [a] life of agony forever."[22] Odian reflected the belief of the tens of thousands of refugees made homeless by Ottoman wartime policies that the British advance into Baghdad offered hope that the massacres and deportations would finally stop. "I began to have ideas about the future. 'When I get to Baghdad,' I mused, 'I'll go to the Armenian church, tell them who I am, enter into relations with the local Armenians and, with their financial help, sort myself out ... Then with British help, I'll go to Basra.'" Other men also wanted to go home. As Odian remembered, "I saw deserting Turkish soldiers ... in the most wretched condition, who had arrived from near Baghdad on their way home."[23]

Those who managed to survive the deportations and war, refugees and soldiers alike, witnessed real changes to their circumstances in the spring of 1917. They were not the kind of changes, however, that Odian imagined would help him and others get home. Aram Andonian was arrested, exiled, and deported like Odian. In exile for over two years, he wrote down his story in late 1919 and had it published that spring.[24] This story of deportation would capture the attention of the British viscount Gladstone who wrote the introduction to the book *The Memoirs of Naim Bey*, which made the case for genocide through eyewitness testimony. It continued the work of Bryce's Blue Book but with an important addition. This eyewitness, Naim Bey, was reportedly a Turkish official who had witnessed the deportations firsthand. These two very different survivor testimonies have been used by historians as evidence to prove that the genocide happened.

But these experiences have served other purposes. Andonian himself went on to direct the Nubar Library in Paris where he collected documents about the genocide, deportations, and Ottoman policy against Armenians and other Christian minorities.[25] As with other survivor testimonies, the authenticity of the representation of atrocities in these accounts and the political motivations of the authors have been called into question, limiting their usefulness as representative proof of genocide. Andonian's own experience of exile, when read in connection with Odian and Naim Bey, reveals other important realities about the massacres beyond the question of guilt. In addition to conforming to contemporary definitions of genocide as systematic attempts to destroy a people, they confirm a pattern of experience with mass atrocity that relies on the institutionalization of remembrance through collecting and retelling stories. Like those of child and women survivors, they also tell that story as a gendered experience of war.

Those in positions of influence did more than chronicle their own survival or offer testimony on the horrors of massacres. Exile meant the opportunity to exercise influence for those deportees of high status in limited but important ways. One of the most important eyewitness accounts of the deportations was written by the Armenian patriarch of Constantinople. Patriarch Zaven der Yeghiayan served from 1913–22, and the account he wrote years later included his observations and journey of exile from Constantinople to Baghdad during the war.[26] While in exile he undertook aid work supported by the church among destitute populations in the occupied regions in collaboration with the British occupying force. Deeply respected among Armenians and the British who occupied the southern Ottoman lands after 1917, he saw himself in the role of intermediary. Helpless to stop the massacres, he attempted to create alliances and bear witness and influence the Allied army of occupation's treatment of minorities. In one instance, he was asked to change the minds of 850 Armenian men in the Baquba refugee camp who had refused to join the British army. As Patriarch Zaven recalled: "I urged them not to allow their relations with the British officers and their government to deteriorate over a mater such as this which was of interest to the entire [Armenian] Nation," and then "they said 'No.'" The patriarch would eventually change his mind to side with the men who had subsequently been disarmed, but not before he sent "several men to Baqubah [*sic*] to settle this matter without any rupture."[27] The patriarch and Armenian philanthropic organizations continued to work with the British to provide funds and resources for refugees in Allied occupied zone during the coming months.[28]

Though clear patterns emerge, deportation created multiple and distinct parallel narratives. Soldiers who encountered refugees had their own stories to tell. Typically considered in a category distinct from survivors, testimonies of those who witnessed the effects of the deportations tell the story of genocide as part of the larger story of the war. Along the "bitter lakes" of Port Said, one British soldier imagined seeing a large camp of up to "1 million Armenians from Turkey … settled down under allied supervision on the banks of the canal." While this number was most certainly an exaggeration – the Egyptian government estimated that it took in only 23,000 refugees – it shows the lasting impression that the appearance of destitute Armenian refugees made on those who had served in the East.[29] For the soldiers who found themselves on the same roads as the deportees, the condition of the refugees shaped their view of the Allied mission and the hopelessness of the humanitarian disaster unfolding around them.

Another soldier related how his unit "commandeer[ed] 300 sheep for the Armenian Refugees who by now had begun to pour into Bijar." He described the region around the village as "a peculiar and motley sight strewn with the sleeping and semi awakened bodies of some 10,000 Armenian refugees who, after 14 days weary march, were enjoying a brief rest before completing the journey to Hamadan." This "strange and pitiful sight" he considered "heaven" compared with what was to come as his unit continued marching along the route. An elderly woman who had been shot was tended to by the unit's medic, but there was little that could be done for others they met along their sixteen-mile journey that day. He described "an endless stream of fugitives all plodding their weary way bringing with them all their portable worldly belongings." For three days this continued along the approximately sixty-mile trek, where he reported seeing forty thousand people. The route was marked every hundred yards or so by corpses stripped naked by marauders, alongside the carcasses of animals that had been used for transport. This soldier's journey on the deportation route continued to reveal the hopelessness of the situation. He recalled seeing a young mother dead. Sitting by the corpse was a toddler, still alive and happy. On his return journey, he saw the corpse of the child laying beside its mother.

In retelling his story, he answered a question he could not pose out loud but must have asked himself countless times about the purpose of the war and its effect on civilian populations. He asserted in his interview that "we could hardly spare these people a drink from our water bottles. Ours was an important mission." As the caravan and the British army crossed paths, they remained part of parallel stories of the war. "It took us three days to ride through them and they too were on the move all the time," this soldier recalled. "As long as I live I will never forget these sights."[30]

Refugee Camp Experiences

Many of the families who survived the experience of deportation found themselves in refugee camps run by the Allied military which occupied the region after 1917. Western-led humanitarian organizations followed on the heels of the occupation and helped set up and run dozens of refugee camps along with a myriad of auxiliary institutions including orphanages, soup kitchens, hospitals, and so-called rescue homes. Reading the stories of survivors who found themselves in these camps, alongside those of military and humanitarian personnel, offers a snapshot of the collective experience of displacement caused by genocide and war.

Levon Shahoian was eleven when his family first arrived at the British-run refugee camp. His family fled its native village in northwestern Iran, trekked over seven hundred miles, and settled, first outside of Baquba, and then in Nahr Umar, a transitional camp outside Basra.[31] Remembering his experiences years later, he viewed his time as a refugee relatively positively. His family had been forced to leave their ancestral village of

Haftevan in the Salmast region of Iran because of Ottoman genocidal policies along the border, and understood the camp as a lifeline. They ended up in the Baquba camp and then were transferred to Nahr Umar. Here he learned English and waited, trusting that the British would make it possible for refugees to resettle in the region. Though it did not happen in the way Shahoian and his family expected, his time at the military-run refugee camp gave them needed relief during the experience of deportation. "It seems as if the deep wounds of the previous years had somewhat healed," Shahoian wrote of his family's time at Nahr Umar.[32] After years of uncertainty and exile in the desert, many refugees felt secure in the heavily guarded camp despite complaints of boredom, inadequate schools, and restrictions on movement. When his brother was arrested for leaving the camp without permission, the family negotiated a way for him to legitimately travel from the camp to the local village to obtain supplies for a small shop the British allowed him to start.[33] For Shahoian's family, the combination of military protection, order, and discipline, combined with resources provided by local and international philanthropic organizations, offered the possibility to start again.

The military had its own war-related reasons for setting up these camps. Lieutenant Dudley Stafford Northcote, a Cambridge graduate from a prominent British aristocratic family, was put in charge of refugees fleeing genocide at a camp set up outside of Baghdad.[34] Northcote had no previous experience with relief work when he took up his post at Baquba. As he told his mother in a letter, looking after refugees was "quite a change from soldiering."[35] By spring 1919, the camp housed 45,000 refugees. Northcote took his job seriously, learning Armenian and participating in the daily life and rituals of the refugees, including Armenian weddings which would come to be a frequent occurrence.[36] But he always knew that ultimately his job would be to "repatriate" refugees. The only question was where. Britain and France were still wrangling over the details of administering Syria, Mesopotamia, Lebanon, and Palestine as mandates.[37] In August 1920, Northcote got the order to start the repatriation project in the British mandate of Mesopotamia, part of modern-day Iraq, and he moved refugees to Nahr Umar. The local population, unsurprisingly, did not like the idea of thousands of refugees making claims to their land. This put the refugee camp in a desperate situation. In the end, government and philanthropic organizations cobbled together funds to aid as many internees as possible who were expelled from the camp.

As the occupation wore on, the British began to see these collaborations as expendable. In 1921, the government announced that the camp would close due to cost. Refugees willing to leave the Basra camp voluntarily were promised a small food ration. Northcote was shocked and publicly refused to send "women and children out of their tents" into the desert. He successfully lobbied the Colonial Office for more time and launched a public campaign on behalf of the refugees.[38] The Lord Mayor's Fund, one of the British philanthropic organizations operating in the region at time, hired Northcote and took charge with the consent of British officials, escorting the refugees to Erivan in the newly established state of Armenia. Transporting thousands of Armenian refugees from the camp in Basra to Erivan where no infrastructure or basic provisions existed to support such a large influx of people with few resources of their own proved nearly impossible. Famine conditions in Erivan coupled with the overwhelming flow of refugees coming in at over one thousand persons per day made it a harrowing experience for the new settlers, who had little comfort or support after the aid workers left.[39]

When the camp finally closed, Shahoian recalled being sent on a barge with his family and their few belongings to Baghdad.[40] After twelve days they made their way to a refugee-run camp called "Gelen" near the banks of the river. Though he missed the feeling of protection and community of the military camp, freedom of movement and access to the resources of a large city would make the difference as his family integrated into life in Baghdad. In his memoir he related his overwhelming feeling of relief that the local population let his family and the hundreds of other refugees stay unmolested and set up camp in a field to restart their lives. He claimed that he would always remember the "hospitable Arabs" who welcomed them "as if we were their relatives" and let them stay in the makeshift camp supplied by the Armenian church in Baghdad.[41]

As for Northcote, he never really got over the experience. When he came back home he sold lace work made by refugees and sent the money back to Erivan.[42] Though aid workers understood that "relief must sooner or later come to an end," the continuing crisis was not easy to forget. British relief organizations throughout the 1920s appealed "to the philanthropy of the people of our Empire to help." The need ultimately overwhelmed anything that private philanthropy, led largely by American and British organizations, could support, with an estimated 130,000 Armenian refugees remaining in the former lands of the Ottoman Empire.[43] Something more was needed, but the British government, which held political control over the region after the invasion of Baghdad in 1917, did not continue to adequately maintain relief efforts in the occupied areas.[44] Meanwhile, war continued despite the armistice signed at Mudros in October 1918 and the Treaty of Sevres signed in August 1920.

The peace treaty with the Ottoman Empire would not be finalized until the signing of a new treaty in Lausanne in 1923, which again shifted the way relief would be delivered, managed, and institutionalized by international institutions.[45] As Northcote's experience suggests, the administration and institutionalization of aid relied on the unsteady collaboration between military expediency, humanitarianism, and accommodations made by the refugees themselves. Humanitarian organizations worked within the confines set up by the military which ultimately shaped the institutionalization of aid. The world of the camp relied on the investment of both military and humanitarian organizations, which allowed a space for temporary aid to have long-term effects.

A failed tool in the attempt to resettle its nearly fifty thousand inhabitants, camps like the one run by Northcote nevertheless provided necessary temporary assistance for those caught in the crossfire of the war and its aftermath in and around Baghdad. Shutting down the camp meant for families like the Shahoians a chance to start again. Eventually, Levon would find work in Baghdad with the military due to his language skills and his time spent in the British-run camps.[46] For tens of thousands of others, the attempt at resettlement by humanitarian organizations, which guided camp actions, would lead to less certain fates in Soviet Armenia or in the Iraq mandate.[47]

Reading Shahoian's story as part of the history of genocide means reconciling how he described displacement as constitutive of new realities which came out of his family's experience with exile. Writing about his experience years later, Shahoian noted how the experience of displacement after the genocide created both a longing for home and an understanding of his community's not entirely insurmountable status as other. How these refugees started their lives again was intimately tied to the many-layered and long enduring experience of genocide that replayed itself countless times across the region. Remaking the Middle East after the war took place in the intimate spaces of families who experienced crimes committed against their communities as a question of survival and accommodation.

Aid workers and internees at other camps made similar adjustments to deal with the uncertainty of the war. Invited by the British military to undertake aid work, the American Red Cross (ARC) quickly established itself in Wadi Surar outside of Jerusalem in the wake of the Allied offensive in 1917.[48] It soon had a network of camps behind the front lines. After the occupation, as had happened around Baghdad, refugees flooded into the occupied zone despite the ongoing conflict. Hospitals, clinics, schools, and workrooms to employ refugees initially served the local population, which comprised mostly Muslim Arabs but also included Greeks, Jews, and Armenians. Eventually, the camp would largely house Armenians who saw the camps as protection from further massacres. ARC managed this mission with help from local, regional, and international organizations. This "quasi-private, quasi-state organization," in one historian's assessment, was part of President Wilson's humanitarian war strategy after the US entered the war in the spring of 1917.[49] Echoing British prime minister Lloyd George's rhetoric, Wilson cited humanitarian responsibility as a wartime obligation. Between June 1917 and 1919 ARC established a strong presence across Europe and in the Middle East, establishing its own "War Council" in Washington, DC to help coordinate relief work related to Allied operations.[50] In and around Jerusalem alone, ARC ran twelve hospitals and sixteen medical dispensaries that served refugee and local populations.

Running a camp in a war zone necessarily required collaboration between the military and humanitarian organizations. Near East Relief, an American-based aid operation without ties to the military, operated in connection with ARC and bolstered the widespread wartime consensus on the importance of US humanitarian intervention. It carried on with this work after ARC's Middle East mission faded. Postwar humanitarianism would come to more fully embrace an evolving secular, apolitical, and international character under the guidance of organizations including NER, Save the Children, Quaker Friends Relief, the Lord Mayor's Fund, and the League of Nations.[51] But in this moment, the ongoing military conflict offered challenges that required a different kind of solution. Tens of thousands of civilians were on the move, criss-crossing battle lines, which required coordination and resources. ARC alone contributed $4.5 million dollars and nearly $1.5 million dollars of supplies to the work.[52] American dollars, coupled with British military infrastructure and ground support and the political will to make humanitarianism part of the Allied war strategy, rendered the front-line refugee camp a necessity of war. Managing refugees in war zones proved more difficult than it had been outside of now-relatively quiet Baquba. At the same time, it made it possible to better control movement along the front and manage how the international community understood the war, its purpose, and the people on whose behalf they claimed to be fighting.

Humanitarian relief workers provided social services which served as a reminder that the war and its effects on civilians continued. Many of the nurses stationed at the camp had previous experience with refugee relief work. As employees of ARC, they understood their job as part of the war effort and the "business" of war-making. "The whole country is a camp and war the main business," remarked ARC nurse Miss Madiera in 1917.[53] The battalion of largely unmarried American- and British-born nurses and assistants found in war work an opportunity to support Allied objectives as trained professionals. Paid substantially less than the men who commanded these units, women ran the day-to-day activities of the camp, from sanitation to health care to education. Many found the work fulfilling, seeking out challenging assignments. "I like my job. It contains great possibilities," commented Rosa Lee, who had come to the camp seeking opportunities as a social worker and freedoms that did not exist back at home. Women workers were indeed given great responsibility.[54] "Only a few days behind the advancing troops," ARC nurses were charged with organizing social services to stem an outbreak of cholera in Tiberias after British general Allenby took the city in late September.[55]

For those living in the camp, relief work meant not only social services but a last resort. When asked when they would return home, one Maronite family from Lebanon informed aid workers of the reality of their situation: "There is nothing there." "We had a hotel. One regiment came and took a little; so it went. It is beautiful here compared to what was there."[56] Though the reply of the aid worker is not recorded in the archive, the idea that a family would want to stay in the "cheerless" camp would certainly have recalled the contradiction of the refugee camp on the front line. Offering aid to refugees in a war zone assumed that a state of normalcy would return eventually. But refugees came not only from the surrounding regions but from places that were hundreds of miles away and occupied by hostile armies. Now in the protection of one occupying force, those interned at the camp gave up freedom for security.

When opportunities arose, attempts were made to return home. At harvest time, for example, "homesick" internees, as aid workers described them, streamed out of the camp to take part. When shelling forced them back they returned to their lot as internees.[57] For those who had no ties to the surrounding region the reality of internment as the only option weighed more heavily. One man from the distant town of Marash understood that by entering the camp he took on subject status. If you kill us," Balthasar Artin told one aid worker, "you kill us. If you save us alive, we live. We are your property."[58]

Conclusion

Reading genocide as collective experience requires studying the representation of genocide in a diversity of testimony literature. This, coupled with representations of genocide in popular culture, literature, and media, and most especially the iterations of survivors themselves (whether in autobiography, poetry, song, or oral testimony) can offer a fuller picture of displacement and survival. These narratives offer new ways of reading the representation of problematic texts about the Armenian genocide, such as Franz Werfel's *Forty Days of Musa Dah* and the Hollywood film *Ravished Armenia*.[59] Are they best read as testimony? Literature? Fiction? Entertainment? Pornography? It depends on the question we ask of the text in relationship to and in conversation with other texts. *Ravished Armenia*, the Hollywood film based on the true-life story of Aurora Mardiganian, who escaped the Ottoman Empire as a teenager, has been recovered today and is being used as evidence of genocide. A new version of the film has subtitles and a dramatic classical soundtrack which do not conform to the original. It is intended to tell the story of the genocide in dramatic form. But it also can be read as unnecessarily blurring the line between fact and fiction to make a political point. In the process, Mardiganian's story gets lost. Interviews with her in her later years revealed how what happened to her was representative of an experience of sexual violence that many women like her must have shared.[60] To access this experience, her story then must be read and reread against and alongside other representations that reflect and even challenge her narrative.

Rather than relegating the category of genocide to the dustbin of history in favour of more elastic legal, economic, and political conceptualizations, scholars have an opportunity to use new tools and apply methods that map genocide across time and place. People experience genocide as either perpetrators, victims, or observers. Understanding the myriad actors, actions, and ideas that constitute genocide as lasting and translatable means moving beyond definitions and recognizing it as a historically bounded event. Genocide can and should be contextualized as a defining modern human experience. This chapter shows one possible way forward: mapping the overlapping journeys of those living in this world. The layering of individual stories of victims, aid workers, the military, and even the perpetrators themselves shows the complex dynamic of genocide and the marks it leaves behind on the social and political landscape. The practice of georeferencing, where historical data is appended with geographical data using ARC-GIS software, for example, now allows scholars to trace the historical spaces occupied by those who left behind personal testimony.[61] The routes people took during deportation to concentration camps and then, for those who survived, the routes they took to get back home are rendered legible in a new way when plotted alongside the sites of resistance, extermination, and relief.[62] Mapping the experiences of survivors using new tools in social science research to trace personal journeys provides a way to read the Armenian genocide as the contested but shared experience of observers, perpetrators, and victims across time and space.

Such an understanding of genocide as *longue durée* raises the stakes by placing perpetrators, victims, and observers in a unified and extended historical frame. This is not a periodization that looks for precursors in earlier events that show the inevitability of genocide, or attempts to read genocide backwards, which risks an ahistorical treatment of events.[63] Extending genocide as experience beyond the moment of atrocity situates genocide as process. It also starts to address the vexing question of comparative genocide.[64] Genocide as an act perpetuated by state and non-state actors is a crime of the twentieth century that has followed us into the twenty-first. We need tools, taken from cultural and social history, to understand its patterns, motivations, and human costs. Simply relabelling it or situating it in a different set of theoretical claims will do little to help our understanding of the act and its aftereffects. To study genocide as experience means analyzing it less as a legal category and political claim on moral conscience and more as a modern human problem. In other words, it is not something that happens to them, but to us. Understanding genocide as our common history makes it harder to view man's inhumanity to man as a series of unfortunate but inevitable events. Most importantly, it makes genocide hard to forget.

NOTES

1 As seen in this volume, Ronald Suny argues for a more narrowly defined understanding of genocide while others, including Norman Naimark and Andrea Graziosi, prefer a more expansive treatment of how we compare and count cases of genocide. Naimark, *Genocide: A World History* (Oxford: Oxford Univesity Press, 2016); Graziosi, "The Soviet 1931–33 Famines and the Ukrainian Holodomor," in *Hunger by Design*, edited by H. Hyrn (Cambridge, MA: Harvard University Press, 2009), 1–19; Ronald Suny, "Debating Famine and Genocide," *Contemporary European History* 27, no. 3 (2008): 476–81.

2 Paul Bartrop and Steven Jacobs have argued for the need to create an inclusive assessment of the "nature and impacts of thought relative to the Holocaust and genocide" over time and across disciplines. *Fifty Key Thinkers on the Holocaust and Genocide* (New York: Routledge, 2011), 4–5.

3 Anton Weiss-Wendt questions the usefulness of the concept because of its use as a political tool by governments and political actors. Anton Weiss-Wendt, *The Soviet Union and the Gutting of the UN Genocide Convention* (Madison: University of Wisconsin Press, 2017); Weiss-Wendt, *A Rhetorical Crime: Genocide in the Geopolitical Discourse of the Cold War* (Newark, NJ: Rutgers University Press, 2018). See also A.W. Brian Simpson, "Britain and the Genocide Convention," *British Yearbook of International Law* 73, no. 1 (2002): 5–64.

4 Raphael Lemkin, *Axis Rule in Occupied Europe* (Washington, DC: Carnegie Endowment for International Peace, 1944).

5 Douglas Irvin-Erickson, *Raphaël Lemkin and the Concept of Genocide* (Philadelphia: Pennsylvania University Press, 2016); A. Dirk Moses, *The Problems of Genocide* (Cambridge: Cambridge University Press, 2021).

6 Michelle Tusan, "Genocide, Famine and Refugees on Film: Humanitarianism and the Great War," *Past and Present* 237, no. 1 (November 2017): 197–235; Tusan, "'Crimes against Humanity': Human Rights, the British Empire, and the Origins of the Response to the Armenian Genocide," *American Historical Review* (February 2014): 69–76; "Promises, Promises: The Strange History of Film and the Armenian Genocide," *Los Angeles Review of Books*, 25 May 2017.

7 This includes economic and political transformations based on new social relations, technologies, and ways of thinking about gender, class, and race. This scholarship has extended beyond World War I studies in British history, where it arguably got its start, to include other wartime experiences. See for example, Paul Fussel, *The Great War and Modern Memory* (Oxford: Oxford University Press, 2013); Jay Winter, *Sites of Memory* (Cambridge: Cambridge University Press, 1998); Susan Grayzel, *Women's Identities at War* (Chapel Hill: North Carolina UP, 2014); Nicoletta Gullace, *The Blood of Our Sons* (New York: Palgrave, 2002).

8 Robert Gerwarth, *The Vanquished* (New York: Farrar Straus and Giroux, 2016); Eugene Rogan, *Fall of the Ottomans* (New York: Basic Books, 2015).

9 Robert Mirak, *Torn between Two Lands: Armenians in America, 1890 to World War I* (Cambridge, MA: Harvard University Press, 1983); Roger Daniels, *Coming to America: A History of Ethnicity and Immigration in American Life* (New York: Perennial, 2002), chapter 7; *North American Armenians* (New Haven, CT: Human Relations Area Files, 1996); Charles Mahakian, *The History of the Armenians in California* (San Francisco: R and E Research Associates, 1974).

10 Jay Winter, ed., *America and the Armenian Genocide of 1915* (Cambridge: Cambridge University Press, 2003); Tusan, "Crimes against Humanity"; Stefan Ihrig, *Justifying Genocide: Germany and the Armenians from Bismarck to Hitler* (Cambridge, MA: Harvard University Press, 2016).

11 Ronald Grigor Suny, Fatma Muge Goçek, and Norman Naimark, eds. *A Question of Genocide* (Oxford: Oxford University Press, 2011).

12 Raymond Kevorkian, *Complete History of the Armenian Genocide* (London: IB Tauris, 2011), 264 (concentration camp map).

13 Michelle Tusan, "The Concentration Camp as a Site of Refuge: The Rise of the Refugee Camp and the Great War in the Middle East," *Journal of Modern History* (December 2021, in press).

14 Annette F. Timm, "Testimony in Holocaust Historiography," in *Holocaust History and the Readings of Ka-Tzetnik*, edited by Annette F. Timm, 37–66 (London: Bloomsbury Academic, 2017).

15 James Bryce, *The Treatment of Armenians in the Ottoman Empire* (Whitefish, MT: Kessinger, [1916] 2010).

16 Hannah Arendt famously disparaged the use of survivor testimony in the courtroom as it did not deal with the question of guilt. *Eichmann in Jerusalem* (New York: Viking Press, 1963). According to Timm, before the Eichmann trial, victim testimony was largely "relegated to the realm of art" ("Testimony," 45).

17 On the use of survivor testimonies and the Holocaust, see Alon Confino, *Foundational Pasts* (Cambridge: Cambridge University Press, 2012); Saul Friedlander, *Nazi Germany and the Jews* (New York: Harper Collins, 2007); Christopher Browning, *Collected Memories: Holocaust History and Postwar Testimony* (Madison: University of Wisconsin Press, 2003); Christopher Browning, *Remembering Survival* (New York: Norton, 2011).

18 Judith Kaplan-Weinger and Yonit Hoffman, "Testimonies of Jewish Holocaust Survivors: Characterizing the Narratives of Resistance and Resilience," in *The Holocaust: Memories and History*, edited by Viktoriia Khiterer, Ryan Barrick, and David Misa, 106–32 (Newcastle upon Tyne: Cambridge Scholars Publishing, 2014).

19 Elizabeth Warnock Fernea, ed., *Remembering Childhood in the Middle East* (Austin: University of Texas Press, 2002). As Robert Fernea puts it in his introduction, children's perspectives often go unrecorded as "histories of ourselves" (1–2).

20 Astrid Aghajanian interview, #17368, Reel 1, Imperial War Museum, London.

21 Thea Halo, *Not Even My Name* (New York, 2001).

22 Yervant Odian, *Accursed Years: My Exile and Return from Der Zor, 1914–1919*, trans. Ara Stepan Melkonian (London: Gomidas, 2009), 135.

23 Ibid., 159.

24 Aram Andonian, *The Memoirs of Naim Bey: Turkish Official Documents relating to the Deportations and Massacres of Armenians*, introduction by Viscount Gladstone (London: Hodder and Stoughton, 1920).
25 http://www.bnulibrary.org/index.php/en.
26 Zaven der Yeghiayan, *My Patriarchal Memoirs*, trans. Ared Misirliyan (Barrington, RI: Mayreni Publishing, 2002), 140.
27 Ibid., 164–6.
28 Assyrians in the camp experienced something similar. The British appealed to religious and secular leaders to help maintain the camp and control humanitarian and military objectives. Brigadier General H.H. Austin, *The Bakubah Refugee Camp* (London, 1920).
29 Norman William Collins interview, #12043, 22 May 1991, Imperial War Museum, London.
30 Private Papers of J Coffey Box 9/25/1.
31 Levon Shahoian, *On the Banks of the Tigris* (London: Taderon Press, 2012).
32 Ibid., 66.
33 Ibid., 56–7.
34 He was the grandson of the Earl of Iddesleigh who, though a loyal political Conservative, had close ties with W.E. Gladstone.
35 Northcote to mother, 3 December 1918. Northcote Papers, British Library, Add MS 57559.
36 Northcote reported speaking Armenian "quite well" by 5 July 1919 in a letter home. Refugee statistics come from Simpson, *The Refugee Problem* (New York: Oxford University Press, 1939), 49.
37 Northcote papers, letter dated 18 July 1919.
38 Ibid., letters from 23 and 24 September 1921.
39 Nassibian, 248–9.
40 Shahoian, *On the Banks of the Tigris*.
41 Ibid., 83–4.
42 Northcote was still employed by LMF in March of 1926 but expresses his wish to "come home." Funding given by Save the Children discussed in letter from 3 February 1922. Northcote Papers.
43 These are Nansen's numbers after the war. The Refugee Survey in 1938 by the Royal Institute of International Affairs estimated the number at between 85,000 and 100,000. Chatham House Archive online. https://www.gale.com/c/chatham-house-online-archive-module-1.
44 Simpson, *The Refugee Problem*, 344.
45 Claudina Skran, *Refugees in Interwar Europe* (Oxford: Clarendon Press, 1995).
46 Ibid., 89–93.

47 League of Nations' refugee commissioner Nansen and US president Woodrow Wilson designated Erivan in the Caucasus as a national homeland for Armenians in 1920. It was proposed that the nation would start as a mandate under European or possibly American control. The mandate never happened and the state of Armenia that eventually emerged was doomed to failure. After two short-lived years of independence it became the Soviet Republic of Armenia in 1922. Today, the region is part of the country of Armenia, which won independence after the Soviet Union collapsed in the early 1990s. Robert Hewsen, *Armenia: A Historical Atlas* (Chicago: University of Chicago Press, 2001), 242. On the history of modern Armenia see Richard Hovanissian, *The Armenian People from Ancient to Modern Times*, vol. 2 (New York: Palgrave, 2004), and Razmik Panossian, *The Armenians* (New York: Columbia University Press, 2006), 246–56.

48 Allenby's headquarters were in Ramleh, thirty miles west of Jerusalem at the time.

49 Julia Irwin, *Making the World Safe: The American Red Cross and the Nation's Humanitarian Awakening* (New York: Oxford University Press 2013), 2.

50 Ibid., 72–3, 139.

51 Keith Watenpaugh, *Bread from Stones* (Berkeley: University of California Press, 2015).

52 Lavinia Dock, *History of American Red Cross Nursing* (New York: Macmillan, 1922), 890.

53 Ibid., 897.

54 Rosa E. Lee, First Report of Wadi Surar Education department, Hoover Institute, American National Red Cross Records, Reel 155, Folder 16.

55 Dock, *History of American Red Cross*, 902.

56 Ibid.

57 Ibid., 906.

58 Ibid., 902.

59 Michelle Tusan, *The British Empire and the Armenian Genocide* (London, 2017), 220–1; Andrekos Varnava and Trevor Harris, "'It Is Quite Impossible to Receive Them': Saving the Musa Dagh Refugees and the Imperialism of European Humanitarianism," *Journal of Modern History* 90, no. 4 (December 2018): 834–62.

60 Timm discusses the erasure of narratives of sexual violence in the reading of Holocaust victim testimony, "Testimony in Holocaust Historiography," 51–5.

61 See Michelle Tusan, "Mapping Genocide and the Refugee Experience during the Great War in the Middle East," recorded talk at https://www.umass.edu/ihgms/event/michelle-tusan-mapping-genocide-refugee-experience.

62 This is done through the process of georeferencing, in which a digital image, such as a scanned map, is appended with geographic information so that GIS

software can "place" the image in its appropriate real-world locations. Attributes illustrated in these maps, such as travel routes, concentration camps, relevant localities, and railroads are manually plotted as data points into a geodatabase in a meticulous process similar to handmade cartography. The georeferenced data can be used to conduct spatial analytics and statistics (for example, to calculate distances or density) or for inclusion in publications and digital/spatial humanities projects. Additionally, the data can be appended in ArcMap with other data points, such as information gathered from historical documents, journals, and testimonies.

63 Ronald Suny, "The Hamidian Massacres, 1894–1897: Disinterring a Buried History," *Études arméniennes contemporaines* 11 (2018): 125–34.

64 Considering genocides in relation to one another has raised the stakes in terms of how we categorize and understand it as event and process. Eric Weitz, *A Century of Genocide* (Princeton, NJ: Princeton University Press, 2003).

9

The Limits of a Genocide Lens and Possible Alternatives

Scott Straus

In this chapter, I reflect on the public and academic conversation about the genocide in Rwanda. I argue that we create important omissions in narrating the history of Rwanda *uniquely* through the lens of the genocide that occurred there some twenty-five years ago – that is, when we make "the Rwandan genocide" the *sole* frame for naming the period of violence in Rwanda in the 1990s.[1]

The genocide in Rwanda has become, after years of labour, documentation, legal proceedings, testimony, and scholarship, a canonical case of mass violence in the twentieth century. That place in world history is deserved. However, whether wittingly or not, the focus on genocide crimes against the minority Tutsi population in 1994 has come to *define* the history of 1990s violence in Rwanda for many students, policymakers, scholars, and other observers. The "Rwandan genocide" typically serves as the sole referent for thinking about mass violations of human rights against Rwandans, *the* marker for labelling the country's violence. To make this point, the government in Rwanda has come to insist, and has largely succeeded in promulgating the idea, that the correct name by which to mark the period is the "Genocide against the Tutsi."

However, while genocide against the resident Tutsi population indisputably took place in Rwanda in 1994, framing 1994 or the 1990s period uniquely around "the Rwandan genocide" or the "Genocide against the Tutsi" does not describe accurately the range of mass violence that occurred in this period. Mass violence against Rwandan Hutu populations took place on several occasions as part of the 1990s struggle for state power, including in 1994. While it is crucial to recognize and memorialize the genocide, narrating the region's history of violence *uniquely* through the lens of genocide has come to occlude, or at least minimize, these other, critical experiences of violence.

At base, this chapter is a call to conceptualize and label Rwanda's history of violence in the 1990s by recognizing the genocide that was committed against the Tutsi population in 1994 while also acknowledging these other experiences of mass violence. In short, my point is: affirm genocide *and* recognize the other mass crimes.

The recent twenty-fifth-year genocide commemoration constitutes a stark reminder of how salient the genocide crimes have become and how invisible the other crimes are. From official commemoration activities in Rwanda to many commemoration efforts outside the country, the twenty-fifth anniversary rarely resulted in an effort to calibrate the history of violence in the region. Rather, the anniversary tended to reproduce a very partial history of violence, only drawing attention to the genocide crimes against the Tutsi population.

Why does this memory disproportion exist? One clear reason is that the post-genocide government in Rwanda has political interests in fostering and policing an inequality in memory. The government's interests have shaped the justice process and the material conditions by which scholarship is produced. Today, we have records from an extraordinary amount of justice procedures concerning the genocide crimes; however, the other episodes of mass violence have not been the subject of any sustained domestic or international justice process. The state has enforced that outcome. Scholarly accounts of the violence against Rwandan Hutu populations are also thin. Gaining permission to investigate these other crimes in Rwanda is virtually impossible. Further, within Rwanda, speaking out about these other crimes can be dangerous. The non-genocide violence thus remains weakly documented and largely unvalidated, and the victims and survivors of these episodes remain unrecognized – at least in public and official commemoration processes.

While political interests drive this outcome, I hypothesize that the concept of genocide also matters. As the "crime of crimes," genocide captures the spotlight and implies a special, untouchable status. Genocide is in a league by itself. Calling attention to other crimes in turn seems easily to trigger accusations of drawing "equivalences," minimizing genocide, or even denial.

Herein lies a deeper challenge for scholars and other observers: how to recognize genocide and its distinctive qualities, while also recognizing other experiences of mass violence? Genocide is a distinctive and distinctly heinous form of violence. Yet the lopsided account of the past that the concept of genocide tends to deliver creates invisibilities and silences that distort histories of violence and that inhibit mutual recognition of multiple forms of mass violations of human rights. As André

Sibomana, the Rwandan priest and human rights activist, said, "Deaths don't compensate for each other; they don't cancel each other out; they simply add up."[2] My focus here is Rwanda, but the argument extends to other cases of genocide.

The Argument

The genocide in Rwanda was a singular, extraordinarily devastating, and in many ways incomprehensible episode of violence. The genocide was one of the most intense mass violations of human rights in the second half of the twentieth century. It was a horror that the world should have sought to prevent and stop, but did not. There were likely somewhere between 500,000 and as many as 800,000 civilian victims.[3] From April to July 1994, the main targets of government-sponsored violence were an identity category, Tutsis, and the violence was state-led, deliberate, systematic, and organized; the purpose was group destruction. The pain this violence caused, the depths to which human beings descended in perpetrating it, and the deforming legacies for survivors and their families are horrendous. I have absolutely no reservations calling the violence that took place "genocide."[4]

However, genocide against the resident Tutsi population of Rwanda and the related murderous violence against opponents of the genocidal government are not the only experiences of mass violence that Rwandans experienced in the 1994 period and through the 1990s, as the struggle for control of the Rwandan territory continued inside Rwanda and neighbouring Zaire (which became the Democratic Republic of Congo in 1997). As I detail in the next section, we can identify several periods of systematic and widespread violence against civilian populations, in addition to the main pattern of genocidal violence. Yet twenty-five years later, these other forms of violence, which, while less intense, less murderous, and not "genocide" (with one possible exception discussed below), remain largely invisible, except to specialists on the region and to dedicated opponents of the current government whose armed forces committed the crimes. The non-genocide crimes remain weakly documented in comparison to the genocide crimes, largely outside public discourse in Rwanda, and unvalidated by way of justice or official commemoration. Within Rwanda, to draw attention to these non-genocide crimes can be politically treacherous and physically dangerous. We are thus left with a severe disproportion in our accounts of past, mass violations of human rights.[5]

Finding careful language to name and frame these other crimes remains a challenge. In drawing attention to these other crimes, one approach has been to suggest that current accounts of the past are fundamentally wrong. Here the language that journalists, political opponents, and sometimes scholars use indicates that the truth is hidden and what we do know is a fabrication. A prominent example of this approach is found in the 2014 BBC documentary *Rwanda's Untold Story*.[6] The titular suggestion of an "untold story" casts doubt on what is already known. The film's opening sequences similarly call into question existing knowledge. "We think we know the story, but do we?" argues the film's journalist and narrator, Jane Corbin, right at the start of the documentary.[7] Her quote is followed directly by an academic who says that "what the world believes and what actually happened are quite different."[8]

The risk with this approach is that it throws the baby out with the bathwater: the approach foments doubt about the knowledge and documentation that has taken place since the genocide; it suggests that what we think we know is untrue. Throughout the documentary, Corbin and her interview subjects question "the truth" about Rwanda. In so doing, the film's editors provide air time to dissidents and critics but offer little space for counterpoints from observers who are critical of the government but nonetheless do not suggest that what we know about the current story is wrong.

One example is the way that the film treats the numbers killed in the genocide. The film mentions the government's claim that a million were killed, more than 90 per cent of whom were Tutsi. The film then provides significant prominence to a scholarly account of deaths in 1994 that claims that only 200,000 Tutsis and 800,000 Hutus were killed.[9] This estimate is a significant departure from most human rights and scholarly accounts. The film does not provide air time to these other serious accounts, in which I believe there is a consensus figure of something between 500,000 and 800,000 Tutsi deaths in the genocide.[10]

To be clear, my argument in this chapter is not that our understanding of the genocide is fundamentally flawed; rather, my contention is that we should also discuss, recognize, study, and account for the other, non-genocide crimes against Rwandans that took place in the 1990s. To be sure, there is much still to learn about the 1994 genocide, but I believe that the fundamental outlines of what happened are known and accurate.[11]

A different approach to drawing attention to the other crimes is to claim that a second "genocide" took place in 1994, one committed by the current ruling party, the Rwandan Patriotic Front (RPF); in this account, the RPF is said to have committed a genocide against Hutus. This approach has a long pedigree, in particular among the political opponents of the current government, especially those opposition figures living in exile.

In a recent book, the journalist Judi Rever has revived these arguments, claiming that the RPF committed a genocide against Hutus in 1994.[12] Rever consistently uses conspiratorial and sensationalistic language to advance her claims; she alleges a "conspiracy of silence" and describes being stalked by state agents across borders as she tries to tell the story of RPF crimes. For example, she writes that the RPF "fill[ed] up fields, swamps and rivers with blood"; she refers to "mass graves, death wagons, and open-air crematoriums."[13]

Most observers of Rwanda refer to this approach as the "double genocide" theory. The idea is that the Hutu-led state committed a genocide against Tutsis in Rwanda in 1994, as the RPF did against Hutus as they fought the civil war and secured power. The appeal of the idea of a "double genocide" has much to do with the power of the concept of genocide. Since "genocide" commands so much attention, one strategy for those who wish to draw attention to these other crimes is to deploy the label "genocide."

However, careful empirical inquiries into this question do not support the idea of a "double genocide."[14] I address the issue below, and similarly argue that "genocide" is not the right label for the crimes committed by the RPF against Hutu civilians in 1994 and 1995.

To reiterate – since these issues are controversial and positions are emotionally held, and I want to be as clear as possible – my purpose in this chapter is to find a way to acknowledge both the genocide committed against the minority Tutsi population, and the mass violence committed against the Hutu population. I seek to do so in a non-conspiratorial, non-sensationalist fashion. I aim not to sow doubt what we know about the genocide. While there are important debates and questions of historical interpretation that remain, I believe the core outlines of the genocide are known. The genocide's scale, intensity, and distinctiveness should be affirmed. But we should also find a way to acknowledge the other mass crimes that took place in this period. The non-genocide crimes deserve to be documented, acknowledged, discussed, studied, and accounted for; its victims should be recognized, and their experience of suffering respected. Further, in narrating the history of mass violence in the country, scholars should look for historical labels that capture the genocide but also acknowledge these other crimes – a task I take up below.

A Wider Lens

René Lemarchand has perceptively argued that Rwanda should be examined from a regional perspective.[15] Lemarchand's alternative approach has much to commend it. Decentred from Rwanda, a vision of the history of violence and atrocity in the region encompasses the successive atrocities in Burundi in 1972, 1988, 1993, and beyond. In 1972, the worst of these episodes, the minority Tutsi-led state orchestrated the destruction of some 200,000 educated and elite Hutu civilians, what Lemarchand has called "selective genocide" and what I have called "mass categorical violence" – large-scale, sustained, group-selective violence against civilians.[16]

The violence in the Democratic Republic of Congo in the 1960s, in the early 1990s, and then the wars of the late 1990s and 2000s left millions dead. The two wars from 1996–97 and from 1998–2004 took the lives of upwards of five million civilians, most of whom lost their lives from the collapse of the state and services in the east. There is also the violence in Uganda, which peaked under Milton Obote in the early 1980s, and that of Idi Amin before him.

Seen in the regional context of the Great Lakes, the Rwandan genocide of 1994 stands out a little less. This is not to deny its particularity or importance, but to recognize that the genocide in Rwanda is not the only episode of extraordinary mass violence in the region. The region is one with multiple episodes of mass violence that have taken place in the span of some four decades. The point is one way to contextualize the 1994 genocide. These other episodes deserve some sustained attention in any historical accounting of mass violence in the Great Lakes region of Africa; they also deserve attention on syllabi in genocide courses.

Lemarchand's overarching claim is that the causal dynamics are regionally interrelated. That is, what happens in Burundi shapes events in Rwanda, and vice versa, and what happens in Congo and Uganda influences what happens in Rwanda, and vice versa. That analysis may be applied to many regions of the world, from North Africa and the Middle East, to South Asia, to West Africa, and beyond. The causal relationships between episodes of violence and the causal mechanisms linking these episodes are less my concern here. Establishing causal processes is challenging; whether and how one episode of mass violence shapes another should be investigated carefully and empirically.

A narrower way to frame the genocide, one I take up here, is to consider it alongside other forms of Rwandan-on-Rwandan violence in the 1990s. Indeed, the genocide took place as part of a broader struggle for power. That struggle for power resulted in a series of interrelated armed conflicts, each with its own associated campaigns of violence against civilians. In other words, in addition to contextualizing the genocide in Rwanda by looking at regional dynamics, I propose an even narrower frame of looking at Rwandan-on-Rwandan violence in the 1990s.

The main macro-level context of the 1994 genocide was a political and military contest, one in which the existing ruling elite (President Juvénal Habyarimana, the entourage around him, and the leadership of his party) sought to keep power in the face of a political, primarily Hutu opposition, and an insurgent Tutsi-led military threat. In that brew and for a variety of reasons following Habyarimana's assassination on 6 April 1994, Rwanda's interim government orchestrated a war against the "Tutsi enemy," prompting an organized, systematic, participatory, and ruthlessly fast campaign of exterminatory violence against the civilian Tutsi population of Rwanda. The genocidal campaign also eliminated high-level political opposition figures, both Hutu and Tutsi, as well as those who aided Tutsis during the genocide.[17]

While the anti-Tutsi genocide was the most intense and murderous, it was not the only pattern of Rwandan-on-Rwandan violence in and around the struggle for power that engendered and followed the genocide. I observe four other major patterns of large-scale violence related to who would control the state in the 1990s. Francisco Guttiérrez-Sanín and Elisabeth Wood define a "pattern of violence" as a "relatively stable and recognizable configuration" of violence, including its repertoire, targeting, frequency, and technique."[18] I will focus in particular on the first two, which claimed the largest number of civilians lives.

RPF Violence against Hutus, 1990–95

First, there is the violence from 1990–95, perpetrated by the RPF and its supporters, primarily against Hutu civilians. This period of violence encompasses three distinct periods: during the civil war prior to the assassination of Habyarimana (1990 to early 1994), the genocide period (April to July 1994), and the period after the genocide when the RPF consolidated its power (August 1994 to mid–1995). I treat the three periods as a single constellation of violence, as they concern the period when the RPF was fighting for and establishing control of Rwandan territory.

The RPF attacked civilians in Rwanda in the first three-and-a-half years of the civil war (1990–94), primarily in the northern prefectures. Some one million Rwandans had fled the northern region by 1993. Their flight was due in part to the war fighting, but some early human rights reporting and RPF deserters indicate deliberate attacks against civilians by the RPF in order to depopulate the region of those presumed to oppose the rebel movement.

The human rights documentation is limited.[19] In *Leave None to Tell the Story* (the seminal Human Rights Watch investigation that documented the genocide crimes as well as some of the RPF crimes), Alison Des Forges cites Rwandan human rights organizations that indicate hundreds of civilians were killed during an RPF attack on the northern city of Ruhengeri in February 1993.[20] How many were killed and how geographically extensive this violence was remains poorly documented.

There is the related violence against Hutu civilians as the RPF advanced against the interim government during the genocide between April and July 1994. The violence here is better documented than the pre-1994 violations. In *Leave None to Tell the Story*, Des Forges alleges that the RPF "killed thousands" of civilians during the course of combat but also as the armed group established control.[21] Citing eyewitnesses, Des Forges describes three main patterns: where the RPF killed civilians who were intermixed with militia, where the RPF called meetings and subsequently massacred civilians, and summary executions of officials, priests, intellectuals, and suspected *génocidaires*.[22] Other human rights reports and scholarly accounts point to similar patterns.[23]

Des Forges estimates that the RPF is responsible for a minimum of 25,000 to 30,000 deaths between April and late July.[24] She finds that "these killings were widespread, systematic, and involved large numbers of participants and victims. They were too many and too much alike to have been unconnected crimes executed by individual soldiers or low-ranking officers. Given the disciplined nature of the RPF forces and the extent of communication up and down the hierarchy, commanders of this army must have known of and at least tolerated these practices."[25]

The most infamous report from the period is the so-called Gersony Report. Robert Gersony was a consultant contracted by the United Nations High Commissioner for Refugees. Alongside a team, he conducted an inquiry inside Rwanda (in 41 of 145 communes) and in refugee camps neighbouring countries to determine the prospects for an early return of Rwandan refugees who had fled the country following the genocide. After his team finished their reporting, Gersony briefed high-level officials at the United Nations who then met with Rwandan officials. According to Des Forges, who documents the process, UN officials agreed to keep the findings confidential, and the United States, which was backing the RPF in Rwanda, concurred.[26]

There is not an official report, to my knowledge. Des Forges describes the findings in detail; Gersony, according to her, concluded that the RPA committed systematic killings between April and August 1994. Gersony, she finds, estimated between 25,000 and 40,000 civilian deaths.[27] A summary of the findings released on the internet is consistent with the details that Des Forges describes.[28] In her recent book, Susan Thomson quotes a member of the Gersony investigating team similarly saying: "What we found was a well-organized military-style operation, with military command and control, and these were military-campaign-style mass murders."[29]

Several Rwandan authors have written about RPF crimes in this period.[30] Eugène Ndahayo writes of "vast massacres" committed by the RPF between 1990 and March 1994.[31] He also lists 18,000 civilians killed in his home prefecture of Gitarama between July and August 1994.[32] Léonard Nduwayo similarly documents massacres and selective killings committed by the RPF in his home commune of Giti.[33] RPF dissident Abdul Ruzibiza, while later recanting some of his book, also claimed deliberate operations of destabilization and killings in 1994.[34]

The RPF is also alleged to have committed massacres in Rwanda after August in 1994 and into 1995. The most well known of these massacres took place in Kibeho against Hutu refugee returnees in April 1995. In this case, several thousand Hutu civilians were killed.[35]

Journalist Stephen Smith, after reporting in Rwanda in 1996 for several weeks, concluded that the RPF was responsible for killing an estimated 150,000 Hutus between July 1994 and April 1995.[36] There are likely other accounts.

To summarize, however one categorizes this period – as one sweep of time from 1990 to 1995 or as three distinct periods within that five-year span – there is credible evidence that the RPF committed systematic and widespread violence against Hutu civilians during the war that preceded the genocide, during the genocide, and after the genocide. Judging from the existing accounts detailed here, I would estimate the number of civilians killed to be, conservatively, in the low tens of thousands, but the total could well reach or exceed 100,000 civilian deaths.

One reason that this mass violence is poorly documented is the lack of justice or accountability mechanisms for it. Even though there have been a few token trials of RPF soldiers, there is nothing in the way of any systematic effort to have justice, official recognition, or accountability for these crimes. This period falls under the jurisdiction of the International Criminal Tribunal for Rwanda, yet no United Nations justice process has taken place; within Rwanda, the *gacaca* process could have covered these crimes, but *gacaca* in practice focused almost exclusively on crimes against Tutsis.[37]

Is the violence against Hutus in this period genocide? While we have still much to learn about the logic of the RPF violence, based on current evidence, I would argue that the violence did not constitute genocide. In social science terms, I would categorize the killings as mass categorical violence: large-scale, repeated, and systematic violence that targets a specific civilian population group (Rwandan Hutus).[38] The hallmark of genocide (in my understanding) is a coordinated effort to *destroy* a specific population group. In this period in Rwanda, I do not see an effort to destroy the Rwandan Hutu population, but rather an organized effort to use mass violence to control and punish it. In legal terms, the violence constitutes crimes against humanity: widespread and systematic violence against civilians. Whatever label one affixes to the violence – and indeed future evidence could lead to different conclusions – many thousands of Hutus were killed, and that should be recognized, validated, accounted for, and memorialized.[39]

RPF *Violence against Hutus in the Democratic Republic of Congo, 1996–97*

The second major pattern of mass violence to consider is that which the RPF and its allies committed following the invasion of what was then Zaire (and became the Democratic Republic of Congo) starting in October 1996. There was extensive violence in the first and second wars in the country, including extensive violence against Congolese, including Congolese Tutsis. My focus here is on the violence Rwandans experienced, but that should not diminish the other patterns and experiences of violence.

After violently securing control of the string of refugee camps along the eastern part of Zaire, Rwandan military officers and troops directed home a large number of refugees. The numbers are uncertain, but the standard estimates are that between 500,000 and 700,000 Hutu refugees returned home, primarily in November and December 1996. But a large number of refugees fled westward, along with them some members of the rump Rwandan military (the ex-FAR), some *interahamwe*, and others associated with the government that orchestrated the 1994 genocide. As they fled westward, Rwandan Patriotic Army (RPA) military personnel alongside some Congolese rebel fighters systematically pursued the refugees and massacred them.

The number of Rwandan refugees killed is imprecise, but is likely in the tens, possibly the hundreds, of thousands.[40] Existing accounts detail repeated, organized massacres of Rwandan refugees. A United Nations mapping exercise elaborately documented the violence.[41] Jason Stearns and Filip Reyntjens have also described the pattern of violence.[42] In addition, there are some first-person accounts.[43]

In its final version, the United Nations mapping report explicitly addressed the question of genocide. The report itself documented more than a hundred incidents of attacks on Hutus inside the DRC in this period. Wrestling with the genocide question, the report found that:

> Several incidents listed in this report, if investigated and judicially proven, point to circumstances and facts from which a court could infer the intention to destroy the Hutu ethnic group in the DRC in part, if these were established beyond all reasonable doubt. The scale of the crimes and the large number of victims, probably several tens of thousands, all nationalities combined, are illustrated by the numerous incidents listed in the report (104 in all). The extensive use of edged weapons (primarily hammers) and the apparently systematic nature of the massacres of survivors after the camps had been taken suggests that the numerous deaths cannot be attributed to the hazards of war or seen as equating to collateral damage. The majority of the victims were children, women, elderly people and the sick, who were often undernourished and posed no threat to the attacking forces. Numerous serious attacks on the physical or mental integrity of members of the group were also committed, with a very high number of Hutus shot, raped, burnt or beaten. If proven, the incidents' revelation of what appears to be the systematic, methodological and premeditated nature of the attacks listed against the Hutus is also marked: these attacks took place in each location where refugees had allegedly been screened by the AFDL/APR over a vast area of the country. The pursuit lasted for months, and on occasion, the humanitarian assistance intended for them was allegedly deliberately blocked, particularly in the Orientale province, thus depriving them of resources essential to their survival. Thus the apparent systematic and widespread attacks described in this report reveal a number of inculpatory elements that, if proven before a competent court, could be characterized as crimes of genocide.[44]

However, the report also argues that countervailing evidence exists; in particular, the report finds that evidence of the "intent to destroy" the Hutu population as such is not definitive. The report notes, among other points, that there were large-scale repatriations.

In my view, of the four episodes of violence described in this essay, the sustained, large-scale violence against the Rwandan Hutu population in the Democratic Republic of Congo is the one that *could* warrant the label of "genocide." The logic of group destruction is the hallmark of genocide, and there is a case to be made that that logic animated the violence after the initial mass repatriations in 1996. Once the RPA and its Congolese allies started to pursue the refugees and other Hutus who fled westward after the repatriation, the dominant strategy was to massacre them. Thus, if one considers the 1997 period after the initial mass repatriation, I think a case for genocide is present.

Whether the label is appropriate or not, a very large number of Rwandans were killed in this period. Yet there has been, at the time of this writing, no justice process and the violence remains unrecognized in official commemorations inside Rwanda, to my knowledge.[45]

Counterinsurgency Violence in Rwanda in 1997 and 1998

There is also the violence that government forces committed in the northwest of Rwanda as part of a counterinsurgency campaign, primarily in 1997 and 1998. Following the repatriation of Rwandan refugees, an insurgency against the RPF-led state intensified in the northwestern part of the country. The state-led counterinsurgency campaign triggered disappearances, murders, population relocations, and other forms of violence and intimidation. While not all the violence was committed by the state's security forces – the insurgents also killed civilians – a good portion was. How many were killed during this period is likely in the hundreds to thousands.[46]

General Repression and Targeted Political Assassinations in Rwanda since 2000

Lastly, there is the general violence and repression that the RPF-led government has exercised since the movement took power. The violence here has the main purpose of intimidation and containing political challenges; political actors and civil society leaders have been assassinated or disappeared, both inside Rwanda and outside the country. The exact numbers remain uncertain. While there is some year-to-year variation, major international human rights organizations, such as Amnesty International and Human Rights Watch, have documented the authoritarian and repressive nature of the state since the mid-1990s.[47]

What to make of this macabre accounting? The main point is that the genocide the Hutu-led state committed against Tutsis in 1994 was not the only episode of large-scale, systematic violence against civilians that took place in 1994 and more generally around the struggle for power in the 1990s. There is much to learn about these other episodes of violence. Their documentation remains sparse, in part because of the absence of public trials or other forms of accountability, and research on them remains thin.

That said, we know enough to know that there was mass, horrific violence. That violence was a major experience for its victims and their families, and their experience should be acknowledged, validated, and memorialized at a minimum. Any accounting of Rwanda's history of violence in the 1990s should include these experiences. If Rwanda's history of violence in the 1990s is reduced only to the "genocide against the Tutsi" – as has now become the standard – then that construction omits large categories of experience and suffering.

In my experience, Rwandans know. They do not forget. If one meets someone who lost family members in 1994, in the mid-1990s, or the late 1990s, they know all too well what happened. They also know that if the RPF committed the crimes, they should not speak outwardly or too loudly about the violence that occurred, at least inside Rwanda.[48] But as outsiders we have a responsibility to speak, and to speak responsibly and carefully, about what many Rwandans fear saying. Speaking responsibly and carefully means not making sensationalist claims, not making conspiratorial claims, and not using language that could be construed to deny the genocide.[49] Our task, I believe, is not to reverse what we have learned about the genocide in 1994, but rather to add to it and to bring in other experiences to create a more balanced and accurate account of mass violence in the 1990s.

Justice and Memory through a Genocide Lens

In the contemporary world, it is now nearly an article of faith among policymakers and human rights advocates that transitional justice is a key ingredient in the aftermath of mass atrocity. Advocates for transitional justice propound many purposes, including the production of a historical record, providing a sense of recognition and possibly reparation to the victims, and deterrence through ending impunity and individualizing guilt. A common aphorism is that without justice there is or will be no peace. We can question the empirical reality of these claims –

we do not know whether truth and justice lead to reconciliation and peace, or whether threats of prosecution deter would-be perpetrators. A minimalist conception of transitional justice holds that it promotes accountability for past, significant violations of human rights. For the purposes of this chapter, I would submit that both the broader and narrower claims for transitional justice exhibit a sound logic; I take them at face value.

If one approaches Rwanda uniquely through the lens of genocide, it is possible to reach the conclusion that the justice and reconciliation efforts, on both the domestic and international levels, are commendable. At the domestic level, after starting a domestic court process, the government initiated the *gacaca* community courts. The result was a dramatic, country-wide effort, resulting in more than a million Rwandans being indicted. At the international level, the ICTR has issued some ninety-three indictments, which led to sixty-two sentences, fourteen acquittals, ten referrals to Rwanda, and a handful of outstanding cases. We can raise questions about each of these processes – *gacaca* was reckless in terms of the human rights of the accused, and the ICTR was inefficient, expensive, and remote. But if one thinks about the question of justice for genocide, in Rwanda and at the ICTR there was a great deal of it.

However, if one embraces the broader history of mass violence that I sketched out in the previous section, then a very different assessment presents itself. With that historical perspective in mind, the justice process in post-genocide Rwanda looks distinctly one-sided. As noted, the *gacaca* proceedings de facto excluded RPF crimes.[50] The ICTR at one point looked into human rights violations that the RPF committed, but no indictment was ever issued – in part because the RPF-led Rwandan state threatened to cut off state cooperation and victims' access to the ICTR. Faced with what would have looked like yet another embarrassing failure, the ICTR relented and focused only on government crimes as part of the genocide.[51]

The same is true for the state's official narrations of the past. The official commemorations of genocide, the national Kigali Genocide Memorial (KGM) in Gisozi, and the various activities sponsored by the National Unity and Reconciliation Commission do not recognize RPF violence against Hutu civilians, as far as I know. The KGM, a place for "remembrance and learning," focuses on the "Genocide against the Tutsi," as well as other genocides around the world, but there is silence on the experience of non-genocidal mass violence that the RPF and its supporters committed against Hutus.[52] Saying as much, after visiting Gisozi, landed political opposition leader Victoire Ingabire in jail in 2010.[53]

The disproportionate account of the past circulates well beyond Rwanda. Consider, for example, the 2019 statement by the United Nations secretary general António Gutteres on the twenty-fifth anniversary of the genocide. Marking the "Genocide against the Tutsi," as one of the "darkest chapters in human history," he expressed a wish to honour those murdered and the resilience of those who survived. He delineates the genocide in this way: "More than 800,000 people – overwhelmingly Tutsi, but also moderate Hutu and others who opposed the genocide – were systematically killed in less than three months." He goes on to implore the world to counter discrimination and hate speech and to encourage understanding, kindness, justice, and reconciliation.[54]

Such recognition is completely appropriate, and indeed the genocide was one of the darkest chapters of recent history. The UN secretary general should acknowledge it and should commit the world to fighting the forces that give rise to it. But there is silence on the episodes of mass violence detailed in the previous section. Why not acknowledge these other forms of mass atrocity and those who survived? To my knowledge, there is no official recognition within the United Nations system of systematic crimes against Hutu civilians during the 1990s period.

These forms of disproportionate recognition persist in scholarship and popular writing. To take one example, a team of scholars and a photographer produced a moving book of testimony of Rwandan women and one man who survived sexual violence in 1994, *The Men Who Killed Me: Rwandan Survivors of Sexual Violence*.[55] The narratives are raw and powerful, but here – as in many accounts – "survivor" means a survivor of the genocide committed against Tutsis.

Recognizing and commemorating the 1994 genocide does not have to be this way. Compare how the Global Centre for the Responsibility to Protect and Médecins sans frontières (MSF) marked the twenty-fifth anniversary. The former remarked how the genocide was a powerful reminder of the world's failure to stop mass atrocities and how the genocide in part spurred the doctrine. Framing its statement around the government's language of the "Genocide against the Tutsi" and condemning the fastest genocide in the twentieth century, the organization – which is committed to ending mass atrocities – made no mention of the RPF mass atrocities in Rwanda or in the Democratic Republic of Congo.[56]

By contrast, consider MSF's statement, which on the one hand described in moving detail the 1994 genocide and how MSF staff reacted. But the statement went further to describe the violence against refugees in the DRC. Referring to how refugees were "hunt[ed] down and slaughter[ed]," MSF estimates that some 200,000 died in 1996 and 1997.[57]

To summarize, there has been an abundance of justice, public recognition, and validation for the genocide crimes against Tutsis, but there is largely public silence – at least in Rwanda and in most of the writing and recognition outside Rwanda (with some exceptions, as noted) – around other experiences of mass violence against Rwandans from the same period.

This disproportionate rendering of the history of violence runs contrary to the ideals of transitional justice. On the question of truth and establishing a historical record, the justice and commemoration processes produce a very partial version of the past, one that omits whole categories of suffering. On the question of acknowledging victims and providing restitution, again only one category of (genocide) victims has received recognition. And on the question of ending impunity so as to break a cycle of violence, the lesson here is that the way to avoid accountability is not to refrain from committing atrocity crimes but rather to retain power.

The Politics of Justice and Memory and the Risks Therein

Perhaps it is not surprising that the Rwandan Patriotic Front government, which is led by and which holds dear the interests of Tutsi anglophone returned exiles – a double minority in the country – would not take punitive measures against its own. Perhaps it is also not surprising that after military victory the state would control the narrative and emphasize a narrative of Hutu perpetrators and Tutsi victims. And perhaps it is equally unsurprising that the ICTR – which, like other international criminal courts, depends on state cooperation – would abandon the idea of an RPF trial. But as scholars and other outsiders we should then recognize, as many Rwandans do, that justice and memorialization are, at least in Rwanda, inherently political. By political, I mean that the justice and memory processes serve the interests of those in power, and those in power exercise a strong hand in which stories get told and how.

At the macro level, the justice process has served the political interests of the ruling authorities in several ways. First, in general, the justice process has utterly defanged any political opposition that the RPF would face. Most of the high-ranking and mid-ranking political and administrative cadre associated with the two historic parties, the MDR and the MRND, have faced charges or prison.

Second, as Anu Chakravarty argues, the scale and scope of *gacaca* meant that many Hutu citizens continually faced the *threat* of indictment; they feared that at any time they could be charged with a crime of genocide, which had the effect of demobilizing potential opposition.[58]

Third, the justice process kept the focus on the atrocities of the Hutu authorities and the Hutu populations, thereby masking RPF crimes and reinforcing the idea that the current government stands as a bulwark against a society and political actors who are prone to committing genocide.

If the justice process is perceived as a political effort to entrench power through discrediting and demobilizing potential opposition, and if indeed the idea of genocide has served in other ways to defang potential opposition, then that presents a dangerous prospect for the country. Such an understanding risks undermining much of the work that has gone into documenting and memorializing the genocide. That is, a number of Rwandans will see the call to remember the genocide not primarily as an act to memorialize a past horror but rather as an effort to valorize one political actor while demonizing another.

There are other risks as well. The most obvious one is that the absence of public acknowledgment, justice, and reparation for the victims of the non-genocide crimes devalues their experience of suffering. Over time, and combined with the political instrumentalization of the memory of genocide, that exclusion likely will breed resentment and serve as an impediment to reconciliation broadly construed.[59] Why, a Rwandan might ask, is only one form of suffering important to recognize? Mutual recognition of past human rights crimes is critical for social repair.[60]

Though harder to document, I have heard in many conversations justifications for violence against Hutus. Those that were killed, so the argument goes, were *génocidaires* or supportive of them. The violence against them then becomes understandable and legitimate, in the eyes of those who voice this argument. I have heard such claims from diplomats, journalists, scholars, and RPF officials and supporters over the years.

For example, in defense of some of the 1994 violence against Hutu civilians in Rwanda, one often hears that the attacks were "revenge killings" that are understandable because RPF soldiers came back to Rwanda to find their families or Tutsis in general massacred. The soldiers found so many dead and did not know who did what, so they killed Hutu civilians. The idea that Rwandan Hutus who fled westward into Zaire (Democratic Republic of Congo) were committed to genocide and therefore deserved to be killed is also a claim one hears.[61] In essence, these arguments are justifications for mass human rights violations – which goes precisely against the spirit of ending the cycle of impunity.

Beyond these more Rwanda-oriented risks, approaching Rwandan history uniquely through a genocide lens tends to create a certain number of assumptions for outsiders. Such an approach favours a Manichean way of understanding history, that is, through a lens of perpetrators and victims. Moreover, such an approach can lead to assumptions about causality. The framing can lead to too strong an analogy with a potted, lay understanding of the Holocaust, which had some important differences with what happened in Rwanda. Those are not my focus here, but they are points worth considering.[62]

The Limits of a Genocide Lens

Why is the history of violence in Rwanda so disproportionate? I have argued that politics is one reason. The RPF, which has ruled Rwanda since its military victory in 1994, has instrumentalized the memory of the genocide, weaving its occurrence and their ending of it into the fabric of power and legitimacy of the post-genocide state. The RPF has many political incentives to tout the memory of genocide, to harness international guilt, to wield justice as a "legal lasso" by which to remove its main political opponents in the name of the rule of law, and to avoid justice and accountability for its own.[63] A Manichean history of violence serves RPF interests.

But the disproportion is so profound and so successful that there must be other sources. Some might credit the RPF's sophisticated information strategy.[64] Others might point to the "genocide credit," meaning that the international guilt in failing to stop genocide gives the RPF a wide margin for maneuver, a margin that the RPF has exploited.[65]

Coercion is also part of the story. The post-genocide political leaders and their supporters have invested heavily in a narrative of the period that emphasizes the "Genocide against the Tutsi." When politicians question that account or seek to broaden it, as did Ingabire, they can be arrested for genocide "denial." Scholars and journalists who offer critical accounts or wider accounts of history similarly can expect derision or charges of genocide denial. When ICTR investigators began to investigate RPF crimes, the RPF-led state suspended cooperation with the tribunal. When a draft of the UN mapping report on atrocities in the DRC suggested that genocide could have been committed, the state threatened to withdraw from all its peacekeeping operations.[66] A particular version of the past serves RPF interests, and the RPF has skillfully and at times coercively acted to make sure the past is told in a particular way.

Lars Waldorf and I found ourselves at the centre of an intimidation effort when we published the edited volume *Remaking Rwanda: State*

Building and Human Rights after Mass Violence in 2011.[67] The book is a collection of essays on post-genocide Rwanda, a volume that drew attention to a number of problems in the country and that emphasized the state's authoritarian nature. Shortly after its appearance, news articles that sometimes personally attacked contributors to the book appeared in the government-sympathetic newspaper, *The New Times*; there also was a website created to attack the book.[68] More consequential, in 2016, the Rwandan Commission for Fighting against the Genocide published a list of "foreigners taking the lead in denying the genocide." Lars and I – as well as other scholars, journalists, politicians, and lawyers – were on that list.[69]

As noted earlier, I have never denied that genocide took place in Rwanda in 1994; indeed, a good part of my career has been devoted to studying the genocide in Rwanda. Yet genocide denial is a crime in Rwanda, and thus this denunciation has to be taken seriously – even if it is a transparent effort to intimidate critics and to silence criticism.

Still, I want to return to the puzzle. The RPF's heavy-handed strategy is not surprising; what is surprising is how successful that strategy has been.

I suspect that at least part of the reason lies in the concept of genocide, and, as scholars of genocide, we should consider the unintended effects of our anchoring concept.

Sitting atop a hierarchy of crimes and drawing immediate analogies to the Holocaust, the concept of genocide evokes a unique kind of horror. Genocide enjoys a status as the "crime of crimes" or as the "ultimate crime."[70] And the Holocaust, perhaps more than any other event in the past century, represents the pinnacle of evil.

The power of the word demands that observers give genocide a particular kind of recognition, a special status where it stands alone and apart from other kinds of crimes of mass violence. That power is one reason why so many actors want to fit disparate patterns of action into a genocide frame.[71]

I agree genocide is a particularly heinous crime, one deserving of special attention. The violent, brutal, furious, and cynical attempt to destroy a group – the very idea of population extermination – is a distinctive and exceptionally pernicious form of violence. Genocide should not be equated with other mass crimes.

But an effect of highlighting genocide can be to blot out other experiences, to make them secondary and less worthy of sustained attention, documentation, justice, and reparation. Genocide's special status, in other words, implies incomparability and untouchability, which in turn renders marginal or even invisible other forms of mass violence. It's as if one cannot say in a single breath, "There was a state-led genocide of Tutsis and extensive RPF crimes against humanity against Hutus." Doing so invites the charge of making "equivalences," relativizing or even denying the genocide, and insulting the memory of the genocide victims. If genocide is so absolute then to speak of related non-genocide crimes becomes tantamount to denialism, and, even worse, if genocide is so absolute then other crimes become justifiable in the name of stopping genocide or preventing new ones.[72]

We are left then with a polarized and polarizing history, one that at a minimum does not serve Rwanda well: either a hugely lopsided and Manichean account of the past that marginalizes non-genocide experiences, or a sensationalizing skepticism about the genocide aimed at bringing recognition to the marginalized crimes.

These effects of genocide on the public (non-political) conversation on the history of violence may not be intentional. They are, I suspect, unintended consequences of the power and evocative connotations of the concept.

Historiographical Assumptions

Seeing Rwanda strictly through a genocide lens has a tendency to create other lacunae. One tendency is to frame Rwandan history tendentiously and teleologically as a story that culminates in genocide. In this instance, genocide is such a powerful and unique endpoint that history becomes backdated to affirm how that endpoint came to be. That is, first colonialism, then the revolution, then the first and second republics were all part of a broad historical sequence whose consummation was the genocide. Similarly, Rwandan history gets told through the eyes of two main historical actors, the "bad" Hutus and the "good" Tutsi victims. Lastly, Rwandan history becomes a normative account, as a history where the observer is led to condemn one set of actors and champion another. In my experience, these are unstated assumptions but ones that flow from seeing Rwanda through a genocide lens.

Perhaps the point is obvious, but Rwanda's long term and near term (as it relates to the genocide) is considerably more complex than a Manichean, teleological account would suggest. Yes, the Germans and Belgians had their impacts, and yes, the racialization of identities and the colonial institutions had implications for how politics played out later in the twentieth century. But Rwanda's pre-colonial period had its effects too. Yes, the Hutu Social Revolution created a racial dichotomy at the heart of Hutu nationalism, and that framing was clearly essential to how genocide came about, as I have argued.[73] But the Hutu revolutionaries acted in response to Tutsi monarchical actions and in a context in which they were not the sole political actors. The list goes on, and crucially it extends to the pre-genocide period in which the RPF actions were important to the overall evolution of events in the country.

Telling Rwandan history through the experience of genocide also reinforces stereotypes and reinforces the idea that ethnic groups act uniformly. In discussions of Rwanda, one often hears of "moderate Hutus," a distinction that implies that Hutus are not by nature moderates. Seeing Rwanda in this way in fact underplays the complex political and social dynamics *among* Hutus that took place before, and also during, the genocide in 1994. A genocide framework does not require these assumptions, but time and again I have seen how such assumptions follow from seeing Rwanda through the lens of genocide.

A final concern with seeing Rwanda through a genocide framework is that it encourages simplistic analogies with the Holocaust. Like Rwanda, the Holocaust was an exceptionally complex event, and the historiography is now deep and full. But in invoking Rwanda through the lens of genocide, some observers suggest that Rwanda happened in ways that are very similar to a cursory understanding of the Holocaust. Hutu political leaders are vilified as Nazis; Rwandan Hutu nationalism is seen as a form of fascism; massacres in Rwanda before 1994 are seen as akin to Kristallnacht; the *interahamwe* are analogized to the SS; and so on.

But Rwanda was different from the Holocaust. I believe in the value of comparison, including in the context of genocide, but I also worry about how comparison can shut down inquiry on Rwanda (and on other genocides), such that observers presume that what happened in Rwanda must be like their understanding of what happened in the Holocaust. Writing several years ago, the eminent scholars of Rwanda, Catharine Newbury and David Newbury, expressed some frustration with the analogy:

> For conditions in Europe of the 1930s to be seen as parallel to those of Rwanda in the 1990s, the following scenario would have had to have occurred: Germany would have to have been ruled by an exclusive Jewish minority for several hundred years; that Jewish minority would have been overthrown 30 years before the Holocaust and throughout that time maneuvered to regain power. France [Burundi in this analogy] would have to have been ruled by a Jewish military government which had killed off some 2 million non-Jews (the figures are adjusted to account for the

> larger size of the French population compared to that of Burundi). Months before the Holocaust, France would have to have witnessed the assassination of a popular, freely elected president (the first non-Jewish leader of the country ever) by a Jewish-dominated army, after which hundreds of thousands of non-Jews would have fled from France to Germany to escape the violence following this assassination. Finally, Germany would have to have been attacked by a Jewish army which subsequently seized some of the most productive areas of the country and drove out some 6–7 million people from the occupied zones (comparable to the one million people who fled from northern Rwanda in the face of RPF attacks in the early 1990s). Absent of such political developments, drawing direct parallels between Rwanda of the 1990s and Germany in the years leading to the Holocaust is problematic. And thus, omitting or eliding Rwandan history in accounting for the particular circumstances of the genocide provides a misleading similarity and a false understanding.[74]

The points here are well taken. The Newburys emphasize the impact of Burundi on developments in Rwanda, as well as the actions of the RPF. They also could make the point about the aftermath of Rwanda. The situations in post-genocide Germany (and Israel) are importantly different from post-genocide Rwanda.

The focus of this chapter is the Rwandan-on-Rwandan violence. The Holocaust analogy might set up a kind of retort to focusing on violence against Hutus that goes along these lines: "Imagine if the firebombings at Dresden were equated with the Holocaust."[75] The Newburys' caution here is again well suited. The Holocaust analogy can limit and distort discussion, as much as it can draw attention to cases of genocide in other parts of the world.

Possible Alternative Rubrics

In the policy world, a sharp move away from a unique focus on genocide has been in evidence in the past fifteen years, from the Responsibility to Protect doctrine to the US government's Atrocity Prevention Board. The terms of reference have become "mass atrocities" and "atrocity crimes."[76] The move was largely taken for practical reasons: a focus on genocide meant that policy efforts to prevent or mitigate such violence happened late in the process (because of the emphasis on showing intent to destroy) and because genocide legally excluded certain categories of targeted groups and did not cover certain kinds of mass violence. Similarly, the mandate of the International Criminal Court encompasses not only genocide, but also crimes against humanity and war crimes.

The government in Rwanda has successfully resisted this shift to mass atrocities. Rather than broaden the discussion of the past to mass atrocities, the government has moved in the other direction. It has promoted and largely gained international acceptance for the concept of the "Genocide against the Tutsi." The recent anniversary was a reminder of how hegemonic this concept of "Genocide against the Tutsi" has become.

As observers of Rwanda, I have argued that we should look for ways to convey the history of violence that clearly affirm the genocide *and* that create space to recognize other experiences of mass violence. Omitting or marginalizing the non-genocide crimes have had the effect of largely excluding the experience of the non-Tutsi population of Rwanda from public and political discussions of violence, memory, justice, and reparation. In the long run, I fear this disproportion of memory will not serve Rwanda well.

One place to start is with labels. Labels are important. What alternatives exist? The Rwandan "crisis" or "conflict" are possibilities, but they are nondescript. In my experience, Rwandans often speak of the "war," but that displaces some of the specificity of widespread and systematic violence against civilians that should be in focus. One could reference the Rwandan "mass crimes," "mass violence," "mass atrocities," or "crimes against humanity." Critics might counter that such labels do not give enough specificity to the crime of genocide that took place.

In line with my argument here, I would put forth a label that affirms the genocide and references other experiences of mass violence. In a recent book on the experience of Médecins sans frontières Rwandan staff and projects, Jean-Hervé Bradol and Marc Le Pape refer to "genocide and mass killings" in their title.[77] Another alternative would be the "Rwandan Genocide and Crimes against Humanity." Or if the state's preferred label is used: "The Genocide against the Tutsi and the Crimes against Humanity against the Hutu." Each of these labels has limitations, but each at least conveys the idea that there were other experiences of mass violence besides the genocide in the same period.

Some might counter that the "Rwandan genocide" is so ubiquitous that changing the label is unlikely. Even so, terminology can change and evolve over time. Either the "Rwandan genocide" should be qualified along the lines suggested above or it should explicitly reference a period in which the other mass violations of human rights that took place in the same period are explicitly acknowledged.

Beyond labels, better documentation of the non-genocide crimes is also in order. There are, appropriately, dozens and dozens of scholarly books written about the 1994 genocide. But to my knowledge, there is not a careful, scholarly account that focuses attention on the drivers and dynamics of the RPF violence, either in Rwanda or in the DRC. There are some accounts from survivors of this violence, from former RPF soldiers, from journalists, and from human rights organizations. I have tried to cite them in this article. These are valuable, but the scholarly deficit is glaring.

Part of that deficit is due to the conditions of possibility for research. A scholar would have a difficult time conducting research on RPF crimes in Rwanda. Moreover, the absence of public criminal justice for the RPF crimes has meant that the legal record is negligible. The continuing opposition by the RPF government is likely to make a future justice process unlikely, at least while the existing power configuration works. Could a truth commission be possible in the future, one that at least documented and even validated these other crimes? That remains a question worth asking.

Additional Implications

There are some additional implications to the analysis for scholars of genocide who might be less focused on Rwanda per se.

The first, as I have argued, is the unintended consequences of affixing the term "genocide" to a period of history. The "genocide" label is a powerful, evocative one. In the Rwandan case, human rights activists, lawyers and judges, and scholars (including myself) have laboured to show that the state-orchestrated violence against Tutsis in Rwanda was "genocide." Yet the downside of such a term is that it comes, or has come in the Rwandan case – with the deliberate help of the state – to *define* a period of history. For the government, the term has instrumental uses, but the rest of us should be cognizant of how the term has the power to eclipse other relevant experiences of violence, even while bringing necessary attention to the genocide itself.

Among scholars of genocide, a dominant question often boils down to: "Is it genocide or not?" Yet such a focus can perhaps unwittingly reinforce the idea that other forms of mass violence do not deserve sustained recognition and scholarly attention, and that in turn dovetails with how histories of violence get told. How can we study and insist on the specificity of genocide while not diminishing the importance of studying other forms of mass violence?

The second implication is how ripe for instrumental manipulation this powerful term is. To invoke genocide has proven in Rwanda's case to be an effective tool in a state's hands. Rwanda contrasts arguably with other canonical cases, such as the Armenian genocide or the Holocaust, where those who lobbied for the term and who later brandished it did not hold power (at least not in Turkey or in Germany). Yet the lesson here is that the concept of genocide is often bound up with politics and power, and that at least deserves some critical reflection from scholars who work on genocide.

Lastly, the silence around the non-genocide crimes has left a vacuum that has been filled by a sensationalist and conspiratorial narrative field that reinforces denialism. Some who wish to draw attention to these non-genocide crimes use language that suggests that what we know about and what has been documented about the genocide is wrong. They also sometimes claim a second or "double genocide" against the Hutus inside Rwanda. They invoke plots and state conspiracies that keep these other stories outside of public discussion. While elements of this counter-narrative are true, in unscrupulous hands the idea of "everything we know is wrong" can encourage or reinforce the idea that the genocide itself is a fabrication of the RPF government and its supporters.

The challenge, I have argued, is to find a way to affirm the genocide that took place, but also to draw attention to the other forms of mass violence that took place in the same struggle for power in Rwanda in the 1990s.

NOTES

1 I would like to thank Andrea Graziosi, Bert Ingelaere, Omar McDoom, Dirk Moses, and Lars Waldorf for comments on earlier drafts. This paper is a revised version of an article published in the *Journal of Genocide Research* under the title, "The Limits of a Genocide Lens: Violence against Rwandans in the 1990s." I presented earlier versions of this work at Monash University, the University of Toronto, Hôtel de Lauzun in Paris, and the Centre for African Studies at the University of Cape Town (UCT); I received helpful comments during each presentation, especially so at UCT. There I was encouraged, rightfully, to address my positionality. Indeed, while I am not Rwandan, I care deeply about Rwanda. I believe outsiders have responsibility in discussing the country. External actors' responsibility dates to the colonial process, extends to the first and second Republics in Rwanda, and to the genocide itself; while these topics are beyond my focus here, external actors shaped Rwanda's history of violence in a variety of direct and indirect ways. Since the genocide,

policymakers, scholars (including myself), lawyers, and memorial professionals have contributed to a narrative field that has elevated the genocide crimes while providing limited visibility to other mass crimes. That is my focus in this chapter. In it, I want to challenge the narrative field that outsiders have helped to construct. As I discuss in the body, I also feel a responsibility to speak out about experiences of mass violence that remain outside the public commemoration and justice processes in Rwanda. Many Rwandans have told me over the years about their experiences or their families' experiences of victimization. Drawing attention to these other crimes can be dangerous for Rwandans living in Rwanda, and thus outsiders, I believe, have some responsibility to bring out what Rwandans have conveyed to them. In this essay, I try to develop a narrative and argument that clearly affirms the genocide crimes but also calls for recognition of non-genocide crimes. I thank Gertrude Fester and Senzeni Ncube for raising this question.

2 André Sibomana, *Hope for Rwanda: Conversations with Laure Guilbert and Hervé Deguine*, trans. Carina Tertsakian (London: Pluto Press, 1999), 117.

3 The number of Tutsi civilian victims in the genocide remains contested. The current government claims that about 1 million Rwandans died in the genocide, more than 90 per cent of whom were Tutsis. I am persuaded that around 75 per cent of the resident Tutsi population was killed in 1994, amounting to between 500,000 and 800,000 Tutsi civilian deaths. That range is a function of how many Tutsis lived in the country prior to April 1994. I discuss the estimate in Scott Straus, *Making and Unmaking Nations: War, Leadership, and Genocide in Modern Africa* (Ithaca, NY: Cornell University Press, 2015), 311–12. My estimate is based on the work of Alison Des Forges, Marijke Verpoorten, and the dictionary of names that the Rwandan survivor organization, Ibuka, put together for Kibuye Prefecture. I discuss these estimates further in note 10.

4 As I discuss later, my criticism of state policy has led some Rwandan officials to label me (and other colleagues) a foreign scholar who denies the genocide. I do not deny, and never have denied, that genocide took place in Rwanda in 1994. My main book on the subject uses the word "genocide" in the title, and the book seeks to explain the dynamics of mobilization and perpetration in the genocide. See Scott Straus, *The Order of Genocide: Race, Power, and War in Rwanda* (Ithaca, NY: Cornell University Press, 2006).

5 I prefer the concept of memory "disproportion" to memory "imbalance." I am arguing here for recognition and attention to the mass violence committed against Hutu populations in the 1990 to 1999 period. I am not arguing that that violence was equivalent to or should balance out the genocide crimes. These other crimes should be recognized in a way that was proportionate to their severity.

6 The film can be accessed here: https://www.bbc.co.uk/programmes/b04kk03t. The idea of a "hidden" or "secret" history occurs elsewhere. See, for example, Abdul Ruzibiza, *Rwanda: L'histoire secrète* (Paris: Editions du Panama, 2005).

7 Corbin introduces the film in this way at 00:20 in the film.

8 The scholar's statement is edited to appear at 00:22.

9 The film quotes Allan Stam as saying that if a million Rwandans died, then, by the estimates he and scholar Christian Davenport have developed, 200,000 Tutsis died compared to 800,000 Hutus; the claim is found at 31:12 in the film.

10 Per note 3, in her seminal book on the genocide, which remains one of the most important, Alison Des Forges estimates that about 500,000 Tutsis were killed while tens of thousands of Hutus were killed in 1994. See Alison Des Forges, *Leave None to Tell the Story: Genocide in Rwanda* (New York: Human Rights Watch, 1999). In a very detailed analysis of Gikongoro Prefecture, using sector-level data, Marijke Verpoorten estimates between 600,000 to 800,000 Tutsi deaths in the genocide: Marijke Verpoorten, "The Death Toll of the Rwandan Genocide: A Detailed Analysis for Gikongoro Province," *Population* 60, no. 4 (2005): 331–67. Both authors estimate that about 75 per cent of the Tutsi population was killed during the genocide, which is a number that corresponds to detailed data from Kibuye Prefecture by Ibuka (see Straus, *The Order of Genocide*). Gérard Prunier also estimates 800,000 killed in *The Rwanda Crisis: History of a Genocide* (London: Hurst, 1998). In a more recent study, Omar McDoom estimates between 475,000 and 531,000 Tutsis killed in the genocide: Omar McDoom, *Why We Killed: Security, Opportunity, and Authority in Rwanda's Genocide* (Cambridge University Press, forthcoming).

11 For English-language research on the genocide, I would point to Des Forges, *Leave None*; André Guichaoua, *From War to Genocide: Criminal Politics in Rwanda*, trans. Don Webster (Madison: University of Wisconsin Press, 2017); Lee Ann Fujii, *Killing Neighbors: Webs of Violence in Rwanda* (Ithaca, NY: Cornell University Press, 2009); Jean-Paul Kimonyo, *Rwanda's Popular Genocide: A Perfect Storm*, trans. Wandia Njoya (Boulder, CO: Lynne Rienner Publishers, 2016); Timothy Longman, *Christianity and Genocide in Rwanda* (New York: Cambridge University Press, 2009); McDoom, *Why We Killed*; Hollie Nyseth-Brehm, "Subnational Determinants of Killing in Rwanda," *Criminology* 55, no. 1 (2017): 5–31. Some decisions at the United Nations International Criminal Tribunal for Rwanda are also a good source, in particular the s for the Military I and MRND trials. There are also a number of important memoirs written by survivors, such as Tharcisse Seminega, *No Greater Love: How My Family Survived the Genocide in Rwanda* (GM&A Publishing, 2019). I also have written on the genocide in *The Order of Genocide* and *Making and Unmaking Nations*.

12 Judi Rever, *In Praise of Blood: The Crimes of the Rwandan Patriotic Front* (Toronto: Random House, 2018).

13 Rever, *In Praise*, 200. She claims the RPF committed genocide on page 232. She also alleges that Hutus in RPF-controlled areas faced risks of "annihilation" (229).

14 Philip Verwimp, "Testing the Double-Genocide Thesis for Central and Southern Rwanda," *Journal of Conflict Resolution* 47, no. 4 (2003): 423–42. As I discuss below, Des Forges in her seminal book, while discussing RPF violence against Hutus, does not invoke the idea of a "double genocide." See also Bert Ingelaere, whose careful observations of and around *gacaca* proceedings affirmed evidence of genocide crimes against Tutsis and crimes against humanity against Hutus. His conclusions similarly refute the idea of a double genocide. See Bert Ingelaere, "Hidden Death: Rwandan Post-Genocide Gacaca Justice and Its Dangerous Blind Spots," in *Genocide, Risk and Resilience: An Interdisciplinary Approach*, edited by Bert Ingelaere, Stephan Parmentier, Jacques Haers, and Barbara Segaert (Basingstoke: PalgraveMacmillan, 2013), 212–30.

15 René Lemarchard, *The Dynamics of Violence in Central Africa* (Philadelphia: University of Pennsylvania Press, 2009).

16 I view genocide as a subset of mass categorical violence; see Straus, *Making and Unmaking Nations.*

17 This summary is based on the sources in note 11.

18 Francisco Gutiérrez-Sanín and Elisabeth Wood, "What Should We Mean by 'Pattern of Political Violence'? Repertoire, Targeting, Frequency, and Technique," *Perspectives on Politics* 15, no. 1 (2017): 21.

19 The pre-1994 human rights reports have some, but minimal, information on RPF crimes in this period, due in part to restrictions that the RPF placed on the human rights investigators' movements; see FIDH, "Rwanda: Violations massives et systematiques des droits de l'homme depuis le 1er Octobre 1990," available at https://www.fidh.org/fr/regions/afrique/rwanda/14463-rwanda-violations-massives-et-systematiques-des-droits-de-l-homme-depuis. See also Des Forges, *Leave None*, 540.

20 Des Forges, *Leave None*, 540.

21 Ibid.

22 Ibid, 541–51.

23 See Amnesty International, "Rwanda: Reports of Killings and Abduction by the Rwandese Patriotic Army, April–August 1994," 14 October 1994, AFR 47/16/94. In that report, the human rights organization describes summary executions, revenge killings, and massacres at called meetings. See also the sources quoted in Filip Reyntjens, *Political Governance in Post-Genocide Rwanda* (New York: Cambridge University Press, 2013), 99–109.

24 Des Forges, *Leave None*, 558.
25 Ibid.
26 Ibid, 555.
27 Ibid., 555–6.
28 The document appears to be a summary of a presentation that Gersony gave to the UNHCR. The document in question, entitled "Summary of UNHCR Presentation before Commission of Experts 10 October 1994," is available here: http://rwandinfo.com/documents/Gersony_Report.pdf, accessed 6 May 2019.
29 See Susan Thomson, *Rwanda: From Genocide to Precarious Peace* (New Haven, CT: Yale University Press, 2018), 86.
30 Sibomana concluded that "the RPF killed a lot of people when it took over the country; no one can deny that. Innocent people died in revenge killings. But so did guilty people." *Hope for Rwanda*, 108.
31 Eugène Ndahayo, *Rwanda: le dessous des cartes* (Paris: L'Harmattan, 2000), 112.
32 Ibid, 118.
33 Leonard Nduwayo, *Giti et le genocide rwandais* (Paris: L'Harmattan, 2002).
34 Ruzibiza, *L'histoire secrete*. Judi Rever's book also relies heavily on interviews with RPF dissidents to advance the book's claims.
35 There is a thorough discussion in Thomson, *Rwanda*, 87–94. See also Terry Pickard, *Combat Medic: An Australian's Eyewitness Account of the Kibeho Massacre* (Wavell Heights, QLD: Big Sky Publishing, 2008).
36 He recounts his analysis and experience in Stephen W. Smith, "Rwanda in Six Scenes," *London Review of Books* 33, no. 6 (2011): 3–8.
37 On the ICTR, see note 49. On *gacaca*, see especially Ingelaere, "Hidden Death," which deals explicitly with this issue of how RPF crimes were not discussed in the community courts. More generally, for a thorough discussion of how *gacaca* worked in practice, see Bert Ingelaere, *Inside Rwanda's Gacaca Courts: Seeking Justice after Genocide* (Madison: University of Wisconsin Press, 2016).
38 I prefer this term to the distinction that Stathis Kalyvas makes between selective and indiscriminate violence in his book *The Logic of Violence in Civil War* (New York: Cambridge University Press, 2006). In his framing, indiscriminate violence is large-scale but not selective. I argue that mass categorical violence is large-scale *and* group-selective. I detail this argument in Straus, *Making and Unmaking*, chapter 1. Judging from current evidence, I conclude that while some of the RPF violence against Hutus in Rwanda was individually selective (specific politicians, priests, civil society leaders, soldiers, and some suspected killers were targeted), most of the time the violence appears to have targeted Hutus en masse. Civilians were killed on a large scale because of their ethnic

categorization. In this sense, the violence was "group-selective," rather than indiscriminate or individually selective.

39 There is also evidence of intra-Hutu violence and score-settling before and during the genocide in 1994, which I do not address here. Judging from existing accounts and my own research in Rwanda, my understanding is that, while such violence existed in different communities, the violence was not widespread or systematic; its scale was much less than the genocide crimes or the RPF violence against Hutu civilians. The extent of such violence during the democratization period and the genocide period is worth further study and inquiry.

40 Jason Stearns discusses the problems with estimates of the number of Rwandan refugees killed and missing. He concludes that "tens of thousands were killed, while more probably died from disease and starvation as they were forced into the inhospitable jungles." See Jason Stearns, *Dancing in the Glory of Monsters: The Collapse of the Congo and the Great War of Africa* (New York: PublicAffairs, 2012), 135–8. By contrast, Kisangani Emizet estimates 230,000 killed; see "The Massacre of Refugees in Congo: A Case of UN Peacekeeping Failure and International Law," *Journal of Modern African Studies* 38, no. 2 (2000): 163–202. Filip Reyntjens also cites the acting United Nations High Commissioner for Human Rights who estimates that 200,000 Hutus could have been killed: Filip Reyntjens, "Waging (Civil) War Abroad: Rwanda and the DRC," in *Remaking Rwanda: State Building and Human Rights after Mass Violence*, edited by Scott Straus and Lars Waldorf (Madison: University of Wisconsin Press, 2011), 132–51.

41 United Nations High Commissioner for Human Rights, "Democratic Republic of Congo, 1993–2003: Report of the Mapping Exercise Documenting the Most Serious Violations of Human Rights and International Humanitarian Law Committed within the Territory of the Democratic Republic of the Congo between March 1993 and June 2003," Geneva, 2010. This is an extensive report that deals not only with the massacres committed against Rwandans but also against Congolese.

42 See Reyntjens, *Political Governance*, 110–15; Stearns, *Dancing in the Glory of Monsters*.

43 For example, Marie Béatrice Umutesi, *Surviving the Slaughter: The Ordeal of a Rwandan Refugee in Zaire*, trans. Julia Emerson (Madison: University of Wisconsin Press, 2004).

44 UNHCHR, "Democratic Republic of Congo," 13–14.

45 On the absence of justice, see Jason Stearns and Frederico Borello, "Bad Karma: Accountability for RPF Crimes in the Congo," in *Remaking Rwanda*, edited by Straus and Waldorf, 152–71.

46 Amnesty International has the best human rights documentation of this period, to my knowledge: Amnesty International reports "Rwanda: Ending the Silence," 25 September 1997, AI Index AFR 47/32/97; "Rwanda: Civilians Trapped in Armed Conflict," 19 December 1997, AI Index AFR 47/43/97; and "Rwanda: The Hidden Violence: Disappearances and Killings Continue," 23 June 1998, AI Index: AFR 47/23/98. See also Filip Reyntjens, *Political Governance*, 115–19. In a careful analysis of "excess mortality," Marike Verpoorten finds that there was particularly high excess mortality in Gisenyi prefecture in the northwest, which she attributes to the effects of the counter-insurgency campaign and the flow of refugees. See Marijke Verpoorten, "Detecting Hidden Violence: The Spatial Distribution of Excess Mortality in Rwanda," *Political Geography* 31 (2012): 44–56.

47 For a good overview of Rwanda's post-genocide state, see Timothy Longman, *Justice and Memory in Post-Genocide Rwanda* (New York: Cambridge University Press, 2017) and Thomson, *Rwanda*. For an overview of human rights reporting, see Human Rights Watch testimony to the United States House of Representatives, https://www.hrw.org/news/2015/05/20/human-rights-watch-testimony-house-foreign-affairs-subcommittee-hearing-developments. On targeted assassinations outside the country, see Human Rights Watch, "Rwanda: Repression across Borders," 28 January 2014, available at https://www.hrw.org/news/2014/01/28/rwanda-repression-across-borders.

48 This is captured well in Ingelaere, "Hidden Death."

49 As suggested earlier, I consider the BBC's "Untold Story" documentary irresponsible. The documentary brought into focus some of the RPF crimes, but it then proceeded to question everything we knew, including the idea that there were more Tutsi victims than Hutu ones during the 1994 genocide period itself. Judi Rever's book *In Praise of Blood* is also irresponsible. As noted, she charges a second "genocide" against Hutus in Rwanda. Her title is unnecessarily provocative, her tone breathless and conspiratorial.

50 Ingelaere, "Hidden Death."

51 On the ICTR, see Thierry Cruvellier, *Court of Remorse: Inside the International Criminal Tribunal for Rwanda*, trans. Chari Voss (Madison: University of Wisconsin, 2010); Leslie Haskell and Lars Waldorf, "The Impunity Gap of the International Criminal Tribunal for Rwanda: Causes and Consequences," *Hastings International and Comparative Law Review* 34, no. 1 (2011): 49–85; Sara Kendal and Sarah M.H. Nouwen, "Speaking of Legacy: Toward an Ethos of Modesty at the International Criminal Tribunal for Rwanda," *The American Journal of International Law* 110, no. 2 (2016): 212–32; Victor Peskin, *International Justice in Rwanda and in the Balkans: Virtual Trials and the Struggle for State Cooperation* (New York: Cambridge University Press, 2008); Victor Peskin,

"Victor's Justice Revisited: Rwandan Patriotic Front Crimes and the Prosecutorial Endgame at the ICTR," in *State Building and Human Rights after Mass Violence*, edited by Scott Straus and Lars Waldorf (Madison: University of Wisconsin Press, 2011), 173–83; and Lars Waldorf, "'A Mere Pretense of Justice': Complementarity, Sham Trials, and Victor's Justice at the Rwanda Tribunal," *Fordham International Law Journal* 33, no. 4 (2011): 1221–77.

52 Kigali Genocide Memorial, https://www.kgm.rw/memorial/exhibitions.

53 She said: "If we look at this memorial, it only refers to the people who died during the genocide against the Tutsis. There is another untold story with regard to the crimes against humanity committed against the Hutus. The Hutus who lost their loved ones are also suffering; they think about the loved ones who perished and are wondering, 'When will our dead ones also be remembered?'" See Chris McGreal, "Is Kagame Africa's Lincoln or a Tyrant Exploiting Rwanda's Tragic History?" *The Guardian*, 19 May 2013.

54 "Secretary-General, Marking Twenty-Fifth Anniversary of Genocide against Tutsi in Rwanda, Urges Leaders to Reject Hate Speech, Discrimination," https://www.un.org/press/en/2019/sgsm19523.doc.htm, 29 March 2019.

55 Anne-Marie de Brouwer and Sandra Ka Hon Chu, eds., *The Men Who Killed Me: Rwandan Survivors of Sexual Violence* (Vancouver: Douglas and McIntyre, 2009). There is also a follow-up book on resilience, *And I Live On: The Resilience of Rwandan Genocide Survivors of Sexual Violence* (Tilburg, Netherlands: Wolf Legal Publishers, 2019).

56 Global Centre for the Responsibility to Protect, "Statement on the 25th Anniversary of the Genocide against the Tutsi in Rwanda," http://www.globalr2p.org/publications/751.

57 Médecins sans frontières, "Remembering the Rwandan Genocide 25 Years On," https://www.doctorswithoutborders.org/what-we-do/news-stories/story/remembering-rwandan-genocide-25-years.

58 Anu Chakravarty, *Investing in Authoritarian Rule: Punishment and Patronage in Rwanda's Gacaca Courts for Genocide Crimes* (New York: Cambridge University Press, 2016).

59 I do not have systematic evidence for this, but I base my claim on interviews, observations, and anecdotal encounters with Rwandans during the past twenty-two years. See also Ingelaere, "Hidden Death."

60 The importance of mutual recognition for memory projects is a key theme in the two-year study called "The Uses and Abuses of Memory" as part of the International Panel on Exiting Violence: see Fondation maison des sciences humaines, International Panel for Exiting Violence, chapter 8, available at https://omnibook.com/view/b4fccb4d-877c-427f-8a12-aae842d203e9.

61 Strangely, the UN mapping report on violence in the Democratic Republic of Congo presents this argument as counterevidence to the idea that RPF and

AFDL forces committed genocide against Hutus in that country. The report states, "The intent underlying the killings could be deemed as collective retribution against Hutu civilians in Zaire suspected of involvement with the ex-FAR/Interahamwe, reinforced by the RPA/AFDL's conviction that upon destroying the camps, all Hutu remaining in Zaire were in sympathy with the perpetrators of the 1994 genocide in Rwanda." See UNHCHR, "Democratic Republic of Congo," 14–15. This reasoning is strange, in my view, because whether the perpetrators saw the violence as retribution should not have bearing on whether the violence should be classified as genocide. The crime of genocide should be determined by the intent to destroy (or what I have called the logic of group destruction). Retribution as motive does not negate the possibility of such an intent.

62 On this point, see Catharine Newbury and David Newbury, "The Genocide in Rwanda and the Holocaust in Germany: Parallels and Pitfalls," *Journal of Genocide Research* 5, no. 1 (2003): 135–45.

63 The concept of a "legal lasso" is the work of Courtney Hillebrecht: see Courtney Hillebrecht and Scott Straus, "Who Pursues the Perpetrators: State Cooperation with the ICC," *Human Rights Quarterly* 39, no. 1 (2017): 162–88.

64 See Bert Ingelaere, "Do We Understand Life after Genocide? Center and Periphery in the Construction of Knowledge in Postgenocide Rwanda," *African Studies Review* 53, no. 1 (2010): 41–59; and Johan Pottier, *Re-Imagining Rwanda: Conflict, Survival, and Disinformation in the Late 20th Century* (Cambridge: Cambridge University Press, 2002).

65 Reyntjens, *Political Governance* and Filip Reyntjens, "(Re-)Imagining a Reluctant Post-Genocide Society: the Rwandan Patriotic Front's Ideology and Practice," *Journal of Genocide Research* 18, no. 1 (2016): 61–81.

66 Colum Lynch, "U.N. Waters Down Genocide Charges against Rwandan Forces in Congo," *Foreign Policy*, 2 October 2010, https://foreignpolicy.com/2010/10/02/u-n-waters-down-genocide-charges-against-rwandan-forces-in-congo.

67 Straus and Waldorf, eds., *Remaking Rwanda*.

68 Remnants of the site and some of the news articles can be found on a website called "friends of evil": https://friendsofevil.wordpress.com/tag/remaking-rwanda. One article in *The New Times* summarized the contribution: "The new book should be seen as the latest project of an association of what may be appropriately called 'Genocide Deniers Inc.' and 'Hate Rwanda Ltd.'" The editors have brought together the works of a wide array of members of these two groups. See Joseph Rwagatare, "Remaking Rwanda: Only Rwandans Can Do it," *The New Times*, 19 April 2011, https://www.newtimes.co.rw/section/read/30356.

69 The Commission's statement may be found here: http://www.igihe.com/amakuru/u-rwanda/article/bamwe-mu-banyamahanga-cnlg-itunga-agatoki-kuba-ku-isonga-y-abahakana-jenoside.

70 For example, the idea of the "ultimate crime," was used by the Public Broadcasting Corporation of the United States, in reference to the Ratko Mladic trial. See https://www.pbs.org/wgbh/frontline/article/what-is-genocide-the-ultimate-crime-explained. The concept of the "crime of crimes" is famously in the title of William Schabas's landmark book *Genocide in International Law: The Crime of Crimes*, 2nd ed. (Cambridge: Cambridge University Press, 2009).

71 Scott Straus, "Contested Meanings and Conflicting Imperatives: A Conceptual Analysis of Genocide," *Journal of Genocide Research* 3, no. 3 (2001): 349–75.

72 The idea of genocide as being an absolutist concept is one that Jean-Pierre Dozon developed at a conference in Paris in March 2019 entitled: "Extreme Violence: International, Rescue, Judge."

73 Straus, *Making and Unmaking Nations*.

74 Catharine Newbury and David Newbury, "The Genocide in Rwanda and the Holocaust in Germany: Parallels and Pitfalls," *Journal of Genocide Research* 5, no. 1 (2003): 140–1.

75 As an example, see a quote from a Rwandan journalist in Chris McGreal's *Guardian* piece referenced above.

76 David Scheffer, "Genocide and Atrocity Crimes," *Genocide Studies and Prevention: An International Journal* 1, no. 3 (2006): 229–50. I also discuss this shift in Scott Straus, *Fundamentals of Genocide and Atrocity Prevention* (Washington, DC: United States Holocaust Memorial Museum, 2016).

77 Jean-Hervé Bradol and Marc Le Pape, *Humanitarian Aid, Genocide, and Mass Killings: Médecins Sans Frontières, the Rwandan Experience, 1982–1997* (Manchester: Manchester University Press, 2017).

Contributors

CAROLINE FOURNET is professor of law at Exeter Law School, University of Exeter.

ANDREA GRAZIOSI is professor of history at the Università di Napoli Federico II, and a past president of the Italian Society for the Study of Contemporary History (2007–11). He is the author of *Histoire de l'URSS*; *Lettres de Kharkov. La famine en Ukraine, 1932–33*; *The Great Soviet Peasant War, 1917–1933*; and *Guerra e rivoluzione in Europa, 1905–1956*. With Oleg Khlevniuk, he founded and edited the series *Dokumenty sovetskoi istorii* (Rosspen).

DOUGLAS IRVIN-ERICKSON is assistant professor, Jimmy and Rosalynn Carter School, and director of the Genocide Prevention Program at George Mason University.

NORMAN NAIMARK is Robert and Florence McDonnel Professor of Eastern European Studies at Stanford University, and a senior fellow at the Hoover Institution.

SCOTT STRAUS is a professor of political science at the University of California, Berkeley.

RONALD GRIGOR SUNY is the William H. Sewell, Jr. Distinguished University Professor of History and professor of political science at the University of Michigan, and emeritus professor of political science and history at the University of Chicago. He is the author of *"They Can Live in the Desert But Nowhere Else:" A History of the Armenian Genocide* (Princeton University Press, 2015); *Looking toward Ararat: Armenia in Modern History* (Indiana University Press, 1993);

and co-editor with Fatma Müge Göcek and Norman Naimark of *A Question of Genocide: Armenians and Turks at the End of the Ottoman Empire* (Oxford University Press, 2011).

FRANK E. SYSYN currently serves as the head of the Toronto office of the Canadian Institute for Ukrainaina Studies. In 1989 he was appointed the first director of the Peter Jacyk Centre for Ukrainian Historical Research at the Canadian Institute of Ukrainian Studies, University of Alberta, where he also serves as editor-in-chief of its Hrushevsky Translation Project. He served as an acting director of the CIUS in 1991–93 and is presently head of the executive committee of the Holodomor Research and Education Consortium. He is co-editor with Andrea Graziosi of *Communism and Hunger: The Ukrainian, Chinese, Kazakh, and Soviet Famines in Historical Perspective* (2016) and co-editor with Andrij Makuch of *Contextualizing the Holodomor: The Impact of Thirty Years of Holodomor Studies* (2015).

ANNETTE TIMM is professor of German and European history at the University of Calgary and the former editor of the *Journal of the History of Sexuality*, for which she introduced the special issue "Transgressive Sex, Love and Violence in WWII Germany and Great Britain" (May 2017). Her publications include *The Politics of Fertility in Twentieth-Century Berlin* (Cambridge University Press, 2010), *Gender, Sex, and the Shaping of Modern Europe: A History from the French Revolution to the Present Day* (co-authored with Joshua Sanborn, 3rd edition, Bloomsbury, 2022), and various articles and book chapters about the history of German population policy. She is also the co-editor of *Not Straight from Germany: Sexual Publics and Sexual Citizenship Since Magnus Hirschfeld* (University of Michigan Press, 2017) and the editor of *Holocaust History and the Readings of Ka-Tzetnik* (Bloomsbury Academic, 2018).

MICHELLE TUSAN is professor of history at the University of Nevada, Las Vegas. Her most recent book is *The British Empire and the Armenian Genocide: Humanitarianism and Imperial Politics from Gladstone to Churchill* (2017). Other publications include *Smyrna's Ashes: Humanitarianism, Genocide and the Birth of the Middle East* (2012); and *Women Making News: Gender and Journalism in Modern Britain* (2005).

ANTON WEISS-WENDT is research professor at the Norwegian Center for Holocaust and Minority Studies in Oslo. He is the author and/or editor of twelve books, including *Documents on the Genocide Convention from the American, British, and Russian Archives* (2019); *A Rhetorical Crime: Genocide in the Geopolitical Discourse of the Cold War* (2018); and *The Soviet Union and the Gutting of the UN Genocide Convention.*

Index

www.ingramcontent.com/pod-product-compliance
Lightning Source LLC
LaVergne TN
LVHW090845220725
816728LV00003B/106

* 9 7 8 0 2 2 8 0 1 1 7 1 2 *